Doctors, Ambassadors, Secretaries

Doctors, Ambassadors, Secretaries

Humanism and Professions in Renaissance Italy

DOUGLAS BIOW

The University of Chicago Press
Chicago & London

DOUGLAS BIOW is associate professor in the Department of French and Italian at the University of Texas, Austin. He is the author of *Mirabile Dictu: Representations of the Marvelous in Medieval and Renaissance Epic* (1996).

The University of Chicago Press, Chicago 60637
The University of Chicago Press, Ltd., London
© 2002 by The University of Chicago
All rights reserved. Published 2002
Printed in the United States of America
11 10 09 08 07 06 05 04 03 02 1 2 3 4 5

ISBN: 0-226-05171-4 (cloth)

Library of Congress Cataloging-in-Publication Data

Biow, Douglas.
Doctors, ambassadors, secretaries : humanism and professions in Renaissance Italy / Douglas Biow.
p. cm.
Includes bibliographical references and index.
ISBN 0-226-05171-4
1. Humanism—Italy. 2. Renaissance—Italy. 3. Italy—Civilization—1268–1559. 4. Italy—Civilization—1559–1789. 5. Italy—Intellectual life—1268–1559. 6. Italy—Intellectual life—1559–1789. I. Title.

DG445 .B56 2002
850.9'355—dc21

2001007087

∞The paper used in this publication meets the minimum requirements of the American National Standard for Information Sciences—Permanence of Paper for Printed Library Materials, ANSI Z39.48-1992.

To

Maura

Simone

Erica

Giulia

&

David

Contents

Preface *ix*

Introduction: *Humanism and Professions in Renaissance Italy* *1*

1. Petrarch's Profession and His Laurel *27*

DOCTORS

2. Three Reactions to Plague: *Marvels and Commonplaces in Medicine and Literature* *47*
3. Fracastoro as Poet and Physician: *Syphilis, Epic, and the Wonder of Disease* *71*

AMBASSADORS

4. Exemplary Work: *Two Venetian Humanists Writing on the Resident Ambassador* *101*
5. The Importance and Tragedy of Being an Ambassador: *The Performance of Francesco Guicciardini* *128*

SECRETARIES

6. Open Secrets: *The Place of the Renaissance Secretary* *155*
7. The Secretarial Profession among Others: *Tasso's Enabling Analogies* *181*

Bibliography *197*

Index *215*

Preface

ITALIANS HAVE AN expression for the way a profession takes hold of them and alters them, and it is not an entirely felicitous one. The expression is "deformazione professionale," which literally means "professional deformation" but is perhaps better translated as affected, or peculiarly shaped by, a profession. My brother-in-law uttered this curious expression one day when I asked him why he kept on using the contorted phrase "a prescindere dal fatto che" [leaving aside the fact that], which actually sounds even more cumbersome in Italian than it does in English. He blamed the way he spoke on his "deformazione professionale." The peculiar way he spoke, he admitted unapologetically, was conditioned by what he did for a living every day as a traveling representative for an international pharmaceutical company. My brother-in-law's point about his professional deformation came back to me some ten years later when I was working as graduate advisor to the Comparative Literature Program at the University of Texas at Austin. While admitting students into the program and taking responsibility for downsizing it during a period of dwindling job opportunities, I gradually realized how much the profession had changed and shaped me. I was no longer the same person I had been when I entered graduate school in 1984. I was now speaking differently, writing differently, thinking differently. I had, I thought, been professionally deformed. As if this were not enough, about the same time that I began charting my way through these matters, the Modern Language Association began publishing *Profession,* a yearly volume in which a host of literary scholars at various levels in the academy not only questioned what they were doing but encouraged others to think seriously about why they were doing what they were doing as professionals in the humanities.[1]

This was more or less the beginning of my interest in the subject of this book. At a time in modern academia when professionalism itself

1. The journal *Profession* began to appear as an adjunct to the *PMLA* in 1990 and is issued yearly with the following pronouncement: "*Profession* is a journal of opinion about and for the modern language profession."

was under scrutiny in the humanities, I wanted to bring this notion of professional deformation back to my period of study. More specifically, I wanted to investigate the ways in which important humanists in the Italian Renaissance took on different professions and were changed by them in the very moment that they may have helped shape those professions in their own time. In working on these issues, I did not mean to construct a rigid parallel between the past and the present. Italian Renaissance humanists were not close kin to students coming out of American liberal arts colleges in the late 1970s or to professors professing in (or against) the humanities at enormous state universities, and they were not transformed by their professions the way I presumed I had been. Moreover, the self-loathing among professionals in the humanities today, witheringly described and analyzed by Stanley Fish, has nothing to do with the hostility humanists occasionally expressed toward some professions in the Renaissance.[2] Nevertheless, I was aware as I embarked on this project that a number of scholars had done much in recent years to connect the Renaissance to the present, situating it—to the extent that they were willing to accept that there was a Renaissance—within the "early modern period" and thus at the origins of our own modern or postmodern one.[3] For many scholars, the Renaissance was important not so much as the bright moment when antiquity was reborn and individualism found widespread nascent expression but as the far darker moment when the modern fragmented self and many modern institutional practices, all of which are viewed with great suspicion, were painstakingly born.

Professions, however, do not have a deterministic hold over a person's identity today any more than they did then. My brother-in-law spoke the way he spoke not just because he exercised a certain profession, but, I imagine, because he was an educated Italian exercising a typically educated Italian's predilection for eloquence, because he was a Sicilian exercising an even more Sicilian predilection for embellishing phrases, and because he was—and is—a particularly articulate person who happens to have an extremely rich vocabulary with which he likes to play in often witty and imaginative ways. Yet my brother-in-law's statement regard-

2. Fish, "Profession Despise Thyself: Fear and Self-Loathing in Literary Studies" and "Anti-Professionalism," in *Doing What Comes Naturally,* 197–214, 215–46.

3. For an overview of the terminological shift, with particular attention to English studies, see Marcus, "Renaissance/Early Modern Studies." Many scholars still rigorously separate the periods and view the Renaissance as roughly covering the years 1350–1600 and the early modern as as roughly covering the years 1550–1800. To avoid confusion, I have adopted the term Renaissance throughout to refer to the 1350–1600 period in Italy.

ing his "deformazione professionale" still has partial meaning and merit. Professions often shape identities, even if it is difficult to know exactly how this shaping process takes place or how to prove it definitively. The connections between identities and professions are manifold, fluid, rarely straightforward—and this is true as much now as it was in the Renaissance. For this reason, when I turned to the Renaissance I found no smoking gun, no humanist openly saying that he or she had been professionally deformed. To my knowledge, no humanist ever marked a passage with the succinct and candid observation that he viewed the world the way he did in part because he had once been a doctor, ambassador, or secretary. Yet as I worked on this book I did find that professions shaped identities even if professions had no clear-cut, deterministic sway over them, and that humanists actively shaped their identities through their work in or discourse about professions. I also discovered, somewhat to my surprise, that while professional identity mattered to many humanists in the Italian Renaissance, it did not fundamentally alter the way they wrote or thought as humanists.

I wrote this book with scholars of literature in mind and as a scholar trained in offering a combination of close and theoretically informed readings of texts. Though they range in strategies, the readings here generally share the literary scholar's concern with such things as textual echoes and allusions; thematic and formal connections or disjunctions; critical theory and genre; the reenactment, displacement, or creation of narrative conventions, codes, and topoi; and the way what is expressed conforms to or is undermined by a particular mode of expression. Concentrating on professionalism has narrowed somewhat the scope of analysis of the works discussed individually at any length; rather than offering a comprehensive, global literary analysis of any particular text, then, this book cuts a swath through several as privileged test cases. Yet the gains associated with this approach I believe outweigh the losses. My focus on professionalism has allowed me to provide a fresh way of looking at canonical texts of literary scholarship, highlighting often less studied aspects in such familiar works as Guicciardini's *Ricordi* and Machiavelli's *The Prince.* It has also allowed me to bring to the attention of literary scholars works often excluded from their close interpretive study, works such as Marsilio Ficino's *Consilio contro la pestilenzia,* Ermolao Barbaro's *De officio legati,* or Torquato Tasso's *Del secretario.* It has thus enabled me to bring familiar and less-known works together in a single unifying historical framework that addresses a topic of broad interest to scholars today, precisely at a time when there has been a growing interest among literary scholars in professionalism in the Renaissance and early modern period and in the humanities generally.[4]

My aim in examining the texts I discuss in this book has not been to reconstruct the individual lives and local culture of the humanist authors who composed them and, by so doing, to seek to explain why as individuals they wrote the way they did. Rather, to the degree that Italian humanists, for all their differences, can be lumped together as shaped by a similar educational program and bound by similar concerns and discursive strategies, my aim was to outline the sorts of commonplaces humanists in the Italian Renaissance collectively generated about the specific professions in question. Historians, and perhaps sociologists, may still find something of interest in the connections made in the various chapters. Historians of medicine may not find advanced here anything new about Fracastoro's theory of contagion, for instance, but they may find it worthwhile to think about the connections I have demonstrated between his poetic and scientific concerns. Similarly, sociologists may find of interest that, as we turn our attention to the pre-industrial period, the humanist criteria for judging what specific professions set the terms for professionalization are distinctly at odds with modern sociological criteria. Medicine, which traditionally fits "the sociological criteria of what professions are and do,"[5] was in fact the profession humanists initially attacked and viewed as least adapted to their program of study, whereas the secretarial profession, largely ignored by modern sociologists, was one that Italian humanists traditionally occupied and eventually invested a great deal of time and energy in shaping as their own.

A number of historical assumptions underpin this study. Historians have linked the success of humanism to the practical needs of a mercantile community that flourished in Italy alongside a court culture and that continued throughout the Renaissance to create possibilities for greater social mobility.[6] At the same time, historians have argued that humanism helped protocapitalism to flourish by advocating a positive attitude toward the acquisition and accumulation of wealth. But historians have not all

4. Works by American literary scholars that consider professionalism in the Renaissance and early modern period include: Rambuss, *Spenser's Secret Career;* Cheney, *Spenser's Famous Flight;* Hoffmann, *Montaigne's Career;* and Bushnell, *A Culture of Teaching.* A groundbreaking study in this area remains Helgerson, *Self-Crowned Laureates.*

5. Larson, *The Rise of Professionalism,* xi.

6. See, for example, McGovern, "The Rise of New Economic Attitudes"; Martines, *Power and Imagination* and *The Social World of the Florentine Humanists;* and Grafton and Jardine, *From Humanism to the Humanities.*

agreed recently on the value of humanism during the Renaissance. On the one hand, for a number of scholars humanism enlightened the ruling elite and those who worked for them, providing them with such things as: a moral education; greater and suppler linguistic skills; a more open, more flexible mind and approach to life in general; taste and style; a Roman ethos that helped foster civic responsibility and the ideal of the citizen orator; and a rhetorical training, particularly a capacity to argue both sides of an issue, that not only generated a skeptical philosophical outlook but also inspired democratic-like discussions and consensus-building.[7] On the other hand, for some scholars humanism was plainly elitist: it excluded women, it taught by rote with a deadening tedium that quashed innovation, it separated educational theory and practice, and it functioned as a kind of domesticating device that essentially served to render docile a large body of people, transforming them into obedient and not very thoughtful bureaucrats adapted to, and most adept at, working for, at best, authoritarian oligarchies and, at worst, despots and the emergent absolutist states.[8] My position in this study is more bright than bleak, though that may have something to do with the selection of authors. By concentrating on a number of major male Renaissance figures, by telling the story of the interaction of humanism and professionalism through case studies, and by highlighting authors who primarily worked for or lived in city-states or republics, I have admittedly stacked the deck. But the picture that emerges from a broad survey of Renaissance writings, ranging from secretarial treatises to works of imaginative literature, is that most humanists, whether they were writing in republics or not, sought to make the *studia humanitatis* a matter of practical interest relevant to their own times, thus bringing together rather than separating theory and practice, the ideology of humanism and the actual uses (at least outside of the classroom) to which it could be put. And as humanists adapted the *studia humanitatis* to suit their needs, they often proved themselves in their writing about and as professionals to be innovative, creative thinkers.

7. Among the wildly different scholars holding various positions alluded to here see: Kristeller, "The Humanist Movement" and "Humanism and Scholasticism in the Italian Renaissance," in *Renaissance Thought,* 3–23, 92–119; Garin, *Italian Humanism;* Gray, "Renaissance Humanism"; Struever, *The Language of History in the Renaissance;* Kahn, *Rhetoric, Prudence, and Skepticism;* Baron, *The Crisis of the Early Italian Renaissance;* Skinner, *Foundations of Modern Political Thought,* vol. 1; Seigel, *Rhetoric and Philosophy in Renaissance Humanism;* and Witt, *"In the Footsteps of the Ancients."*

8. This is the position advanced by Grafton and Jardine in *From Humanism to the Humanities,* particularly xi–xvi. Their thesis has often found a more receptive audience among literary scholars than among historians.

This study adopts the conventional dates for humanism in Italy. It begins with Francesco Petrarch (1304–1374) as "the first to formulate a program and a goal for humanists," even if, as Ronald Witt points out, "he was preceded by two generations of scholars and literary men with interests in and attitudes toward the ancients much like his own."[9] I have also adopted the term "protohumanist" to identify writers who have been traditionally claimed by both medieval and Renaissance scholars, writers such as Giovanni Boccaccio (1313–1375), held up by some scholars as one of the founders of humanism and claimed by others to be thoroughly medieval in outlook. Witt has done much to challenge our assumptions regarding when humanism began, and he has urged us to do away with terms such as "prehumanists" or "protohumanists."[10] I have nevertheless relied heavily on the traditional historiographical model in this study. My aim is not to redefine the timeline of humanism, to reexamine why or when humanism began and ended, but to investigate through test cases the relationship of humanism to professionalism and, more precisely, to disclose how professionalism is expressed in a number of canonical works of Renaissance literature. Furthermore, I have included in this study figures some Renaissance scholars might not consider humanists. Guicciardini and Machiavelli, for instance, were not humanists in the way Leonardo Bruni or Pietro Bembo or Baldesar Castiglione were, but they were certainly indebted to humanism as a cultural program that shaped the way they wrote and thought.[11] Considering these examples, it is important to stress from the outset that the writers studied in this book were indebted to humanism to varying degrees and in different ways. Some, such as Petrarch, Ficino, Barbaro, and Tasso, were at the center of humanist culture; others, such as Guicciardini, Machiavelli, and Boccaccio, are said to have been influenced profoundly by it. Humanism, then, is treated in this study as a very diffuse and malleable set of values and rhetorical practices that appealed to a broad strand of society in Renaissance Italy. Given the breadth of humanism's appeal, by including rather than excluding Boccaccio, Machiavelli, and Guicciardini, I can offer a richer and deeper understanding of how the Renaissance drew on humanist culture to shape professional identity.

9. Witt, *"In the Footsteps of the Ancients,"* 81.

10. Ibid., 18–20.

11. Felix Gilbert's classic study, *Machiavelli and Guicciardini,* argues this point; see 297–300 on Guicciardini adopting and revising humanist history writing. Black, in "Machiavelli, Servant of the Florentine Republic," 72–78, makes a strong case for viewing Machiavelli as a humanist.

If the discourse of humanism shaped the way the authors discussed in this book wrote either about or as professionals, the reverse, I maintain, was also true. The engagement of Renaissance Italian humanists with professions had an impact on their humanism insofar as they were forced, when writing about professions or as professionals, to bring the rather abstract ideals of humanism as a pedagogical program into the real world. For when humanist pedagogues articulated the *studia humanitatis,* they wanted both what Montaigne deplored, a well-filled head, and what he admired, a well-constructed one, but in neither case did they actually imagine concrete professions for their students to practice, except to become, in some vague way, members of the ruling elite. The writers considered in this book, by contrast, grappled with the problem of yoking humanist ideals to the real needs of real people practicing professions in the world. The result was not a rejection of humanism, which instead proved remarkably resilient in providing Italian humanists with ways of writing about professions and as professionals, but a modification or qualification of it. The humanist investment in professional identity did not therefore redefine humanism any more than professional experience radically formed—or better yet, to borrow from the opening term of this preface, "deformed"—humanists themselves. Yet as Italian Renaissance humanists wrote about and as professionals, many were significantly shaped by the "available professional channels and tasks"[12] into which their talents were occasionally drawn. In the context of this book, then, humanism provided a kind of unity of knowledge, a shared sensibility and approach, that bound people together and allowed for both innovation and change when those were deemed necessary or appropriate, and that allowed different people to shape themselves through a common discourse and disciplinary mode even as they wrote about or engaged in radically different professions.

12. See Kristeller, "The Humanist Movement," 13, my emphasis: "It was the novel contribution of the humanists to add the firm belief that in order to write and to speak well it was necessary to study and to imitate the ancients. Thus we can understand why classical studies in the Renaissance were rarely, if ever, separated from the literary and practical aim of the rhetorician to write and speak well. This practical and professional connection provided a strong incentive towards classical studies and helped to supply for them the necessary manpower for their proper development. For I cannot help feeling that the achievements of a given nation or period in particular branches of culture depend not only on individual talents, but also on *the available professional channels and tasks in which these talents can be drawn and for which they are trained*. This is a subject to which cultural and social historians apparently have not yet paid sufficient attention."

In writing this book on professions and humanism, I was aided, appropriately enough, by a number of colleagues across the humanities and by fellowships for professional development. For financial assistance, I would like to thank the National Endowment for the Humanities for a year-long fellowship, as well as the University of Texas at Austin for a Faculty Research Assignment and a Summer Research Assignment. These fellowships gave me the opportunity to do most of the initial research and writing in Italy over a thirteen-month period, and I am extremely grateful to William J. Kennedy, Eduardo Saccone, Wayne A. Rebhorn, and Nancy S. Struever for writing on my behalf. I owe a special debt of gratitude to Gloria Meraz for her help in working through issues of professionalism early on; to Nancy S. Struever for being an engaging, helpful, and supportive interlocutor, and for inviting me to discuss aspects of Guicciardini's ambassadorial work at the Johns Hopkins University, Charles Singleton Center for Italian Studies in Florence; to Giorgio Patrizi for inviting me to present preliminary thoughts on Machiavelli before a group of Renaissance scholars assembled by the Folger Institute and the Centro studi sulle società di antico regime "Europa delle corti" at the Università di Roma, La Sapienza; to the Medieval and Early Modern Studies Program, the Historical Center for the Health Sciences, and the Colloquium on the History of Law in Western Society for inviting me to present and discuss chapters 2 and 5 at the University of Michigan; and to Tom Willette, Andrea Cammelli, Penny Marcus, Diane Hughes, Michael Schoenfeldt, Brenda Preyer, Julia Hairston, and Marcello Simonetta for their guidance and encouragement.

My thanks as well to colleagues at the University of Texas at Austin: Guy Raffa for his insights into the connections between the sciences and literature; Daniela Bini for her unflagging support and help with translations of the Italian; Marc Bizer for sharing with me his excellent work on Du Bellay and Renaissance secretaries; Timothy Moore for more than kindly checking and correcting my translations of the Latin; Michael Harney for checking my Spanish translations; and Martha Newman and Caroline Castiglione for their sound advice. All errors in translations, I hasten to add, are my own. I am especially indebted to Alison Frazier, an astonishing historian and scholar of the Renaissance, who read through the manuscript once (part of the Introduction even twice) and gave me insightful feedback at a crucial moment. My greatest debt of gratitude is once more to my friend and colleague Wayne Rebhorn, an always impeccable reader and scholar of the Renaissance, who helped me shape this project from the start and puzzle my way through it at every stage. He scribbled (that is the correct verb, I believe) copious comments on the margins of my manuscript, all of which were very much to the point and found their way into my book as it evolved. He made the difference, as he knows only too well.

I am extremely grateful to Alan Thomas, executive editor at the University of Chicago Press, for taking an interest in this project and seeing that it improved over time. My thanks as well to Albert R. Ascoli, William J. Kennedy, and a third reader for the Press, who made detailed, challenging, and perceptive comments, some of which, they will find, I incorporated directly into my prose. Randy Petilos ushered the book through the Press and answered graciously and quickly all my queries; Leslie Keros and Evan Young did a splendid job of editing and preparing the manuscript for publication; Martin White did a wonderful job of compiling the index. I am also grateful for the assistance I received at a number of libraries that provided me with access to their collections: the Biblioteca Nazionale di Firenze, Villa I Tatti, Newberry Library, New York Academy of Medicine, New York Public Library Rare Books Collection, Biblioteca dell'Archiginnasio di Bologna, and Harry Ransom Center. The staff at the Interlibrary Loan office at the University of Texas at Austin kindly tracked down a host of recondite books and articles for me, and I appreciate all their help. Portions of chapter 6, now much revised, originally appeared in the essay "From Machiavelli to Torquato Accetto: The Secretarial Art of Dissimulation," in *Educare il corpo, educare la parola nella trattatistica del Rinascimento,* edited by Giorgio Patrizi and Amedeo Quondam (Rome: Bulzoni, 1998), 219–38, and are used by permission of Bulzoni Editore.

Finally, my parents did not have an actual hand in the making of this book, but they did indirectly influence it in that most Renaissance of ways: through their example. My stepfather, the late Robert M. Feely, a lawyer who seemed to relish spending Saturdays and Sundays in the office, used to remark that a legal training helped sharpen a mind by teaching people how to argue both sides of the coin; but he also insisted on the value of a humanistic education in general, which he maintained was the best preparation for the law. For her part, my mother, Margot H. Feely, used to sharpen her skills as a professional editor in the publishing world by continually correcting my grammar and diction. When the time came for me to make a living and choose a career, which I tried to put off as long as I reasonably could, my parents, both educated in the humanities, stood as influential models of professional development and commitment. My thanks as well to my mother-in-law, Gabriella Cassini Muratore, for her faith and support, and my brother-in-law, Roberto Muratore, for his assistance and persistence in Rome. This book is dedicated, as I promised it would be, to my three daughters, but it is also dedicated to my son, who was born while I was writing it, and to my wife, who has sustained me in both my life and my profession.

Introduction

HUMANISM AND PROFESSIONS IN RENAISSANCE ITALY

Humanism was a rich and varied educational and cultural program during the Italian Renaissance, a period that ran from approximately the mid-fourteenth to the end of the sixteenth century, a period framed in this book by the opening and closing chapters, on Petrarch's *Coronation Oration* (1341) and Tasso's *Del secretario* (1587) respectively.[1] By and large, humanism was a program of study dedicated to the revival of the classics and the belief that a careful reading of ancient letters proved beneficial to humankind, ethically, politically, and spiritually. In the strictest sense of the term, humanists were students, scholars, and teachers of the *studia humanitatis,* whose subjects were grammar, rhetoric, poetry, history, and moral philosophy.[2] Humanists did not study or teach these subjects in a particularly systematic way, and the boundaries between them were often blurred. One central, unifying subject within the *studia humanitatis* was rhetoric, the art of speaking well and persuasively. Within this framework, the search for eloquence underpinned the humanist program in Italy, a search that led humanists to study and imitate, as well as uncover the lost or largely neglected works of, ancient authors in Greek and Latin. Yet it was also a search for an eloquence as much wedded to wisdom as it was highly politicized. While humanists admired not just the form in which ancient authors eloquently expressed their ideas but the ideas themselves, their admiration for classical letters was by no means slavish.

1. My brief overview of humanism is indebted to the studies in preface, notes 6 and 7; to Greene, *The Light in Troy,* chaps. 1–5; and to the articles collected in Rabil, ed., *Renaissance Humanism,* above all those in vol. 1 dedicated to humanism in Italy.

2. This is the classic formulation from Kristeller, *Renaissance Thought,* 10.

They struggled with *both* the form and the content of classical literature, investing it with a new energy and understanding peculiar to their own time, needs, and sensibilities. And as humanists imitated and emulated classical literature, they occasionally brought to light their own sense of its (and their own) historical specificity and contingency.

As they devoted themselves to unearthing, correcting, and studying ancient letters, humanists developed new ways of viewing the past and contributed significantly to the discipline of history and modern philology. Placing the language and thoughts of classical writers in their proper historical context, reconstructing the texts they uncovered through careful textual comparison, emendation, and analysis, Italian humanists envisioned classical antiquity not as a seamless temporal extension of their own moment in time but as a distinctly different period conditioned by its own specific, historically determined circumstances. The revival of interest in classical culture led not just to a discovery of abandoned ancient texts but to a new understanding of the relation of the present to the past they unearthed and situated in time. This experience of understanding the present in relation to a more clearly defined past conceived as distinct and different could prove exhilarating, as humanists forged connections across time and recognized shared ways of viewing the world, just as it could prove liberating, as humanists questioned the accepted universal validity of a classical author's thought by viewing it as the product not of a timeless authority but of a particular person embedded in a distinct moment in history. At the same time, in measuring the present against the past, humanists occasionally lamented the loss of virtue in their own period and yearned to have lived in the classical one, when virtue flourished and greatness was properly rewarded with glory and fame. The humanist interest in the past was thus fraught with tensions: humanists dethroned authorities yet cherished them, simultaneously rooted authorities in a distant, different past and felt a deep sense of familiarity with and affinity to them.

The humanist interest in the past was not just scholarly but also practical, for the classics provided humanists with models for self-expression and for living the good and virtuous life. Time and again, humanists claimed that the examples found in the classics of ancient Rome, and eventually the examples found in ancient Greece, taught moral values and civic responsibility in the active life, the *vita activa*. This was by no means an uncontested claim, however, and over time the humanist faith in exemplarity—itself partly an outgrowth of, though by no means a reductive imitation of, the Roman faith in exemplarity—underwent a crisis.[3] From the outset, the exemplary figures of the past posed an immediate moral problem. The exemplars of ancient Rome and Greece, for all their heroic stature and greatness, remained pagans, and their lives were rarely uniformly virtuous. Emulating such examples, no matter how great they were, becomes difficult if their lives do not offer up values that are deemed worthy of emulation and do not cohere within a stable, unified narrative. The worth of exemplars as models rests on the assumption that their lives are imitable, but not every aspect of their lives was. In addition, and perhaps more importantly, the humanist understanding of the past as a uniquely situated moment in time complicated the applicability of the classical exemplar's life to action in the present. If the past is distinct and different, even the slightest shift in conditions threatens the usefulness of the exemplar's life as a reliable model for comportment and action in the present. Imitating the lives of ancient exemplars therefore did not come without risks; it required prudence—though prudence, understood as practical wisdom, was often paradoxically thought to be learned from the lives of exemplars themselves. The various problems arising out of the humanist treatment of exemplarity did not mean that humanists completely lost their faith in it as a way of making the pagan past useful for present practice, but they did become more skeptical, more cautious about its reliability, and they became increasingly aware of the need for a complex, nuanced approach.

Guided by the classical culture they admired, humanists also believed that their educational program, somewhat like the Greek ideal of *paideia,* offered humans the opportunity to maximize their potential for personal growth. In the process humanists helped give rise to a Renaissance notion of selfhood that was at once liberating and problematic. Typically, humanists advocated that the self was not a given but something shaped, consciously molded to allow for the greatest possible freedom in self-development. As Giovanni Pico della Mirandola (1463–1494) memorably expressed it in the famous opening to his *Oration on the Dignity of Man* (1486), humans possessed the protean ability to fashion themselves into whatever they desired; they were capable of elevating themselves to angelic heights or lowering themselves to the level of brutes. In this way humans distinguished themselves from all other creatures and found their worth, their *dignitas,* in that they had no clearly defined or fixed value;

3. On the crisis of exemplarity in the Renaissance, see Grafton, "Renaissance Readers"; for an extended treatment in primarily works of imaginative literature, see Hampton, *Writing from History*. Concentrating on humanist hagiography, Frazier has complicated the humanist treatment of exemplarity in her "Reforming Hagiography."

the particular privileged place of humans was, oddly enough, to have no particular place at all, no predetermined, specified position in the cosmos. For this reason the self needed to be disciplined from an early age, cultivated, educated. Yet, while the protean nature of the self—its flexibility, as it has been characterized[4]—opened up possibilities for human development, it also rendered at times painfully obvious that human identity must now be viewed and treated as open-ended, dynamic not static, a sort of continual work in progress that could potentially take on any of a number of forms. One could indeed become a beast in behavior—in Machiavelli's terms a lion or a fox. By extension, a number of concerns grew out of this humanist notion of the protean self: if all selves are made, not born, then all selves may be viewed as constructs or fictions and therefore as potentially fraudulent; and if all selves are made, not born, then all selves may be construed as just masks (personae), covering over an abyss at the core, with an absence at the center of selfhood.[5] Given these concerns, humanist literature often lavished attention on selfhood, and it is often marked by a self-reflexive turn. It thus hardly mattered whether humanists were writing about poetry or courtiership, history or romance, they tended to find some way of inserting themselves into their writings, calling attention to themselves in one form or another, however candidly or obliquely, as they fashioned their own identities in discursive form.

Just as there are enormous differences between the *studia humanitatis* of the Renaissance and modern notions and practices of humanism, so too there are vast differences between the professions of the present and those of the past. During the Renaissance, for example, Italians trained in the liberal arts and with a classical education occasionally referred to the occupation of the secretary [*secretario/segretario*] as a "professione." They did so in part because they held the position of the secretary in higher esteem than we normally do today. Being a secretary required not just the mechanical, routine work of writing, sealing, and cataloging letters but the learned rhetorical expertise needed to compose those letters, as well as the knowledge of a host of other disciplines, including—but not limited to—the ability to write poetry, which was often presented in Italian treatises on the subject as necessary for secretarial training and

4. Greene, "The Flexibility of the Self."

5. On these issues in general in the European Renaissance, with a focus on England, see Greenblatt, *Renaissance Self-Fashioning*; but see also, for a critique, Goldberg, "The Politics of Renaissance Literature"; and Martin, "Inventing Sincerity."

professional success.[6] By calling the occupation of the secretary a "professione," humanists helped elevate its status as an intellectual art to the level of the then more established professions, over and against which the profession of the secretary was at the time publicly defining itself in discourse and as a discursive practice itself. In Italy, having a profession did not necessarily mean one had to have a higher institutional degree. One could be a "gentleman" with a liberal education who lived within a community that sought to monitor itself closely and to claim its own jurisdiction, and who exercised a profession, such as—in point of fact—the profession of the secretary.[7]

The meanings associated with the term "professione"—a concept that even today is notoriously difficult to pin down[8]—ranged widely in Renaissance Italy and often differed from our own. Although "professione," as Maria Malatesta argues, was "a polysemic term," certain traditional meanings dominated in the Middle Ages and beyond.[9] Conventionally, having a "professione" in the Middle Ages meant being part of a religious order. One "professed" one's faith publicly and made, by virtue of that profession (here understood as a proclamation), a commitment to the other members of the order and, of course, to God. But having a profession could also denote, as Malatesta points out, "two distinctive semantic fields: a wider area comprising various forms of public confession or avowal (in the sense of professing an idea, a religious faith, a doctrine); and a more restricted field in which it referred to any occupation, whether intellectual or manual."[10] We find these concepts reiterated throughout the Renaissance. In keeping with these meanings, for example, the famous and authoritative *Vocabolario degli accademici della Crusca* (1612) offers the following definition after the lemma "professione": "Instituto. Lat. *institutum*. . . . Per esercizio, e mestiero. Latin. *ars*. . . . Per solenne promessa d'osservanza, che fanno i religiosi regolari."[11] These two meanings of "professione" as an "art" or as a religious order predominated in lexicons through the Renaissance and well into the early eighteenth century.

6. The notion that the secretary needed to have a knowledge of poetry became a topos of secretarial treatises; see Bizer, "Letters from Home."

7. Nor should we underestimate the importance of print in disseminating this "new professionalism"—see Burke, *The Fortunes of the "Courtier."*

8. See Abbott, *The System of Professions,* 318.

9. Malatesta, "Introduction," 1–23. My thanks to Andrea Cammelli for calling my attention to this study.

10. Ibid., 6.

11. *Vocabolario,* 654. The definition remains substantially the same in the later versions I consulted.

By the time Tommaso Garzoni (1549–1589) wrote his monumental *La piazza universale di tutte le professioni del mondo* at the end of the sixteenth century, the term "professione" had become so saturated with meaning that the author could indiscriminately mix high and low forms of work: the beggar with the butcher with the banker. Garzoni wrote his *Piazza universale* in a period when the earlier, focused, humanist debates over the relative merits of certain arts (principally defined as a dispute between the arts of medicine and of law) had culminated in the "professional *mentalité* of late Renaissance culture." This mentality, George McClure argues, brought about a "triumph of professions in late Renaissance culture" and gave rise not only to Garzoni's cornucopian collection but also to a host of other wide-ranging texts "rooted in the growing rhetorical claims of professional identity and experience."[12] In point of fact, Garzoni's enlarged 1587 edition of the *Piazza universale,* which first appeared in 1585, culminates with the profession of the humanist as the one that contains, rather than being contained by, all the other professions listed before it in the book:

> I thought that I had thoroughly embraced and included in my book all the professions and especially the most illustrious ones. But some lettered persons have revealed to me that I have left out the humanist, a profession among the most noble and honored. I had, however, thought to have included the profession of the humanist partly in the section on grammarians, partly in the section on rhetors, partly the section on historians, and lastly, if there were need, under the area of poets. But these people tell me that the humanist is a *je ne sais quoi* more than all this, or better yet a composite of all these professions, and that the above mentioned four are the cornerstones of the profession of the humanist.[13]

Well before Garzoni wrote his *Piazza universale,* Renaissance humanists understood the polysemic nature of the term "professione" and occasionally used the word with its full semantic range in mind. The term "professione," for example, embraces a host of concepts in Castiglione's *Il libro del cortegiano* (1528), an extremely influential text reworked into its final four-book shape between 1521 and 1524 and often used as the model for treatises addressing professional concerns.[14] On the one hand, "professione" in *Il cortegiano* can broadly indicate a state of mind, a habit,

12. McClure, "The *Artes* and the *Ars moriendi,*" 95, 124, 121.

13. Garzoni, *La piazza universale,* 1526. My translation.

14. See for example Patrizi, "Il *Libro del Cortegiano*"; and Burke, *The Fortunes of the "Courtier."* For the influence in England, see Javitch, *Poetry and Courtliness*; and Whigham, *Ambition and Privilege.*

a general practice: "And they of all men run the risk who make a profession [*che vogliono far profession*] of being very amusing" (2.36.3–4);[15] on the other, it could narrowly designate the notion of a special concern, as when Castiglione (1478–1529) describes the elaborate care some courtiers take regarding their appearance: "others attend to [*altri fan professione di*] their teeth, others to their beard, others to their boots, others to their bonnets, others to their coifs" (2.27.39–41). "Professione" can further indicate a public avowal, in the sense of professing knowledge of a subject ("Then, in those things wherein he knows himself to be totally ignorant, I would never have him claim ability in any way [*non voglio che mai faccia professione alcuna*]"—2.38.39–41), but it can also signify an "art," understood in the narrowest sense as a specific job, with reference particularly to a work involving manual rather than necessarily intellectual labor. More generally, "professione" indicates an ability to perform certain tasks: "There are of course some who know their own excellence in one thing and yet make a profession [*professione*] of something else, though something in which they are not ignorant; and every time they have an occasion to show their worth in the thing wherein they feel they have talent, they give evidence of their considerable ability. And it sometimes happens that the company, seeing this ability of theirs in something that is not their profession, think they must be able to do far better in what is their profession" (2.39.35–41). However, Castiglione also uses the term to denote intellectual labor within a culturally defined discipline, such as the priesthood or the law: "And, what is more, these offenders against God and nature are men who are already old, who make a profession [*fan professione*], some of priesthood, some of philosophy, some of sacred law" (3.40.29–31; see also 3.45.12). Finally, "professione" could signify a discipline in the widest sense of the term, as the product of any practice that required master-pupil training, from that of the wrestler to the philosopher: "Therefore, whoever would be a good pupil must not only do things well, but must always make every effort to resemble and, if that be possible, to transform himself into his master. And when he feels that he has made some progress, it is very profitable to observe different men of that profession [*di tal professione*]" (1.26.1–5).

The most important use of the term "professione" in *Il cortegiano,* however, occurs at its first mention. Toward the beginning of Book 1, Federico Fregoso proposes the game that will then be selected as the

15. All references are to the 1929 Sansoni edition of Castiglione, *Il cortegiano.* Translations are the 1959 Anchor edition translated by Charles S. Singleton.

activity for the evening. In doing so, he declares to the general assent of all attending:

> In all Italy it would perhaps be hard to find an equal number of cavaliers as outstanding and as excellent in different things, quite beyond their principal profession of chivalry [*profession della cavalleria*], as are found here, wherefore, if there are anywhere men who deserve to be called good courtiers and who can judge of what belongs to the perfection of Courtiership, we must rightfully think that they are here present. So, in order to put down the many fools who in their presumption and ineptitude think to gain the name of good courtiers, I would have our game this evening be this, that one of this company be chosen and given the task of forming in words a perfect Courtier, setting forth all the conditions and particular qualities that are required of anyone who deserves this name. (1.12.11–23)

By chivalry, Federico Fregoso presumably means the military profession of "cavalleria," the profession of the equestrian knight. Consequently, Castiglione soon reminds us—much as he reminds us throughout *Il cortegiano* (1.44.45, 46.2; 2.8.8; 3.4.49)—that "the principal and true profession [*la principale e vera profession*] of the courtier must be that of arms" (1.17.1–2).[16] Yet Castiglione also indicates that it is the burden of the group gathered in the evening to reveal all the other professions appropriate to the perfect courtier (1.21.29–32).[17] In the course of identifying the plethora of professions in which the courtier inevitably excels, Castiglione further reveals that the profession of arms symbolizes the vestige of what it meant to be a courtier in times gone by. The profession of arms is a symbolic trace of the antiquated courtier, whom Castiglione inscribes into his text yet means to efface by emphasizing not the courtier's capacity to fight but his ability to speak. In defining what makes a courtier chivalrous, Castiglione privileges throughout his *Il cortegiano* not arms but "those studies which we call the humanities [*studii che chiamano d'humanità*]" (1.44.2). We are given an explicit indication of this in book 1, when a man who has made it solely his "mestiero" [business, 1.17.36] to fight is flatly ridiculed as a bore. The courtier whose profession is that of arms alone is lacking in the profession of chivalry. He is a brute, without refinement, and he should be shunned by the group of true courtiers, who are "gentlemen." He may know how to ride a horse and fight in battle but not how to

16. See Woodhouse, *Baldesar Castiglione,* 88.

17. "And even as we read that Alcibiades surpassed all those peoples among whom he lived, and each in the respect wherein it claimed greatest excellence, so would I have this Courtier of ours excel all others in what is the special profession of each" (1.21.29–32).

hold civil conversation in polite company. He lacks, at the very least, *sprezzatura*.[18]

In considering the role of professions in *Il cortegiano,* we need to recall as well that Castiglione's aim is not so much to paint a portrait of a perfect courtier with all his various professions as to establish and recognize through the fashioning of that portrait a class of good professional courtiers. Nor in the fiction of the text are we confronted with a single perfect courtier; rather, we see the portrait of a group that is making every effort to define its professional status and importance by consensus.[19] Castiglione's *Il cortegiano* simultaneously presents two portraits and two frameworks. First, there are the courtiers intent on painting the portrait of a perfect courtier, and then there is Castiglione, who is painting the larger portrait of the courtiers themselves (with all their obvious imperfections) as they attempt to legitimize their role in relation to the absent prince. In the process, Castiglione presents the courtier—in modern sociological terms—as indeed a professional. He envisions courtiers as possessing their own knowledge and training grounded in the "studii che chiamano d'humanità." These studies would comprise not only a thorough knowledge of Greek and Latin but, as Wayne Rebhorn points out, far more general fields of learning and expertise. This knowledge grounded in the "studii che chiamano d'humanità," which grows out of both bookish studies and lived experience, is at once theoretical, embodied in "the Hellenistic ideal of well-roundedness and elevated amateurism," and practical, drawn from "the more Roman and earlier Greek notion of education as training for service to the state."[20] In addition, courtiers have specific tasks, which would entail not so much arms as the education of the prince and the provision of counsel. At the same time, courtiers have a jurisdictional claim over a rival profession: that of the educator, the *maestro di scuola*. They have their own ethical concerns rooted in the demands of their professional work as educators and counselors of the prince. Along with this, they have subtle mechanisms for identifying themselves as a group of professionals and for excluding others from their ranks. *Sprezzatura,*

18. Needless to say, Castiglione himself was better versed in the profession of letters than of arms, on which see Hale, "Castiglione's Military Career." On Castiglione's career as a diplomat, see Guidi, "Baldassar Castiglione et le pouvoir politique."

19. This point is emphasized most in Castiglione scholarship by Saccone, especially his "Grazia, Sprezzatura, and Affettazione in the *Courtier*" and "Trattato e ritratto." A number of scholars have taken Castiglione's depiction of the perfect courtier as a master of many abilities to be, as Hale puts it, an indication of his "scorn of professionalism of any sort" (Hale, "Castiglione's Military Career," 162).

20. Rebhorn, *Courtly Performances*, 197. See also Lipking, "The Dialectic of *Il cortegiano*."

which Eduardo Saccone links to the exclusionary function of irony in society, "is the test the courtier must pass in order to be admitted to this club, to obtain the recognition of his peers."[21] Finally, courtiers have wide public appeal. Rhetorically, the *meraviglia* they elicit is the response Quintilian and Cicero deemed necessary to even begin to engage and consequently persuade a public (*Institutio Oratoria,* 8.3.5–6).[22] In short, Castiglione's courtiers have everything it takes to impress a public and other professionals that they have a profession. They have concrete tasks and mechanisms for identifying courtiers as professionals with their own abstract yet practical knowledge, all of which has absolutely nothing to do with the profession of arms. They have their own form of work, which competes with and preempts the work of the educator of princes and even that of the professional soldier. And they have their own strategies of self-promotion, which are rooted in rhetorical practice but owe much to poetic practice as well.[23]

Though Castiglione may in his text explicitly identify the professions of the courtier, it is ultimately courtiership itself as a profession that he implicitly seeks to describe. Castiglione noticeably states as much in the earlier version of *Il cortegiano* when he makes, in the preface later discarded, the following significant pronouncement:

> However, among the other things that have come about in recent times, beyond which we have no news of, we see now emerging this sort of man that we call the courtier, a profession [*professione*] quite widely exercised throughout all Christendom: indeed, since there have always been many obedient servants to princes and great lords—some dearer, others less dear, some ingenious, others foolish, this one favored because of his valor in arms, that one for his knowledge of letters, another for his physical beauty, and many for none of these reasons but only for a certain hidden conformity of their nature; only recently has a profession [*professione*] been made of this court service, if we can call it that, only recently has it been refined to an art and a discipline.[24]

The omission of this paragraph from the final prefatory letter, added in probably 1527, should not be taken to indicate that Castiglione's conception of the courtier as a professional has changed in the final, authorized

21. Saccone, "Grazia," 60.

22. Quintilian, *Institutio Oratoria*: "Recteque Cicero his ipsis ad Brutum verbis quadam in epistola scribit, *Nam eloquentiam, quae admirationem non habet, nullam iudico.* Eandem Aristoteles quoque petendam maxime putat." On the response of *meraviglia* in *Il cortegiano,* and its different functions, see Rebhorn, *Courtly Performances,* 47–51.

23. On the poetic practice of the courtier, see Javitch, *Poetry and Courtliness.*

24. Castiglione, *Lettere,* 1.193. On this see Saccone, "Trattato e ritratto," 5–7. See also Woodhouse, *Baldesar Castiglione,* 70 and 189, on the "new professionalism" of the *Cortegiano.*

version of *Il cortegiano.* Rather, Castiglione's refusal to ever discuss the work of the courtier as a profession in the final version may be taken as part of a narrative strategy that imitates poetic practice by privileging, as Daniel Javitch argues, the "ability to conceal aspects of [a] subject and delay by indirection, the recognition of . . . meanings."[25] Refusing to state the obvious—to state the obvious would indeed be a sign of *affettazione*—Castiglione omits any explicit reference to the courtiers as professionals in the final version. The "good" courtiers, who both understand and practice the art of *sprezzatura,* can nevertheless recognize each other as such. Though Castiglione calculatingly refuses to say so in the final version of *Il cortegiano,* the "good courtiers," in addition to exercising a multitude of professions, clearly have a profession of their own, a new profession, and it is this profession that Castiglione largely describes, rather than prescribes, through the debates of a court community at Urbino.

Sociologists studying professions, however, have not concerned themselves much with works such as *Il cortegiano.* Sociologists focus primarily on the postindustrial period and, above all, the twentieth century, since most date professionalism—if not its emergence, then at least its rise—from the appearance of extended market economies and widespread possibilities for real social mobility. The paucity of well-defined institutional frameworks within which sociologists can securely place professions and systematically evaluate the nature of professional training—other than the institutional frameworks of the university and the church—perhaps accounts for the scant attention they have paid to professions and professionalism in Renaissance and early modern Europe.[26] Yet as many professions of the Renaissance flourished outside institutional frameworks, they generated on a large, measurable scale "discursive practices," to borrow Charles Goodwin's terms, "used by members of a profession to shape events in the domains subject to their professional scrutiny."[27] Italian

25. Javitch, "Poetry and Court Conduct," 874.

26. Consider, for example, the comprehensive study *I professionisti,* ed. Maria Malatesta, which focuses almost entirely on the nineteenth and twentieth centuries. My thanks to Andrea Cammelli for bringing this work to my attention. Historians of Renaissance and early modern continental Europe, however, have increasingly paid attention to professions and issues regarding vocational choice. See for example Cipolla, "The Professions"; Vasoli, "Le discipline"; Fiorato, ed., *Culture et professions en Italie;* McClure, "The *Artes* and the *Ars moriendi*"; Bec, "Lo statuto socio-professionale"; de Caprio, "Aristocrazia e clero"; Douglas, "Talent and Vocation"; Garin, *La disputa delle arti;* Gilmore, "*Studia Humanitatis*"; Martines, *Lawyers and Statecraft*; the entire section on "Humanism and the Professions" in Rabil, ed., *Renaissance Humanism,* 3.310–79; and Fragnito, "Buone maniere e professionalità." For England, see now O'Day, *The Professions.* George McClure has informed me that he is currently engaged in a book-length study on the rhetoric of professions from Petrarch to Glissenti.

27. Goodwin, "Professional Vision," 606.

Renaissance humanists such as Castiglione were aware of the formative nature of their professions, much as they were often aware that their own language in the vernacular was in a state of formation and that they were not only forging their own identities in language but forging for posterity a language itself. In addition, Italian Renaissance humanists were keenly aware that many of their professions, so many of which originated in the Middle Ages but which they were sometimes reconceptualizing as new, were not grounded in institutions, guilds, or government statutes and licensing procedures. Many of their professions, bound to courts, communes, and principalities, were instead grounded in a communal, self-authenticating discourse that both periodically defined and policed their notion of a particular profession as a meaningful form of work.

In this light, Andrew Abbott's structural and relational theory of professions can help put into context the conditions for the development of professions in Renaissance Italy. According to Abbott, professions, which are always necessarily in a formative state, are historically determined activities that form at any given time an interconnected system. Within these systems, professions are continually disputing jurisdictions, which Abbott defines as a profession's claim to control—partially or completely—a certain form of work. As professions evolve and compete amongst themselves, they may gradually relinquish one or another jurisdictional claim. In particular, this relinquishment occurs when a certain form of work has become increasingly routine. Professions then generally delegate that routine work to subordinate groups under their supervisory control. New forms of work in turn create new professions, as well as new forms of competition within the system of professions. Moreover, a profession's ability both to seize and to enforce its jurisdictional claim is, according to Abbott, directly related to the strength of its appeal to a body of abstract knowledge and its perceived applicability. That specialized knowledge—which is often but not always academic—must be adaptable to cultural shifts; flexible enough to embrace new forms of technical and intellectual advances; and held in high prestige, both within the system of professions and, significantly, by the interested public at large. The competition among professions within a system is thus often acted out in the public arena, for a profession cannot simply claim jurisdictional control over a form of work if the public does not legitimize that claim by confirming its confidence in a particular profession's body of abstract knowledge as both appropriate and useful. A profession must therefore not only compete within a system for jurisdictional control, but also rhetorically persuade an interested public, through a variety of mechanisms, that its body of abstract knowledge and applicable practice is most suited to a certain form of work. Mechanisms for persuasion no doubt change over time, but one factor influencing a profession's success, we can infer from Abbott's model, is its ability to make use of innovative technologies to disseminate and persuasively advance its ideas.

Humanism offered aspiring professionals a number of advantages during the Renaissance, not the least of which being that, with its emphasis on rhetoric and oratory, it taught people how to persuade—according to Abbott, a skill central to a profession's success. A profession seizes control by convincing the public that its knowledge is highly sophisticated yet appropriate and useful for lived experiences. In this regard, humanism proved to be admirably suited to the needs of a simultaneously courtly and mercantile society that was beginning to place a host of diplomatic and administrative tasks, some of them quite complicated, under professional control. Lisa Jardine and Anthony Grafton have argued that Scholasticism, rather than humanism, was "far better adapted to many of the traditional intellectual and practical needs of European society"; that Scholasticism effectively "trained men for employment in powerful and lucrative occupations" in the "professional faculties of law, medicine and theology"; and that Scholasticism "even taught the future estate manager, government clerk or solicitor how to keep books, draw up contracts and write business letters"—in short, that Scholasticism brilliantly "equipped students with complex skills and fitted them to perform specialized tasks."[28] But thanks to its wide public exposure, its strong ties to the new and growing mercantile class and court society, its commitment to disseminating its program of study through the then novel medium of print, and its strategy of applying abstract knowledge, especially through exemplarity, to shape ethical and civic behavior, humanism ultimately proved to be better situated to persuade the public that its program of education, rather than Scholasticism, was the most appropriate to the tasks at hand within the burgeoning mercantile economy and entrenched courtly society. From the outset, humanism was at once abstract and applicable, theoretical and practical—at least, so humanists persistently and persuasively maintained. The success of humanism, in other words, is to be found not just in its program of instruction, which so many in the Renaissance deemed rewarding and pleasurable,[29] but in its perceived applicability, which served professionals well. For if what professions need

28. Grafton and Jardine, *From Humanism to the Humanities,* xii–xiii.
29. Grendler, *Schooling in Renaissance Italy,* 407.

KING ALFRED'S COLLEGE LIBRARY

to succeed are effective strategies for self-promotion, humanism proved itself in Italy to have great public support as a pedagogical program that promised to mold young men who held or sought diplomatic and administrative posts within growing civic and court communities, both of which actively supported humanism and were shaped by it. Humanism, as a program of instruction, thus occupied the status of "abstract knowledge," in Abbott's terminology, to which professionals appealed in their attempt to bolster their status and thereby publicly, as well as persuasively, claim jurisdictional control over certain kinds of work.

This book focuses on the professions of doctor, ambassador, and secretary, but it is important to point out that there were certainly other professions that could have been discussed, beginning with the profession of notary, the profession most closely linked with humanism early on and the one out of which it initially grew, as numerous scholars have maintained. Paul Oskar Kristeller advanced this argument long ago, when he noted that "the humanists of the Renaissance were the professional successors of the medieval Italian *dictatores,* and inherited from them the various patterns of epistolography and public oratory, all more or less determined by the customs and practical needs of later medieval society."[30] As Witt bluntly puts it, "humanism, from Lovato's generation to the early fifteenth century, was an enterprise of notaries."[31] Yet another important language-based profession, the legal profession, obviously had close ties with humanism, and numerous humanists were employed as schoolmasters and, eventually, as university professors.[32] There are yet other professions that engaged humanists and occupied their attention as well as their skills, among them theology. Yet I have chosen to focus on doctors, ambassadors, and secretaries, and for essentially two reasons. First, I want to move from a profession humanists initially resisted to one they enthusiastically embraced. This narrative strategy has the negative

30. Kristeller, *Renaissance Thought,* 12–13. See also Seigel, *Rhetoric and Philosophy in Renaissance Humanism,* 200–225; and Witt, "Medieval *Ars Dictaminis,*" "Medieval Italian Culture," and *"In the Footsteps of the Ancients,"* esp. 90–93; also Skinner, *Foundations of Modern Political Thought,* 1.29–31, 71–83, 101–4.

31. Witt, *"In the Footsteps of the Ancients,"* 92.

32. On lawyers and humanism, see Gilmore, *Humanists and Jurists;* Skinner, *Foundations of Modern Political Thought,* 1.201–7; and the synthesis by Schoeck, "Humanism and Jurisprudence." On humanist schoolteachers, see Grendler, *Schooling in Renaissance Italy;* but also, for a more polemical approach, Grafton and Jardine, *From Humanism to the Humanities.* The term *humanista* was in fact first coined to describe the professional teacher of the *studia humanitatis* and largely retained that meaning. See Campana, "Origin of the Word 'Humanist'"; Kristeller, *Renaissance Thought,* 110–11.

effect of overstating the humanist break with Scholasticism and (at the risk of reiterating self-aggrandizing humanist rhetoric) reinforcing the value-laden notion that the Renaissance represented a crucial advance over the dark period of the Middle Ages. However, it also has the positive effect of immediately clarifying how humanists consciously marked out differences and really did define themselves over and against longstanding rival practices. Although in hindsight we can say that humanism had medieval antecedents and developed side by side with Scholasticism as one intellectual mode among others, many humanists, such as Castiglione, saw themselves as doing something new in a new historical period. Second, I focus on doctors, ambassadors, and secretaries because I want to examine three professions that grew up and flourished at different moments of the Italian Renaissance, so as to provide a connected yet overlapping analysis of the interaction of professionalism and humanism. The chapters in this study may therefore be read separately, each standing on its own, but I have structured it to progress in stages, unfolding over a period of approximately two and a half centuries.

I begin with the profession of medicine. By the fourteenth century, medicine was an institutionalized, degree-conferring discipline already firmly established within the Italian university system. According to Darrel Amundsen and other historians, it is during this period that we can actually begin to "speak of the development of a clearly defined medical deontology [ethics of duty] and professional ethics, appreciated (at least in theory) by those within and those outside the profession."[33] The humanist interaction with the profession of medicine, however, did not begin until late in the fourteenth century, and it blossomed only in the second half of the fifteenth. From medicine I then turn to two important professions that grew up outside the academy and were codified and exercised by humanists at the height of the Renaissance in Italy. The first is the resident ambassador, a uniquely Italian invention of the fifteenth century and a profession peopled almost from the start with humanists, who both wrote about and exercised it as trained orators.[34] The second is the secretary, a profession that was defined gradually toward the latter half of the sixteenth century in a spate of highly influential Italian treatises and has long been associated in modern historiography with Renaissance humanism.[35]

33. Amundsen, *Medicine, Society, and Faith,* 291.

34. The fundamental study on this remains Mattingly, "First Resident Embassies" and *Renaissance Diplomacy*.

35. See for example Kristeller, *Renaissance Thought,* 102: "the vast majority of humanists exercised either of two professions, and sometimes both of them. They were either secretaries of

Focusing on these three professions, I trace through case studies the involvement of humanists in the formation of professional identity and in professions themselves during the Italian Renaissance, beginning with their resistance to the profession of medicine in the fourteenth century and ending with their highly engaged investment in the profession of secretary in the sixteenth century.

The professions of doctor, ambassador, and secretary differ with regard to their interaction with humanism. Early on, humanists, and in particular Petrarch, proved hostile to medicine, which was a well-established profession long before humanism as a program of study ever came into being. Yet as more and more doctors desired to participate in that program of study and wished to be viewed as learned humanists, they also increasingly concerned themselves with locating the source of their ideas and their professional identity in the authority of a revered classical past. Often, humanist doctors placed themselves squarely in an agon with that classical past, seeking not only to imitate but to emulate their ancestors. Like the work and duties of the doctor, the work and duties of the ambassador were clearly well-defined before humanism ever fully came into being as a program of study. Yet, from the outset there was no rejection on the part of humanists of the profession of ambassador, as there had been of that of doctor. Rather, the humanist interest in oratory sparked interest in the work of the resident ambassador in particular because he was conceived as an orator designated to represent a sovereign power for an extended period of time. Then, as humanists wrote about the work of the resident ambassador and, in the process, directly or indirectly about themselves, they drew on their knowledge of ancient history and rhetoric and repeatedly fashioned their ambassador over and against the classical culture they revered yet simultaneously sought to perfect and overcome. The growth of humanism and the development of the professional identity of the ambassador are thus closely connected throughout the Italian Renaissance. Secretaries, like ambassadors, also existed long before humanism as a program of study ever came into being, but the duties of the secretary were never explicitly articulated in discourse until the mid-sixteenth century, when they were in part defined, and debated, by Italian humanists. A number of these authors, true to humanist practice, created a definition of their profession in a historicizing manner, often seeking a classical analogue for the profession of secretary in their own

---

princes or cities, or they were teachers of grammar and rhetoric at universities or at secondary schools."

time. However, if in theory secretaries in the late sixteenth century were expected to have humanist training so as to compose eloquent letters, in praxis, as servile functionaries working often within elaborate bureaucracies, they were not expected to reveal an open, questioning breadth of mind, and they certainly bore little resemblance to the great humanist secretaries of the Italian quattrocento or early cinquecento, secretaries such as Bembo, who was often privileged in these treatises as a figure of exceptional success. In this respect, this book ends at the point where a tendency becomes evident in humanist education away from liberating minds and ideally inculcating vigorous, intellectual inquiry, and toward assuring professional success for those who wished to undertake specific administrative tasks in a dutiful way, tasks such as those undertaken by the secretary.[36]

Italian humanists also had different views of the professions of doctors, ambassadors, and secretaries as avenues for social mobility. For the most part, humanists did not overtly view the profession of doctor as the key to success, though doctors did make exceptional gains in acquiring prestige and reputation during this period, and humanists came to respect and value the profession. Often enough doctors wished to be viewed as humanists to help elevate the status of their profession—to make the profession of medicine appear, as they had for so long tried to make it appear, less a mechanical and far more an intellectual art. Predictably, humanist discussions of the profession of ambassador do not entertain fantasies of upward social mobility; they are largely conservative in nature, written to and for men of a somewhat elevated class. Ambassadorships, and particularly important ones, it was assumed, would be restricted to persons of already some social standing. Humanists, however, did envision the profession of the secretary as a real ladder to success. Ideally, a humanist who became a secretary could improve his social rank and move from one status to another. The treatises on the secretary are filled with just such claims, and some of them even entertain the possibility that the secretary could eventually take over and displace the master he served. Italians writing about the secretary fashioned a profession for a society in

36. Tracing the crisis of the prior glory of humanism and, more generally, the role and function of intellectuals in Italy in the late cinquecento, see Rosa, "La chiesa e gli stati regionali nell'età dell'assolutismo," 257–317; de Caprio, "Aristocrazia e clero"; and virtually all the studies on the secretary referred to below in chapter 6, note 1. However, Anthony Grafton argues for the enduring importance and richness of humanism in the sixteenth and seventeenth centuries, as well as its contribution to the intellectual advances of the time. See Grafton, "New Science."

which the opportunities for social mobility within the growing secular and ecclesiastic bureaucracies of the late Renaissance were on the increase, opportunities the humanist secretary was expected to take advantage of. As one might expect, not a few hopes were dashed along the way.

While focused primarily on doctors, ambassadors, and secretaries, this study begins with a chapter on Petrarch and his coronation oration. I begin with Petrarch because he defined for many what it meant to be dedicated to the *studia humanitatis,* and in his coronation oration he first publicly articulated for those who came after him what it meant to have a profession in the context of the humanist project he inaugurated. Petrarch's oration, "with all its mingling of elements old and new," is not just "the first manifesto of the Renaissance," as Ernest Hatch Wilkins maintained.[37] In its conspicuous reliance on pagan authorities, the coronation oration is also the first great manifesto of humanism, which privileged such authorities in its search for eloquence and as part of a larger program of rhetorical education.

The bulk of my study then turns to the professions of doctor, ambassador, and secretary, examining them in three separate sections, each composed of two chapters. The first chapter of each section offers a diachronic view of the interaction between humanism and the profession in question by presenting case studies that cover a significant expanse of time. For the most part, these initial chapters establish how the professions I discuss were viewed, used, and reconstructed by humanists, who may or may not have worked within them. In these chapters I treat, among others, such humanists as Marsilio Ficino (1433–1499), who wrote a treatise on the plague in 1479 (chapter 2); Ermolao Barbaro (ca. 1454–1493), a Venetian humanist who wrote about the work of the resident ambassador from probably 1489 to 1490, after returning from a year as the Venetian representative to the court of Ludovico Sforza in Milan (chapter 4); and Niccolò Machiavelli (1469–1527), who drafted *The Prince* soon after being dismissed as secretary from the Second Chancery in Florence in 1512 (chapter 6). The second chapter of each section then provides a more detailed profile of a humanist who was influenced by his professional practice or whose work as a humanist helped fashion the way a profession was viewed. They are: Girolamo Fracastoro (ca. 1478–1553), who wrote a medical poem titled *Syphilis* over a twenty-year period, from 1510 to 1530 (chapter 3); Francesco Guicciardini (1483–1540), who began his *Ricordi* during his tenure as ambassador to Spain from 1512 to

37. Wilkins, *Making of the "Canzoniere,"* 300.

1513 (chapter 5); and Torquato Tasso (1544–1595), the humanist poet who published a treatise on secretaries in 1587 (chapter 7).

In the first section, on "Doctors," chapter 2, "Three Reactions to Plague: Marvels and Commonplaces in Medicine and Literature," begins with a famous scholastic physician, Gentile da Foligno (d. 1348), revealing how deeply embedded the profession of medicine was within the university system and Italian society at large. Then, after discussing Boccaccio's sarcastic yet ambivalent treatment of doctors in his *Decameron* (1349–50), it concludes with Ficino, in whom humanism and the profession of medicine were brought together in a truly fruitful way. Gentile da Foligno, who wrote some of the earliest *consilia* about the plague, represents the kind of scholastic physician the medical profession was producing just before the Renaissance. He also represents the kind of physician Boccaccio felt so deeply ambivalent about when he opened his *Decameron* with a description of how ineffective doctors had been in combating the plague. In the *Decameron,* we are in fact provided with the perspective of a protohumanist, one who has begun to participate in the Petrarchan contest with doctors, which may be understood, according to George McClure, as a contest motivated by "professional rivalry."[38] By contrast, Ficino, who wrote about the plague somewhat more than a century after Boccaccio, rejected this early humanist contest with doctors. On the contrary, Ficino envisioned himself as both a practical physician and a moral philosopher, a doctor and a humanist. When he wrote about the plague in his *Consilio contro la pestilenzia* (1481), he therefore drew on his knowledge of both scholastic medicine and classical literature. On the one hand, Ficino offered the familiar medical advice that people should live moderately during the plague; on the other hand, he observed, as one might expect a humanist doctor and translator of Plato's dialogues would have observed, that Socrates had survived the plague precisely because, according to Ficino, Socrates was throughout his life a moderate man. In Ficino, we thus find the perfect synthesis at the end of the fifteenth century of the doctor influenced by humanism and the humanist influenced by the profession of medicine.

Chapter 3, "Fracastoro as Poet and Physician: Syphilis, Epic, and the Wonder of Disease," profiles Girolamo Fracastoro, renowned humanist physician and author of *De contagione et contagiosis morbis* (1546), a medical text often considered to have anticipated modern germ theory, and

38. McClure, "Healing Eloquence," 331. See also his fine *Sorrow and Consolation in Italian Humanism.*

of *Syphilis sive morbus Gallicus* (1530), one of the most famous neo-Latin poems of the century. This chapter considers how Fracastoro's novel conception of contagion in his medical works was fundamentally rhetorical in its character, while his poetry inversely owed much to the medical discourse of his time, in particular to treatises on syphilis and the plague. Fracastoro's *Syphilis* draws heavily on, yet finally distances itself from, Lucretius's *De rerum natura* and the Lucretian perception of diseases as always rationally explicable. In the Lucretian scheme of things, the worst thing one could do was wonder over the causes of such diseases, as people did over the plague that struck Athens and decimated its population around 430 B.C.E. The passion of wonder, however, dominates Fracastoro's poem, just as it did his scientific medical studies, for *Syphilis* imitates not just the *De rerum natura* in its themes and didactic structure, but the *Aeneid* as it appropriates the Virgilian representation of epic wonder and discovery. To wonder over syphilis constitutes the first step toward understanding disease cognitively and appreciating it aesthetically as a matter of both scientific and poetic interest. The result is that Fracastoro makes *Syphilis* a hybrid form, a scientific poem, just as he created a kind of poetical science in *De contagione*. The medical profession and the humanist interest in classical literature and rhetoric are thus brought together in Fracastoro's works.

In the second section, "Ambassadors," chapter 4, "Exemplary Work: Two Venetian Humanists Writing on the Resident Ambassador," focuses on the treatises of Ermolao Barbaro and Ottaviano Maggi (d. 1586), the first completed at the very end of the fifteenth century, the second toward the middle of the sixteenth. Both Barbaro and Maggi viewed the work of the resident ambassador through the myth of Venice, and as a result they expressed in their otherwise very different treatises a shared vision of the resident ambassador as a tireless, self-sacrificing participant working for the good of the state. Both Barbaro and Maggi also saw their own identities as humanists to be intimately bound up with the images of the resident ambassador presented in their treatises. Barbaro, who was the first humanist to write on ambassadorial work, broke with humanism in one way by refusing to look to the classical past that he knew so well for models for the diplomatic practices of his own time. Instead, he grounded his examples of ambassadorial work in specifically Venetian diplomatic practices and, above all, in his own and his father's performance. By contrast, Maggi's treatise, composed almost seventy years later, is a more completely humanist performance and endows the perfect ambassador with all the bookish knowledge a humanist might ever wish to acquire. Unlike Barbaro, Maggi cannot use himself as an exemplar of ambassadorial work because he had never served as an ambassador. However, as he idealizes the profession and makes Odysseus a model for ambassadorial work, Maggi offers that figure as a disguised reflection of himself as a worldly and resourceful hero. Despite their differences, then, both Barbaro and Maggi identify with the profession defined in their treatises as well as with the same sovereign power they served, and they both reveal a typically humanist faith in exemplarity as a reliable way to shape the ambassador's comportment in the present and for the future.

Chapter 5, "The Importance and Tragedy of Being an Ambassador: The Performance of Francesco Guicciardini," centers on Guicciardini's *Ricordi,* the earliest versions of which were composed while he was the Florentine ambassador to Spain (1512–1513), precisely during the years when the Florentine Republic fell and the French lost their hold over northern Italy. More than any other humanist of his time, Guicciardini in his *Ricordi* questioned whether the models of classical antiquity could function as reliable guides to action in the present. Yet Guicciardini believed, as did a number of humanists of his generation and class, that he could offer practical advice drawn from his own personal experience. Guicciardini's early *Ricordi* grew out of a desire to offer advice on the basis of flexible rules he derived in part from his personal experience as ambassador to Spain. Moreover, Guicciardini's memory of his experience as an ambassador to Spain became more and more crucial to him as he reworked his *Ricordi* later in life and increasingly reflected, in proverbial form and sometimes with real pathos, on diplomacy in general. In the very earliest ricordi, for example, Guicciardini shared an optimistic, humanist faith in Quintilian's vision of the orator, and hence the ambassador, as a good man who speaks well. Yet as Guicciardini learned that he was not trusted with information by the Florentine government while working in Spain, and as he became more and more disillusioned in his marginalized status as a representative of a beleaguered republic at King Ferdinand's dazzling, powerful court, his vision changed dramatically, becoming more pessimistic and tragic. By the time he composed his final versions of the *Ricordi,* the ambassador, far from being a diplomat "in the know," appears as an actor who may be conscious at all moments that he is acting and that his performance is what matters most, but he is also tragically aware that he is, in truth, a performer operating in the dark. Thus, as Guicciardini reflected on his work as an ambassador, he did not become more skeptical as to whether he could derive lessons from it. Rather, he continued to do just that. However, those lessons became more skeptical in nature as he came to understand that ambassadors could never be sure why they had even been sent on their diplomatic missions in the first place.

In the final section, on "Secretaries," the sixth chapter, "Open Secrets: The Place of the Renaissance Secretary," addresses in general the subordinate status of secretaries in Renaissance Italy and the strategies of secrecy and silence they employed. It was in large measure by being secretive and silent, and by knowing how to persuade through secrecy and silence, that the Renaissance secretary not only proved his worth to his master but acquired a secure place in that master's cabinet. Thus, throughout the Renaissance, and particularly in the many treatises written by Italians from the mid-sixteenth to the early seventeenth century, the typical secretary was portrayed not only as a humanist who could write polished letters, but as a deferential, tight-lipped servant. Strangely enough, in the sixteenth and early seventeenth centuries, a few writers envisioned Machiavelli as just such an exemplary secretary worthy of imitation. For them, *The Prince* was the product of a man not only versed in the *studia humanitatis,* but trained as a secretary. Machiavelli did, in fact, write about secretaries in chapter 22 of *The Prince,* and in that work he also elaborated on thoughts formulated earlier in his secretarial letters and reports sent back to the Chancery. However, though he was influenced by his work as a secretary when he wrote *The Prince,* and though he even dedicated a small portion of it to a discussion of the secretaries the prince had to choose, Machiavelli the author of *The Prince* is hardly the exemplary secretary that some later made him out to be, nor does he resemble the kind of secretary described in chapter 22 of his own text. Far from behaving with the reticence expected of secretaries, the Machiavelli who writes *The Prince* is deliberately assertive in his work and does what no good humanist secretary was ever supposed to do: he discloses secrets. In this respect, the Machiavelli who wrote *The Prince* was very much the exception to the rule regarding how a secretary, understood as the "keeper of secrets," was expected to behave during the Italian Renaissance.

The final chapter, "The Secretarial Profession among Others: Tasso's Enabling Analogies," primarily explores the tension between the past and the present in the formation of the profession of secretary in late Renaissance Italy. My focus is on Torquato Tasso's compact and influential treatise on secretarial work, *Del secretario.* At the outset, like many humanists, Tasso turns to the classical past for models for the secretary. In particular, he holds up Cicero's *De oratore* and *Orator* as models for writing about the profession of secretary. Yet Tasso abandons these models, finding it difficult, if not impossible, to join the two separate rhetorical strategies underlying Cicero's treatises in his own. Moreover, like many humanists writing on secretaries, Tasso holds up Cicero, and in particular the Cicero who wrote letters, as the authoritative model for the secretary's writing. Every secretary, we are given to understand early on in the treatise, should imitate Cicero and keep volumes of his letters close at hand. However, Tasso has problems with his own advice, since for him classical Rome in no way resembles late-sixteenth-century Italy, and the liberty-loving letter-writer of Cicero's republic is not at all like the slavish, self-effacing letter-writer of the princedoms in which Tasso lived. The world for Tasso has changed so dramatically that any analogy constructed between the past and the present was always going to be flawed in some way. Yet for Tasso, even if the secretary lacks a secure classical precedent, his authority remains great, not only because he knows how to imitate Cicero, as every humanist should, but because he knows how to be silent and slavishly self-effacing in the increasingly centralized bureaucracies of late Renaissance Italy.

Though the writers treated in this book clearly differed in many ways, they shared a number of interests typical of humanists, and they collectively brought these interests to bear on their writings as professionals or about professions. Throughout the Renaissance, humanists tended to make their reflections on almost any given topic an occasion for self-reflection and even self-promotion. Not surprisingly, a number of humanists in this book, though certainly not all, were actually fashioning themselves in the very moment that they wrote. Petrarch wrote about his own poetic achievements in his coronation oration, and he envisioned himself in it as a romance hero buffeted by Fortune and driven by his love for the laurel, the very laurel that symbolically embodied not only the fame Petrarch sought in his quest for poetic glory but the name of his beloved. Writing about himself in a different way, Ficino in his treatise on the plague transformed the gay and ironic Socrates into a more sober and melancholic version of himself. In his poem on syphilis Fracastoro viewed himself as an epic hero curing others of a deadly disease, and he named himself as one of the great innovative physicians of all time in his treatise on contagion. Barbaro overtly fashioned a flattering portrait of himself in his treatise on ambassadorial work, while Maggi created a less conspicuous parallel between Odysseus as an informed, worldly traveler and himself as a mid-level diplomat following his patrons about Europe on their various ambassadorial missions. In his *Ricordi,* Guicciardini subtly distinguished his work as a wise diplomat from that of the bungling Florentine politicians, who nevertheless had the good sense to elect him to be their representative to King Ferdinand in Spain. Finally, Machiavelli inscribed himself into his treatise on princes as a "quondam segretario," drawing on things learned as secretary to the Second Chancery, and he no doubt hoped that some prince might one day appoint him as one of the very "a secretis" [secretaries] defined in chapter 22 of *The Prince.*

Throughout the Renaissance, humanists typically called attention to classical culture and often vied with it in their writings. This too is a characteristic feature of a number of the figures discussed in this book. Petrarch, for instance, did so, but he was deeply conflicted about the ancient world and its value: he cited only pagan sources in his coronation oration, yet he modeled it on the medieval sermon; he revived the ancient custom of crowning the poet laureate in what he perceived to be a period of cultural decline, yet he also aimed to humble Roman culture by delivering his coronation oration at the Capitoline precisely on Easter Sunday. Ficino was less ambivalent about the value of classical culture when he wrote his treatise on the plague: he clearly had Plato's texts in mind when he wrote his *Consilio,* and he eschewed any sort of humanist rivalry with pagan culture. By contrast, Fracastoro hoped he might surpass the ancients and win fame for himself in his treatise on contagion, and he selectively imitated Virgil's *Aeneid* and Lucretius's *De rerum natura* in *Syphilis,* his medical poem. Barbaro in his treatise on ambassadors implicitly pits Venice against classical Rome: Venice had evolved a form of government superior to any in classical antiquity; for Barbaro Venice was, teleologically speaking, what Rome would be in its perfected form. Maggi in his treatise on ambassadors imitated Plato and Xenophon and Cicero, yet he also imagined that he had surpassed the ancients by touching on matters never discussed by them. Guicciardini invoked Quintilian's definition of the orator as the good man who speaks well when, as an ambassador, he wrote the first version of his *Ricordi,* but he eventually came to believe, in later versions of the *Ricordi,* that the lessons of antiquity could not become durable rules for surviving in a world governed by the whims of Fortune. Machiavelli also drew parallels between the present and the past in *The Prince,* but not when he spoke about secretaries, perhaps because secretaries, as Machiavelli and other humanists conceived of them in the Renaissance, had not existed in antiquity. Finally, in his *Del secretario,* Tasso expressed the profoundly historicized view that the secretarial profession was a new one created for and in a new period, and he argued as well that there was no single classical text that could define the profession in a fully satisfactory way or provide completely reliable models for the letter-writing work of secretaries.

Most of the writers discussed in this book relied, as humanists throughout the Renaissance tended to do, on exemplarity as the means both to edify and to persuade others. Petrarch, newly crowned poet laureate in Rome, urged others to follow his example and scale Mount Parnassus; by doing so he hoped to forge a new and more elevated identity for poets in his own time. Ficino looked to Socrates as an exemplary model to teach people how to survive the plague, yet by transforming Socrates into a version of himself, Ficino was also inviting people to behave like him. Barbaro stressed in his treatise that examples teach far better than precepts, and he repeatedly held up himself and his father as models of proper diplomatic behavior. Maggi located the exemplary ambassador in his Venetian patrons and singled out Odysseus, a sly version of himself, as a model worthy of imitation. Guicciardini in his *Ricordi* undercut the humanist faith in exemplarity yet recognized that examples were still needed as guides to diplomatic behavior. Finally, Tasso pinpointed his father as the one modern secretary worthy of being set alongside the great ones of antiquity, and he repeatedly referred to, while subtly undermining, the figure of Cicero as the humanist secretary's supreme model for letter-writing. The writers discussed here, then, like countless humanists in the Renaissance, were deeply engaged in the professions they wrote about or exercised, and like those humanists they fashioned versions of themselves in their writings, established or undermined comparisons between the present and a revered classical past, and constructed compelling examples of comportment not only for those living in the present, but for those who would one day come after them.

There is one final, important element that binds together many of the authors discussed in this book, and that is their collective investment in the literary. As it focuses on the dialectical interplay of professions and humanism in Renaissance Italy, this book underscores the fundamentally literary dimension of a number of texts singled out for study, primarily by analyzing them in terms of the different authors' rich manipulations of genre. Thus, Petrarch in his coronation oration structures his quest for the laurel crown through the genre of romance. He arguably does this so that poets, in exercising their profession, can be seen to operate—as wandering romance heroes tend to operate—outside of conventional, traditionally organized social frameworks. In Petrarch's vision, poets, moved by their own personal desire as they exercise their profession, will continually prove themselves in the world as they aspire, like romance heroes, to ever greater heights of fame and glory. They will thus make their *otium,* their private though still productive play with language, their *negotium,* their life's endless labor accomplished for the public good, despite all the obstacles that Fortune has placed in their path. Boccaccio, perfecting the novella form in his *Decameron,* emerges as the master storyteller who self-consciously co-opts the professional physician's capacity to heal by putting into practice, in a manner that physicians never effectively could, the prevailing medical wisdom that one should combat the plague by telling delightful stories. Fracastoro is equally committed to the literary: he employs a poetics of scientific wonder in a didactic epic poem on syphilis, a new and wondrous disease for which he recounts a pastoral myth about an irreverent shepherd who scorns the ancient pagan gods. Like Fracastoro, Maggi is drawn to the literary: he urges ambassadors to read Homer carefully, and he positions himself through his identification with Odysseus as a romance-epic hero who has acquired prudence through his extensive travels. By contrast, Guicciardini imagines his unhappy lot as a marginalized ambassador in terms of the genre of tragedy; he arguably uses tragedy not only to sometimes distance himself from but also to shape with real pathos his plight as the often uninformed representative of an indecisive Italian republic at the court of a powerful king, a king who had mastered the art of dissimulation and European diplomacy. Finally, Tasso describes the secretary in a way that strikingly resembles his characterization of the epic poet in both the proem to his *Gerusalemme liberata* and his two discourses on the art of poetry.

The writers in this study, then, codify, appropriate, and transform the professions they embrace not only by approaching those professions as humanists, but also by looking at those professions, both directly and indirectly, from the vantage point of literature. In keeping with this predilection, this book therefore opens with Petrarch, who in his oration not only provides an image of himself as a poet worthy of the laurel crown, but introduces the work of the poet as an activity that at once claims and denies a certain professional status for itself. The work of the poet is an activity that is thoroughly engaged with the world, boasts a venerable history and the solid support of a learned king, and has its own distinct jurisdictional claim and cultural authority, yet it presents itself as standing outside and above a host of other institutionalized professional activities because of its unique indebtedness to discursive play, the kind of play typically associated with, and structurally embodied in, romance. This book then closes with Tasso's Platonized image of himself as the poet who, while occupying an established profession at the court in Ferrara, claims knowledge of all the other professions described in his epic poem, including, though certainly not limited to, the three examined in the chapters that follow: the doctor, the ambassador, and the secretary.

One

PETRARCH'S PROFESSION AND HIS LAUREL

Along with the right to perform the work as it wishes, a profession normally also claims rights to exclude other workers as deemed necessary, to dominate public definitions of the tasks concerned, and indeed to impose professional definitions of the tasks on competing professions. Public jurisdiction, in short, is a claim of both social and cultural authority.

—ANDREW ABBOTT

The Coronation Oration: Romancing a Profession

The day is April 8, 1341, the place Rome. Petrarch delivers his coronation oration to "a large multitude and with great joy" (*Fam.* 4.8; 196) in the halls of the Senatorial Palace on the Capitoline.[1] It was a ceremony that he had carefully constructed. His speech is titled after the medieval sermon type called the "Collatio," which normally consisted of a public reading and interpretation of the sacred scriptures among monks, and it

1. The epigraph that heads this chapter is from Abbott, *The System of Professions,* 60. The best study of the oration, to which I am indebted, remains Wilkins, "Coronation of Petrarch," in *Making of the "Canzoniere,"* 9–69. I draw from Petrarch, *Le familiari, I–XXIV,* with translations, only slightly modified on occasion, from Petrarch, *Letters on Familiar Matters;* references in my text are to book, letter, and page number in the English translation. All references to the original Latin version of the coronation oration are provided in my text, and they are taken from Petrarch, *Opere latine,* 1256–83; but see also Godi, "La 'Collatio laureationis' del Petrarca." The translation of the coronation oration is from Wilkins, "Petrarch's Coronation Oration," in *Making of the "Canzoniere,"* 300–313. For the *Privilegium* and *Seniles,* I have used *Librorum Francisci Petrarche impressorum annotatio.* On the coronation oration, see also Trapp, *"The Poet Laureate,"* 95–105; Calcaterra, "L'incoronazione," in *Nella selva del Petrarca,* 109–18; and Gensini, " 'Poeta et historicus.' " My thanks to Marcello Simonetta for bringing Gensini's article to my attention.

begins with a quote he then proceeds to explicate in the light of other writings, point by point. But Petrarch does not choose a verse from Holy Scripture; nor does he refer to sacred writings in the compilation of quotes that occupy about a quarter of his text. With the exception of himself, Petrarch scarcely mentions or cites from any Christian writer, and the verse he begins with, the verse that runs as the main thread throughout the speech, is drawn from the third book of Virgil's *Georgics*. He takes his cue from a didactic pagan text about farming and from a book within it that teaches how to work livestock. Why the *Georgics*? And why on this "festive day" (3.2; 302) choose a verse from a book that ends with a plague that lays waste the land? After all, Petrarch is ostensibly celebrating with his oration an ascent to Parnassus, not a descent into death, despite all the inherent difficulties he claims he faces in making this voyage for both himself and the community:

> "Do you not see what a task you have undertaken in attempting to attain the lonely steeps of Parnassus and the inaccessible grove of the Muses?" Yes, I do see, oh my dear sirs; I do indeed see this, oh Roman citizens, "Sed me Parnasi deserta per ardua dulcis / raptat amor" [But a sweet longing urges me upward over the lonely slopes of Parnassus] as I said at the outset. (5.5–6; 304)

Ascents according to Petrarch often require descents at the same time.[2] This concept has roots in antiquity but was traditionally linked in the Middle Ages to Christ's descent into humility, beginning with His death and harrowing of hell as preparation for His ascent to the throne of heaven. This concept of simultaneous descent and ascent was certainly familiar to Dante, who used it as a master narrative in the *Commedia*. There Dante's wayfarer progresses toward heaven as the way down through hell becomes part of a continuous yet circuitous upward voyage to God. As the pilgrim spirals through the three realms of the otherworld, his journey corresponds in allegory to Christ's harrowing of hell, resurrection, and enthronement.[3] This same Christianized concept of ascent and descent underpins Petrarch's coronation oration. Petrarch has chosen to celebrate his crowning precisely on Easter Sunday, the day on which Christ rose from his tomb and ascended victorious after his descent into hell, as well

2. This concept was voiced in Petrarch's letters, such as *Fam.* 1.6, 36: "The higher a wayfarer ascends, the closer he comes to his descent. To put it differently, by ascending he in a certain way descends [*quodammodo ascendendo descendit*]. The same thing is happening to me." The concept also underpins *Fam.* 4.1, the so-called letter about the "Ascent of Mont Ventoux."

3. On this, see Freccero, "Pilgrim in a Gyre," in *Dante: The Poetics of Conversion,* 70–92.

as the day on which Dante's pilgrim, after having entered the inferno on good Friday, emerges to ascend to a Christianized Parnassus on top of Mount Purgatory, where he is crowned and mitered. However, unlike Dante, Petrarch has not journeyed through hell and purgatory with Virgil as his guide. He has entered, after admittedly a tiresome trip, ancient fallen Rome, where Virgil, "the very father of poets" (3.3; 302), once lived and wrote. Now Virgil's symbolic son—not Dante but Petrarch—has come to receive his laurel crown. And this crown, far from being one goal among many, is *the* final goal for Petrarch. Rather than being otherworldly and reaching toward God, Petrarch's ascent is terrestrial, and it aims to stop at the pinnacle of Parnassus. If Petrarch has been reborn on Easter day, he has been putatively reborn within a narrative structure far different from the comic and eschatological one within which Dante had placed his wayfarer.

As Petrarch begins his ascent toward Parnassus to become the laureate poet, he symbolically descends as well. The age in which he lives is old, he observes, so old that it has forgotten the virtues of its former glory and customs for "more than twelve hundred years" (6.1; 304). Even the Capitoline, which marks the center of Rome, is "decaying" (*Fam.* 4.7, 193), Petrarch tells King Robert in a letter that describes his crowning. Like the romance hero who must set out on a quest to regenerate the senescent land typically stricken by a plague, Petrarch, notwithstanding his detractors, has chosen to come to the center of the decadence of his own age—Rome—and revitalize his country by renewing an ancient custom in a time of decline: "I am moved also by the hope that, if God wills, I may renew in the now aged Republic a beauteous custom of its flourishing youth" (6.2; 304). So too, like the typical romance hero, who functions first as an individual inspired by love and then as an agent of the community, Petrarch has set out on a quest, driven by "amor" [love]. He quests for a prize that will confer on him great "personal glory" (5.7, 10.2; 304, 307) and will thereby allow him to bring to life a dead culture. Descending to ascend, Petrarch will win fame for himself and renew Rome and Roman culture as he renews their ancient custom, rejuvenating both so that they may come to life once again. In doing so, Petrarch claims he will lead men and women, who have grown weary in a time of decline, toward Parnassus along an arduous yet uplifting path:

> I will say only this: while there are some who think it shameful to follow in the footsteps of others, there are far more who fear to essay a hard road unless they have a sure guide. Many such men I have known, especially in Italy:

> learned and gifted men, devoted to the same studies, thirsting with the same desires, who as yet—whether from a sense of shame, or from sluggishness, or from diffidence, or, as I prefer to think, from modesty and humility—have not entered upon this road. Boldly, therefore, perhaps, but—to the best of my belief—with no unworthy intention, since others are holding back I am venturing to offer myself as guide for this toilsome and dangerous path; and I trust that there may be many followers [*me in tam laborioso et michi quidem periculoso calle ducem prebere non expavi, multos posthac, ut arbitror, secuturos*]. (8.1–2; 306)

Like romance heroes who must face trials and tribulations so that others may one day follow and attain personal goals of great social value, Petrarch has been tried and tested to the full in his adventures (or so he claims in his oration): "How hard and inexorable fortune has been to me, with what labors she has oppressed me from my youth up, how many blows I have endured from her" (3.1; 302). Buffeted by fortune, Petrarch seeks to achieve the impossible: "Everyone, to be sure, who has made trial of the poetic task knows what impediments are placed in his way by the bitterness of fortune" (3.3; 302). For this reason, Petrarch has chosen to cite from the *Georgics* and from a book that ends with the plague. If Orpheus's loss underpins the disease in the fourth book, Petrarch, descending to ascend Parnassus, has come to Rome to recall his own homeland, now reduced to a senescent wasteland, from the depths of its own massive cultural loss. Like the death-defying Orpheus, who embodies so many qualities that Northrop Frye associates with romance,[4] Petrarch speaks in his oration to a forgetful, decaying world, but he also aims to revitalize an entire culture through his work as a "divinely inspired" poet (2.7; 301). Without the inspired poet there would be no possibility of regeneration for all those who toil in the world. The occupation of others thus indirectly depends on the revivifying Orphic song of the poet whose profession Petrarch here hails. So Petrarch feigns that a concerned friend might well ask him: "What is all this, my friend? Have you determined to revive [*renovare*] a custom that is beset with inherent difficulty and has long since fallen into desuetude? and this in the face of a hostile and recalcitrant fortune?" (5.2–3; 304). This is Petrarch's romance quest and "labor." His struggle with Fortune, which has brought him to wander about in his "amor" for the sake of studying and in his effort to

4. Frye, *Secular Scripture,* 97–157, in which chaps. 4 and 5, on descent and ascent, would be particularly relevant here.

avoid the "impediments placed in his way" (3.3; 302), has finally led him, after so many adventures, back home.

By opening his oration with the *Georgics* as the work most dedicated to "labor" (2.11; 302), Petrarch thus aims to validate within the quest-structure of romance the "profession of the poet" as a heroic form of work worthy of award and respect in a time of cultural decline. However, though Petrarch may have explained the need for the poet in society in the first half of his oration, he does not explain the true "nature of the profession of the poet" (9.2; 306) until the middle; and then, when he does, Petrarch is brief, though characteristically ambiguous. At the thematic and structural center of his oration, before closing with his discussion of the virtues of the laurel as the appropriate prize for his work in "the office and the profession of the poet" (9.4; 306), Petrarch writes:

> It would take me too long to discourse upon this theme; but if time were not lacking and I did not fear to weary you I could readily prove to you that poets under the veil of fictions have set forth truths physical, moral, and historical—thus bearing out a statement I often make, that the difference between a poet on the one hand and a historian or a moral or physical philosopher on the other is the same as the difference between a clouded sky and a clear sky, since in each case the same light exists in the object of vision, but is perceived in different degrees according to the capacity of the observers. Poetry, furthermore, is all the sweeter since a truth that must be sought out with some care gives all the more delight when it is discovered. Let this suffice as a statement not so much about myself as about the poetic profession, for while poets are wont to find pleasure in a certain playfulness, I should not wish to appear to be a poet and nothing more [*hoc non tam de me ipso, quam de poetice professionis effectu dixisse satis sit, neque enim, quamvis poetarum more ludere delectet, sic poeta videri velim, ut non sim aliud quam poeta*]. (9.6–8; 307)

The profession of the poet, it would seem, has it both ways. On the one hand, Petrarch praises poetry in the face of the customary objection that it is a lie. Defending poetry, he relies on the justification, familiar in the Middle Ages and Renaissance, that allegorical readings disclose deep hidden truths encoded in works of fiction. On the other hand, Petrarch proceeds to confirm the impression that poetry consists of merely gaming with words—a position embedded in the very structure of romance[5]—

5. The seminal study on this is Parker, *Inescapable Romance.*

when he renders the activity of the poet playful too ("ludere delectet," 9.8). Given that Petrarch begins the oration by informing his audience that he will speak in "the manner of poets" (1.1; 300) and then proceeds to insist that "the manner of poets" (9.8) is to play, we may infer that to "play" (9.8) with "subtle figures" [obliquis figurationibus, 9.4; 306] constitutes the manner of all poets at all times, including Petrarch in his oration. His collatio, after all, is a poetic one, as he announces from the outset: "Today, magnificent and venerable sirs, I must follow in my speech the ways of poetry, and I have therefore taken my text from a poetic source. For the same reason I shall do without those minute distinctions that are usually to be found in theological declamations" (1.1; 300).

In titling his oration a collatio, Petrarch calls attention to the fact that he adopted a loose oratorical form. In keeping with the notion that it was closely connected to communal monastic life, the collatio was conceptualized as a sort of conversation. As we read in the commentary to the famous *Collationes* of John Cassian (A.D. 360–435), the first abbot and founder of the abbey of Saint-Victor at Marseille, "Collationes are so called from talking about things [*conferendo*], as everyone knows."[6] The form of the collatio might seem improvisational, yet it was intellectually rigorous. Through conversation, *confabulatio,* it provided for a mode of inquiry where dark passages of scripture were placed under scrutiny and often enough examined in relation to one another. On occasion, a collatio could espouse the value of play in the context of higher religious concerns. Cassian, in the last of his twenty-four collationes, reminds us of the value of play when he tells the story, eventually repeated by many after him, of St. John's response to a follower:

> It is said that the blessed John the evangelist, while he was gently stroking a partridge with his hands suddenly saw a philosopher approaching him in the garb of a hunter, who was astonished that a man of so great fame and reputation should demean himself to such paltry and trivial amusements, and said: "Can you be that John, whose great and famous reputation attracted me

6. Cassian, *Opera omnia,* 477 n. a, from which I cite the following: "Collationes a conferendo dictas nemo nescit. Hinc Smaragdus abbas (*In cap.* 40 *Regulae D. Bened.*): Collatio, inquit, est confessio, collocutio et confabulatio, ubi de Scripturis divinis, aliis conferentibus interrogationes, conferunt alii congruas responsiones; et sic quae diu latuerant occulta, conferentibus fiunt perspicua. Isidorus lib. iii *de Summo Bono* (Cap. 15): Cum sit, inquit, utilis ad instruendum lectio, adhibita tamen collatione majorem intelligentiam, praebet. Melius est enim conferre, quam legere. Collatio autem docibilitatem facit. Nam propositis interrogationibus cunctatio rerum excluditur, et saepe objectionibus latens veritas approbatur. Quod enim obscurum, aut dubium est, conferendo cito perspicitur." See also the references under the lemma "collatio" in Du Cange, *Glossarium mediae,* ad loc.

also with the greatest desire for your acquaintance? Why then do you occupy yourself with such poor amusements?" To whom the blessed John: "What is it," he said, "that you are carrying in your hand?" The other replied: "a bow." "And why," said he, "do you not always carry it everywhere bent?" To whom the other replied: "It would not do, for the force of its stiffness would be relaxed by its being continually bent, and it would be lessened and destroyed, and when the time came for it to send stouter arrows after some beast, its stiffness would be lost by the excessive and continuous strain, and it would be impossible for the more powerful bolts to be shot." "And, my lad," said the blessed John, "do not let this slight and short relaxation of my mind disturb you, as unless, sometimes relieved and relaxed the rigor of its purpose by some recreation, the spirit would lose its spring owing to the unbroken strain, and would be unable, when need required, implicitly to follow what was right." (Coll. 24, chap. 21)[7]

As St. John informs his interlocutor, play as a form of relaxation was central to the well-being of humans, all of whom sometimes need to slacken their efforts in order to better return to more serious goals. Aristotle's term for play as temporary relaxation was *eutrapelia*. Glending Olson has traced the importance of this concept, which had a long history in classical culture, throughout the late Middle Ages, where it received extended treatment at the hands of Roger Bacon (ca. 1214–1294), St. Thomas Aquinas (1224/25–1274), and Nicole Oresme (ca. 1325–1382), among others.[8] However, while it might be advocated within a collatio such as Cassian's, play was not appropriate to the form of the collatio itself, however conversational in tone the collatio might appear to be. The form itself was lax but certainly not playful.

Although medieval writers valued play as relief for the tired mind, body, and spirit, they did not advocate play, so conceived as the relaxation of the mind, as a goal itself. Such a notion went against not only Aristotle's original concept of *eutrapelia* but every subsequent concept of play that was indebted to it. As Olson succinctly asserts in his study of the concept of *eutrapelia* in the Middle Ages, "the moral problem is to give play its due without turning it into an end itself."[9] Hence Aquinas, in referring back to Cassian, rightly subordinated play to the felicity of contemplation: "The activity of playing looked at specifically in itself is not ordained to a

7. Cassian, *Opera omnia,* 1313–15; translation from Cassian, *Select Library of Nicene and Post-Nicene Fathers,* 540–41. See the discussion of Olson, *Literature as Recreation,* 91–92, who cites Cassian.

8. Olson, *Literature as Recreation,* 90–127 in general.

9. Ibid., 99.

further end, yet the pleasure we take therein serves as recreation and rest for the soul, and accordingly when this be well-tempered, application to play is lawful" (IIa–IIae, q. 168, art. 2.3).[10] God, as creator, might "play" as a "theologia ludens,"[11] but humans, with their unquiet hearts, may only play to revive their spirits as pilgrims on their journey to God,[12] as they travel from the region of unlikeness to likeness. For this reason, Petrarch, in his ascent of Mount Parnassus, carefully makes a point of declaring that play is only the poet's manner, and that to be a poet is in itself not enough.

It is one thing to acknowledge what Petrarch claims poets ought to do, though, and quite another to come to terms with what Petrarch actually does in a collatio that subtly draws on the quest-structure of romance. For in his collatio, which is composed by someone who claims that the profession of the poet is indeed his profession, Petrarch does more than exemplify play as a manner of speaking. At times he elevates play, in the sense of playing with possible imagined meanings, as an end. No sooner has Petrarch described the nature of the poet than he begins to discuss the various veiled meanings associated with the laurel branch as the appropriate reward for his labors in his oration. The fragrance of the laurel described by Virgil signifies for Petrarch "the good repute" (11.4; 309) and "glory" (11.5; 309) sought by poets through the medium of "spirit" (11.5; 309) rather than the "body" (11.5; 309). The shade of the laurel, described by Horace, symbolizes the repose poets garner from "labor in studying" (11.8; 310). The fabled incorruptibility of the laurel signifies the immortality achieved through fame and the preservation of the poets' work. And its sacredness, propitiousness as a provider of true dreams, longevity, and indestructibility further signify for Petrarch the reverence in which all men and women should hold poets, the truth contained in their writings, and the immortality they achieve. In his poetic oration, Petrarch thus not only acquires the laurel as the end of his labor by playing with figural language; he has transformed the laurel itself into the multifarious symbol of the professional poet's play with figures.

Rather than debasing poetry in his oration with so many fanciful readings of "subtle figures" (9.4; 306) encoded into the image of the laurel

10. Aquinas, *Summa Theologiae.* Olson (*Literature as Recreation,* 98) discusses this quote from Aquinas in detail.

11. See, for example, Giuseppe Mazzotta's rich discussion of this notion in Dante's poetry, which brings together theology and aesthetics in its treatment of play. Mazzotta, *Dante's Vision,* 219–41.

12. Olson, *Literature as Recreation,* 99, 101–2.

in pagan literature, however, Petrarch extolls play, both the writer's and the reader's, as a serious activity worthy of pursuit for one in his—the poet's—profession. Part of the renewal of poetic practice as defined in Petrarch's collatio, then, necessitates a renewal, and therefore a redefinition, of professionalism itself. For if to be a professional traditionally did not include the activity of discursive play and romance wandering, Petrarch makes every effort at elevating the profession of the poet and his or her serious gaming to the status normally accorded the priesthood. In title and form Petrarch strategically evokes the tradition of the collatio as a medieval sermon but then conspicuously—indeed playfully—departs from it. He cites, after all, not from Scripture as he goes about defining in so many oblique ways the value of the laurel, but from, as he prefers to call it, the "scripture" of the pagan poets (1.1; 300). By doing so, Petrarch both differentiates and renders equal in "social and cultural authority" his profession of the poet with the competing and established profession of the priesthood, a profession Petrarch eschewed throughout his lifetime, even though he did probably take minor ecclesiastical orders in order to receive benefices and to maintain his financial independence.[13]

It was not only the clerical profession that Petrarch largely rejected for himself. He repeatedly refused to identify the profession of the poet with any one discipline, and he purposely located the poet in solitary places, far from the cities and courts customarily associated with established professions. In a letter to his friend, the Florentine statesman, protohumanist, and papal secretary Francesco Bruni (ca. 1315–ca. 1385), with whom he often corresponded in his old age, Petrarch wrote:

> So that you may realize, my friend, how far I am in my opinion and in reality from this judgment of yours, I am not any of all the things you attribute to me. What then am I? A scholar? Not even that, but a backwoodsman, a hermit in the habit of mumbling something dull amidst the lofty beeches, and—the height of arrogance and rashness!—handling a frail pen beneath a laurel sprout, not as fruitful in results as fervent in labor, more in love with letters than rich in them. I am indifferent to sects, greedy for the truth. Since the search for it is arduous, I, a lowly and feeble seeker without self-confidence, often embrace doubt itself in place of truth to avoid becoming entangled in error. Thus, slowly I have become a squatter in the academy, one of many, and the latest in the humble throng, granting myself nothing,

13. See the seminal study by Dionisotti, "Chierici e laici," in *Geografia e storia,* above all 61; and Wilkins, "Petrarch's Ecclesiastical Career," in *Studies in the Life and Work of Petrarch,* 3–32. As Trinkaus (*In Our Image and Likeness,* 2.661–62) succinctly puts it, Petrarch "could well be religious without being a religious."

> affirming nothing, doubting all but what I consider a sacrilege to doubt. Here, then, is your Hippias [Greek Sophist, ca. 460–375 B.C.E., appearing in various Platonic dialogues, two bearing his name], who once dared to profess all things in philosophical circles; with you he professes nothing beyond the anxious search for truth, nothing beyond doubt and ignorance.[14] (*Sen.* 1.6, 27–28)

To play, wander, err, descend and ascend at the same time, professional poets need solitude. They need not just a conceptual space but a physical one, a room of their own. For within the physical space of solitude provided by such retreats as Vaucluse, which in turn becomes for Petrarch a psychological space of doubt and ignorance in the search for truth, the poet playfully exercises his or her profession. And Petrarch's labors as a poet—always present in the image of the laurel that in his oration symbolized through "subtle figures" (9.4; 306) the rewards of his profession—would be with him to his dying days. Not by chance, Petrarch entered Rome for his crowning on the anniversary of his meeting with Laura,[15] whose name embodies not just the rewards Petrarch seeks as he exercises his profession as a poet, but the conflicts he feels within himself as he ascends, albeit descending, in his romance-quest to reach the heights of Mount Parnassus.

Petrarch's Professionless Profession

Not long after being crowned, Petrarch began to reflect on his coronation. He soon wrote back to King Robert, who had tested him and found him worthy of the prize, that he had been the first to receive the laurel in his age. "This custom of the laurel crown," Petrarch wrote,

> which has not only been interrupted for so many centuries, but here actually condemned to oblivion as the variety of cares and problems grew in the republic, has been renewed in our age through your leadership and my involvement. I know many other outstanding talents throughout Italy and in foreign countries which nothing would have kept from this goal except for its long disuse and the ever suspect novelty of the affair. After my personal experience with it I am confident that the novelty will wear off in a short time and the Roman laurel will be vied for through competition. For who could seriously hesitate when King Robert is one of the patrons? It will be

14. Petrarch, *Letters of Old Age*. Page references in my text are to the English translation.
15. Wilkins, "Coronation of Petrarch," 61.

of help to have been first [*primum*] in this competition in which I do not consider it to be inglorious even to be the last. (*Fam.* 4.7, 193)

Technically speaking, Petrarch had not been the first to receive the laurel. Others, such as the Paduan historian, politician, and playwright Albertino Mussato (1261–1329), had been crowned, and Petrarch knew this when he composed his *Privilegium laureae,* his diploma, which accompanied the oration and presented him as the first to resuscitate the ancient Roman tradition.[16] The *Privilegium,* which "was obviously a classicizing adaptation of the medieval academic graduating ceremony," as Wilkins observed, conferred on Petrarch a diploma; the title of Master; the authority to practice his rare "profession" in all places and at all times, to crown other poets, and to read, dispute, and interpret ancient letters; and "the right to enjoy those 'privilegia immunitates honores et insignia' commonly enjoyed by professors [*professores*] of liberal and honorable arts."[17] Yet in his *Privilegium,* as in his letter to King Robert, Petrarch felt it important to imagine that he was the first to receive the laurel, especially after having been tried and tested to the full by a wise and worthy king. He needed this illusion. It was one more feature of the romance mode through which Petrarch viewed his crowning, not only directly after his coronation but throughout his life. Even in his unfinished letter to posterity, Petrarch described in romance fashion how the two letters inviting him to be crowned at Paris and Rome miraculously arrived—"mirabile dictu" [wondrous to say, *Sen.* 18.1]—on the very same day (see also *Fam.* 4.4, 188: "Because the affair does indeed seem almost incredible [*incredibilis*]").

At various points in his life, in both proud moments of self-glorification and introspective, confessional moments of self-reproach, Petrarch viewed his coronation through the structure of romance: he recalled at moments

16. Mussato's crowning took place in Padua in 1315.

17. Wilkins, "Coronation of Petrarch," 65. On the *Privilegium,* see also Gensini, " 'Poeta et historicus,' " 178–79, 191; Calcaterra, "L'incoronazione," 113. The *Privilegium* refers not only to the "poete officium" (twice) but also to the poetic profession as one that is exceedingly rare, valuable, and worthy of award: "hisdem privilegiis imunitatibus honoribus et insignibus perfrui debere quibus hic vel usque terrarum uti possunt vel posse sunt soliti liberalium et honestarum artium professores eo que magis quod professionis sue caritas ['raritas' in Basel, 1554] uberioribus eius favoribus et ampliori beneficio dignum facit." As a number of scholars point out, the *Privilegium* conferred on Petrarch not only the title of poet but also that of historian, though it still seems weighted (it strikes me) in favor of the former: "Quondam in nostra republica historici ac precipue poete maxime viguerunt." All citations in my text from the *Privilegium* are taken from Petrarch, *Librorum Francisci Petrarche,* [24 v] v, though I have emended slightly according to Petrarch, *Opera omnia,* 3.1254–56.

how young and inexperienced he had been; how much he had wandered about before he could ever reach his goal; how he had been tested by the wisest of all kings; how he was driven by love in his lonely quest; how the laurel bestowed on him great personal glory; how he was alone in his endeavor; how his choice of Rome constituted a homecoming; how courageous he had been in accomplishing this feat and how much he labored both before and after he received the laurel; and, of course, how his crowning constituted a form of cultural renewal in a time of decline. This last point was reiterated forcefully in the *Privilegium,* which echoes the language of the oration and was surely composed in part by Petrarch. "This poetic honor," the senator Orso dell'Anguillara would have declared, "certainly in our age (and not without pain we say), we see has fallen into oblivion [*oblitum*] up until now, and I am not sure whether it is because of the dullness of the talents or the ill-will of the times [*sue ingeniorum tarditate seu temporum malitia*]. . . . Clearly, however, we have heard that excellent poets are crowned on the Capitoline as if they were triumphators. That ritual has fallen into such disuse in our age that, over the last 1,300 years, right on up to now, one does not read of someone receiving such an honor. Thinking about this the most excellent man and most ardent examiner of such studies since his boyhood, Franciscus Petrarcha. . . ."

In his *Privilegium,* as in his oration, however, Petrarch did not believe, despite claiming to be the "first" [primum], that he was fashioning the identity of a poet independent of practical professional life. Instead Petrarch fashioned his identity in his speech and diploma over and against contemporary professional ceremonies and institutionalized practices, borrowing from both in the very moment that he revised and reinvented them. Not surprisingly, in the process Petrarch chose to define his profession as poet against two dominant institutions that often determined professionalism in the early Renaissance: the church and the university. After all, Petrarch chose to have the "typical medieval graduating ceremony" of his coronation take place not at the University of Paris, which had offered him the honor of receiving the laurel, but at the Capitoline in Rome, on the exact spot, Petrarch believed, where Cicero—who is repeatedly cited in his oration—had publicly spoken to Caesar centuries before. In orchestrating this remarkable event and delivering for the occasion an innovative oration, Petrarch was not in any way being narrowly antiprofessional or anti-institutional.[18] Far from it,

18. Nor can Petrarch be deemed antiprofessional in the way Stanley Fish conceives of the term in present-day usage, as "basically an up-to-date twentieth-century form of the

throughout his life Petrarch actively interacted with professions, including the three professions discussed in this book, all of which Petrarch appropriated or made use of, in one form or another, in his poetry and prose.

For example, in a letter to Giovanni Dondi (ca. 1330–ca. 1390), an important physician and professor of medicine at Padua, Petrarch claims that his dear friend's concern for his ill health fills him with good humor. But in point of fact Petrarch does not joke, or rather, in "writing jokingly to a friend," he does not seek to elicit laughter from his interlocutor (*Sen.* 12.1, 438). Petrarch's jocularity constitutes a *ludus* in the classical sense of a contest. It is humor with a barb, part of a skirmish between two disciplines, no more nor less than his earlier *Invective contra medicum,* a work that, as Eugenio Garin claims, grows out of the *disputa delle arti* of the times.[19] "My controversy with doctors," Petrarch wrote in another instance, "is indeed great" (*Fam.* 15.6, 264). For Petrarch, physicians transformed the "silent arts" of medicine, as Virgil had characterized it (*Aen.* 12.397), into a vociferous form of scholastic disputation. In exercising their profession, doctors feigned to know everything except the one thing they professed to know (*Sen.* 5.4), precisely in the moment that they tried to demonstrate their eloquence by spouting out phrases from Aristotle, Cicero, Seneca, and Virgil. It was bad enough that one often had to die in physical pain. It was particularly injurious to have to hear doctors talk at your bedside in the most inept and inelegant of ways. For Petrarch, doctors lacked eloquence; they quarreled incessantly about matters of little consequence; they used language in a painfully inarticulate manner, agitating the soul; and they lacked what they most needed in the context of a rhetoric of intervention: decorum.[20] By contrast,

---

traditional hostility to rhetoric" (Fish, *Doing What Comes Naturally,* 219). Petrarch, far from being antirhetorical, was rhetorical through and through, with Petrarchan rhetoric here understood in Nancy Struever's terms as an epistemological program that fostered debate and inquiry. According to Struever, Petrarch advocated a rhetoric that recognizes its own historical engagement; that does not mystify its procedures as pure but nonetheless takes seriously analytic and philosophical investigation; and that involves moral work and privileges variety and flexibility. See Struever, "Petrarchan Ethics: Inventing a Practice," in *Theory as Practice,* 3–56, and "Petrarch's *Invective contra medicum.*"

19. Garin, *La disputa delle arti,* xlv–lviii. See also Thorndike, "Medicine versus Law at Florence"; and in particular, McClure, *Sorrow and Consolation in Italian Humanism,* 50, and his fine "Healing Eloquence." See also the brief but cogent remarks of Kristeller, "Philosophy and Medicine in Medieval and Renaissance Italy."

20. Struever, "Petrarch's *Invective,*" passim. Petrarch's polemic with medicine is particularly well-studied. Along with the works cited, see the concise overview by Martinelli, "Il Petrarca e la medicina," 205–49. In addition to the *Invective,* see *Fam.* 5.19, 6.3, 12.5, 14.3, 15.5, 15.6, 21.10, 22.12, and *Sen.* 3.5, 3.8, 5.3, 5.4, 12.1, 12.2, 13.9, 15.14, and 16.3.

Petrarch believed that *his* words could have a salutary effect. As George McClure demonstrates, in a revival of the classical literature of sorrow and consolation, Petrarch sought to reconstitute the rhetor as a *medicus animorum* in opposition to physicians, who concerned themselves with the superfluities of the body rather than the transcendent realm of spirit.[21] In counseling one person after another in the art of dying as a solemn giving up of oneself to God, Petrarch saw his role as physician to the spirit. It was Petrarch who could recommend cures for the soul: "The famous physician being sent to you will accomplish, God willing, what I would like to do; I myself shall follow as soon as possible since you consider this too a likely remedy. In the meantime, I have decided to insert in this letter a unique cure I find popular with doctors—if you accept it in good faith, do not expect sounder advice from any Hippocrates! It is composed more or less of these ingredients. First of all, you must willingly entrust yourself and your concerns to divine judgment" (*Fam.* 9.1, 1–2).

Though Petrarch was never actually a physician, he did from time to time occupy the office of ambassador as part of his understood obligation to patrons;[22] from his private letters one can see how he calculatingly made use of his work in various diplomatic missions for his own rhetorical purposes. In one letter (*Fam.* 5.3), for example, amid his descriptions of the decadence of Naples after the demise of King Robert, Petrarch did not take the opportunity to describe the political makeup and power structures of the realm to which he has been sent by Pope Clement VI

21. McClure, *Sorrow and Consolation in Italian Humanism,* 18–72 in general.

22. Muscetta, "Crisi e sviluppi," 18, succinctly writes: "È chiaro che in questo rapporto di parità e di collaborazione c'era una contropartita. Essa non emerge da quelle pagine apologetiche ma certamente da tutto l'epistolario del poeta, che a Milano (come ad Avignone prima, e a Venezia dopo) assolse missioni ufficiali e talora importanti di ambasciatore." On Petrarch's political activities, see Dotti, *Vita di Petrarca,* in general the chapter "L'attività politica," 281–317, but more specifically on his ambassadorial work the sections "Missione a Venezia" (288–291) and "Missione a Praga" (313–17); and Wilkins, *Life of Petrarch,* 54, 62, 136–37, 152–53, 173–75. Needless to say, Petrarch never served as a resident ambassador, a position that was not created until the fifteenth century, but he did acknowledge that he functioned as an ambassador in diplomatic missions according to the then understood notion of ambassadorial work. Petrarch's term for this ambassadorial activity, as it would be throughout the Renaissance, was "legation." See, for example, *Fam.* 18.16, 70, where he acted "not as a simple participant in the distinguished legation [*preclare legationis*] but as its leader by special appointment"—*Fam.* 19.13, 103: "concerning his embassy [*legatione*] to Caesar." See as well *Fam.* 22.13, 240, and his summary of his missions in *Sen.* 17.2, 650: "Once I was sent to Venice to negotiate the reestablishment of peace between the city and Genoa, and I used up a whole month of the winter; later, in behalf of peace in Liguria, three months far away from civilization with the Roman prince [Charles IV], who was reviving, or to put it more correctly, abandoning the hopes of the—alas—collapsed empire. . . ."

and where he had once been tested as a young man worthy of the laurel crown.[23] All this important diplomatic information Petrarch has privately placed, as he indicates to Giovanni Colonna, in other letters: "And you will have to share some of the blame if from the information that I sent at some length in other more confidential letters you do not keep the Roman Pontiff better informed" (*Fam.* 5.3, 235).[24] Nor did Petrarch describe in this letter his diplomatic work in negotiating the release from prison of Colonna's three friends. Petrarch instead used the occasion afforded by his diplomatic journey to offer a series of satirical characterizations of the men who had seized power in Naples and to extract from the moment moral insights into life. At the end of his letter, which marks the climax, Petrarch writes:

> Perhaps three of four times I have visited the prison known as Camp Capua, where I saw your friends who have lost all hope except in you since the rightness of their cause which should have been their primary protection has thus far proven damaging to them. As everyone knows, it is most dangerous to try to uphold a just cause before an unjust judge. It might be added that there is no greater enemy for unfortunates than the man who haughtily enjoys the spoils of their belongings, since he naturally would like to remove those who may find occasion to demand the return of what is rightfully theirs. Thus, cruelty always follows upon avarice, and it might also be noted that when there is a pirating of one's inheritance there is always the potential danger of loss of life. It is certainly a difficult lot of man not to be able either to be poor in safety or to regain his riches! If ever this happened to anyone it is now happening to your friends, for as captives there is no one who has not had some portion of their personal belongings plundered. How could such grasping plunderers possibly be concerned about the liberty or safety of someone who seems to be closely connected with their own poverty? Therefore they would have been safer had they possessed nothing. But the situation is such that they made bitter enemies with serious harm to themselves. I saw them in fetters; oh shameful sight! oh unstable and onrushing wheel of Fortune! However, just as there is nothing more ugly than that kind of captivity, in the same manner

23. On this mission, in which Petrarch was "sent to Naples with a letter from the Pope urging the release of the three prisoners [from the family of the Papini]," see "Mission to Naples," in Wilkins, *Life of Petrarch,* 39–44. The mission proved unsuccessful. See also *Fam.* 5.4, 238; 5.6, 249; *Sen.* 10.2, 368.

24. As Witt remarks: "Although he attempted to apply his familiar style to oratory . . . he took no risk with official or business letters. Correspondence between princes and city-states, which offered a wide field for displaying one's eloquence, remained largely untouched by the new style. Petrarch himself occasionally demonstrated his ability to compose in the medieval style when called upon to write a public letter on behalf of a government" (Witt, "Medieval *Ars Dictaminis,*" 32).

there is nothing more elevated than the minds of the prisoners. (*Fam.* 5.3, 236)

Petrarch's diplomatic work here functions in the service of ethical inquiry, self-reflection, and a deeper understanding of humankind in the face of great personal trials and suffering. We know very little about Petrarch's work in negotiating the release of these three prisoners. We do, however, know a great deal about Petrarch's moral concerns, as he abstracts the plight of the prisoners to arrive at more general observations regarding the transitory nature of Fortune, human suffering, and the inherent pettiness and dignity of humankind in an often unjust world.

By contrast, Petrarch, preferring to remain a "private man,"[25] repeatedly rejected the office of the secretary offered to him by different popes on no less than four separate occasions,[26] and he attributed little value to the office when he merely mentioned it in passing in one of his lyric poems. In *Canzoniere* 168, a sonnet that details once again Petrarch's solitary pining away for Laura, the secretary is just a substitute, a stand-in for another whose words he simply transmits:

Amor mi manda quel dolce pensero
che secretario antico è fra noi due,
et mi conforta et dice che non fue
mai come or presto a quel ch'io bramo et spero.

Io, che talor menzogna et talor vero
ò ritrovato le parole sue,
non so s' il creda, et vivomi intra due:
né sì né no nel cor mi sona intero.

In questa passa 'l tempo, et ne lo specchio
mi veggio andar ver la stagion contraria
a sua impromessa et a la mia speranza.

Or sia che po: già sol io non invecchio,
già per etate il mio desir non varia,
ben temo il viver breve che n'avanza.[27]

25. Ibid., 31.

26. The offers came from Pope Clement VI in 1347 and 1351, and Pope Innocent VI in 1359 and 1361. See on this in particular Wilkins, *Studies in the Life and Works of Petrarch,* 16–17. On the importance of Petrarch's break with the *ars dictaminis,* see the fine study by Witt, "Medieval *Ars Dictaminis,*" 1–35. On Petrarch's refusal to be a secretary, see *Sen.* 1.2, 3, and 4, and especially on his refusal to adopt the chancery style, *Fam.* 13.5, 189–90.

27. Petrarch, *Petrarch's Lyric Poems.* The translation is only slightly modified.

[Love sends me that sweet thought which is an old secretary between us and comforts me and says that I was never so close as I am now to what I yearn and hope for.

I, who have found his words sometimes false and sometimes true, do not know whether to believe him, and I live between the two: neither yes nor no sounds whole in my heart.

In the meanwhile time passes, and in the mirror I see myself nearing the season that is contrary to his promise and to my hope.

Now come what will: I am not the only one who is growing old, and my desire does not vary at all with age; but I do fear that what remains of life may be short.]

"Love," the "dolce pensero," not the secretary, here consoles. The words conveyed belong to Love, and they "speak" to the poet through the agency of the secretary because for Petrarch written words in letters were said to speak. But the secretary, who bears the message and figurally represents the message according to early commentators, ostensibly does little. "He sends that sweet and amorous thought, the ancient secretary," the humanist Giovanni Andrea Gesualdo writes in his 1553 commentary to the *Rime,* "which, from the moment that he entered into the amorous interplay, is between those two . . . that is, between [the lover] and Love, because the secret sent by love is the thought."[28] According to Gesualdo, the "secretario," acting as a supplement for the sweet thought of Love, merely becomes the message passed on in "secreto." At first glance, there would seem to be little in the role of this "secretario" other than to bear witness in privacy to the words of love as a "sweet thought." And yet without the "secretario," without the agent of writing who bears the message of love, the poet cannot exist in a dialogue with the absent Love. The poet fails to hear the words that console him and therefore lacks the hope that he will one day obtain the object of his desire. More to the point, without the secretary, the poet never enjoys the "sweetness" of Love's thought, which operates as a substitute for the fulfillment he lacks—Laura and, by extension, the glory of the laurel. It would seem, then, that to climb the heights of Mount Parnassus, the professional poet

28. I cite from Petrarch, *Il Petrarcha con l'espositione di M. Gio. Andrea Gesualdo,* 195. I would like to thank William J. Kennedy for providing me with copies of the commentaries. On Petrarchan commentaries, and specifically a discussion of Giovanni Andrea Gesualdo, see Kennedy, *Authorizing Petrarch.* For subtle appropriations and complex revisions of Petrarch's figure of the "secretario" in French Renaissance verse, see Bizer, "Letters from Home," esp. 160–63.

sometimes needs a professional secretary, if only to provide him with the message of hope that will sustain him through the rest of his life.

Petrarch may therefore have composed a collatio much as a priest might do, yet he wrote a collatio that was by no means a medieval sermon delivered to monks. He may have received the laurea and with it the right to teach as a university professor, but throughout his life he preferred to remain, as he put it, a "squatter in the academy." Petrarch may have thought of himself as a kind of doctor, but only as a doctor of souls (*medicus animorum*) and for the friends of his own choosing; he may have functioned as an ambassador when sent on missions by patrons, but in the process he used the office to reflect privately on moral concerns. He may have recognized the importance in general of secretaries in society and included one as a figure of thought in a poem, but he preferred to help others secure the office that he repeatedly rejected and that had been offered to him by different popes. Time and again, Petrarch refused to transform the profession of the humanist poet first fashioned in his oration into any single established, official profession. In this respect, Petrarch functions as an impressive contrary to the writers discussed in this book. He emerges as an innovator because he characterized his new profession of poet as a kind of professionless profession, privileging the contrasting ideas that he himself held a profession—the profession of poet—yet that he was tied down to and restricted by no other in any concrete or lasting official way. Petrarch's shadow undoubtedly loomed large in the Renaissance. Yet humanist doctors, ambassadors, and secretaries often greatly valued their professions, and to varying degrees humanists over the next two and a half centuries helped construct those professions in discourse as they simultaneously looked back to classical antiquity and fashioned themselves in their own time. Professional identity and humanism were indeed closely intertwined throughout the Italian Renaissance.

Doctors

Two

THREE REACTIONS TO PLAGUE

Marvels and Commonplaces in Medicine and Literature

> The players, meanwhile, had finished and gone; their leader bowing and scraping, kissing his hands and adorning his leave-taking with antics that grew madder with the applause they evoked. After all the others were outside, he pretended to run backwards full tilt against a lamp-post and slunk to the gate apparently doubled over with pain. But there he threw off his buffoon's mask, stood erect, with an elastic straightening of his whole figure, ran out his tongue impudently at the guests on the terrace, and vanished in the night.
>
> —THOMAS MANN

Traditionally in classical medical thought it was considered the job of doctors to familiarize the unfamiliar as they went about reading the signs of disease in the world. A memorable statement along these lines comes from Hippocrates in his opening discussion of epilepsy, when he attacks the magicians and quacks who have obstinately read and treated the disease as something wondrous:

> I am about to discuss the disease called "sacred." It is not, in my opinion, any more divine or more sacred than other diseases, but has a natural cause, and its supposed divine origin is due to men's inexperience, and to their wonder at its peculiar character. Now while men continue to believe in its divine origin because they are at a loss to understand it, they really disprove its divinity by the facile method of healing which they adopt, consisting as it does of purifications and incantations. But if it is to be considered divine just because it is wonderful, there will be not one sacred disease but many, for I

will show that other diseases are no less wonderful and portentous, and yet nobody considers them sacred. (1.1)[1]

Hippocrates here addresses in synthetic form a matter of serious professional concern for physicians. Interpreting, labeling, classifying, and above all explaining wondrous diseases provided a means by which physicians could publicly demonstrate, if not actively flaunt, their professional expertise in the moment that it was being visibly tested and, at times, earnestly questioned. This was the case in the late Middle Ages and the Renaissance, as physicians were forced to confront the wondrous new diseases of plague and syphilis and, as a result, to demonstrate and sometimes defend the social value of their knowledge and expertise as professionals. Indeed, medieval and Renaissance doctors could, and certainly did, interpret novel diseases such as plague as a miraculous sign of God's displeasure or the result of universal causes, both of which were ultimately beyond medical understanding and thus outside the prescribed area of a physician's professional inquiry. However, natural causes could be rationally explained, and physicians, including those writing on the plague, consequently "distinguished the remote, universal, superior and celestial causes from the near, particular, inferior and terrestrial ones."[2] With regard to the near and particular causes of the disease, doctors largely assumed that they theoretically embraced all possible diseases and cures within their elaborate system of knowledge, a knowledge acquired through extensive professional training.

While interpreting, labeling, classifying, and explaining diseases was a matter over which physicians in the Middle Ages and Renaissance felt they had jurisdictional claim as professionals, they did not come up with new modes of conceptualizing and treating new and wondrous diseases. Nancy Siraisi and Michael McVaugh, for instance, argue that "the new disease environment" of plague and eventually syphilis contributed to a "long medical Renaissance," a scientific and cultural revival that evolved in two broad "phases," from the twelfth to the early fourteenth century, and then from the mid-fourteenth to the end of the sixteenth century. This long medical Renaissance should still be distinguished from the medical Renaissance—or what scholars often refer to as the "medical humanism" or "medical hellenism"—of the sixteenth century, when physicians brought fully to bear on their field of professional inquiry a number of humanist techniques of study, among them a highly critical

1. *Hippocrates,* 139–41. The epigraph heading this chapter is drawn from Mann, *Death in Venice,* in *Death in Venice and Other Stories,* 61.

2. Arrizabalaga, "Facing the Black Death," 251.

approach to medieval and Arabic texts and sources and a philological approach to ancient texts of medicine now read directly in the original Greek.[3] Yet during the period of "continuing growth and development" of the medical profession in the late Middle Ages and Renaissance,[4] the increased recognition of and scientific interest in not just new but wondrous diseases brought challenges to the existing intellectual systems of medical knowledge. Those systems were not, however, in any way displaced.[5] The medical Renaissance, like the Renaissance in the arts and literature, was a period of innovation *within* tradition. Rhetorically speaking, it was marked by an interest in novelties and a commensurate concern for cultural commonplaces. The notion of a wondrous disease, which was of growing concern to doctors,[6] also proved of interest to some writers of imaginative literature in the Middle Ages and the Renaissance, who instead wished to defamiliarize the familiar as they, like their medical counterparts, went about reading and writing about the signs of the world. Doctors and poets thus shared a common concern in the late Middle Ages and the Renaissance not only for semiotics (doctors in diagnosis, poets in representation) but for all that is wondrous.

To contextualize the profession of medicine as it was practiced and viewed from the fourteenth to the late fifteenth century, and to provide through case studies a structured overview of how the profession of medicine, after an initial period of resistance, became a discipline of interest to humanists in northern Italy and was actively studied by them, I examine in this three-part chapter how a scholastic doctor (Gentile da Foligno), a protohumanist storyteller (Giovanni Boccaccio), and a humanist philosopher and physician (Marsilio Ficino) reacted to plague. I begin with Gentile da Foligno, the first northern Italian to write extensively on the plague. His observations on the pestilence, which changed radically over a very short time, were at once atypical, in that unlike other contemporary

3. Siraisi and McVaugh call for a "long medical Renaissance" broken down into two "phases," without dismissing the distinctiveness of the medical Renaissance of the sixteenth century ("Introduction," 9–14). Arrizabalaga, Henderson, and French (*The Great Pox,* 69) further distinguish the "medical hellenism" from the 1490s on from the "Latin medical humanism" of the fifteenth century in general; the latter came about "as a result of the recovery of the *De medicina* of Cornelius Celsus, whose followers considered him to be 'the physicians' Cicero' (*Cicero medicorum*) and who took his work as a model of Latin writing."

4. Siraisi and McVaugh, "Introduction," 9.

5. On the interest in wondrous diseases in the Renaissance, along with marvelous cures and effects, see Siraisi, "The Hidden and the Marvelous," in *The Clock and the Mirror,* 149–73, as well as more generally Daston and Park, *Wonders and the Order of Nature,* 135–72, for a discussion of medical and natural wonders.

6. See in particular Daston and Park, *Wonders and the Order of Nature,* 136–37, 144–46, 159–60.

physicians he viewed the plague as a marvel, and typical, in that he offered the customary medical advice on how to combat it. Gentile also functions in my discussion as a representative figure of the scholastic medicine over and against which humanist physicians would define themselves in the sixteenth century. I then turn to the *Decameron,* where Boccaccio levels an early humanist attack against doctors. My twofold focus here is on Boccaccio's carnivalesque treatment of two pigs, whose death in the introduction is perceived as a wonder because it defies current medical beliefs about the transmission of diseases, and his carnivalesque treatment of Doctor Simone, who naively believes in the marvel of a world in which all social categories can be magically erased. I then conclude with Ficino, who draws heavily on scholastic medicine yet does not participate in the Petrarchan contest with doctors. To be a doctor constituted a respected profession for Ficino, and his *Consilio contro la pestilenzia* (1481), which repeatedly refers to Gentile's *consilia,* represents an attempt to link the profession of Ficino's own father[7] with that of his humanist son, the practical physician with the practical moral philosopher, the "mechanical" labor of medicine with the Petrarchan belief in the humanist as the *medicus animorum.* By the time Ficino composed his *Consilio,* however, plague was not a singular disease that elicited awe but just one more marvelous disease among others. The first and last sections of this chapter, which focus on early plague literature composed by scholastic and humanist physicians, thus frame a fiction writer's view of the medical profession and its inefficacy in dealing with the pestilence in Renaissance Italy. Taken together, these three sections reveal how plague, once perceived as a marvel by Gentile da Foligno and Boccaccio, gradually became a commonplace in the minds of physicians in the Italian Renaissance.

Gentile da Foligno, the Medical Profession, and the Novelty of Plague

Gentile da Foligno, illustrious doctor, commentator, and teacher of medicine in northern Italy, died in Foligno in 1348 while trying to combat the

7. Ficino, *Consilio contro la pestilenzia,* 55: "our father Master Ficino, singular physician, who cured the greater part of the diseased who came to him." Translations throughout are mine. On Ficino as physician philosopher, see in particular McClure, *Sorrow and Consolation in Italian Humanism,* 132–54, but also the introduction to Ficino, *Three Books on Life,* 18–19. For some interesting thoughts on the *Consilio* in the light of Mary Douglas's work, see Calvi, *Histories of a Plague Year,* 64–68.

plague.[8] Earlier, in the course of assisting the officials of Perugia and its citizens, he wrote a number of *consilia* about the pestilence, each of which recommended preventive and curative measures and articulated various possible causes for the disease. The first and longest, the *Consilium contra pestilentiam,* was written for the city and university of Perugia; the three shorter subsequent *consilia* were composed for the College of Physicians of Genoa; probably the city of Naples; and the College of Physicians of Perugia.[9] Together these four *consilia,* written "for the common good of all," represent some of the earliest in what would eventually develop into a steady stream of treatises on the plague in the late Middle Ages and the Renaissance.[10] Cumulatively, Gentile's *consilia* trace an awareness on the part of a learned eyewitness, trained in both the practical and the theoretical medicine of his time, not only of the severity of the pestilence in the year of its arrival in northern Italy but eventually of its absolute novelty. At first Gentile used the plague for "scholastic disputation"[11] and found in it nothing out of the ordinary,[12] but his opinion changed dramatically as he compared it to earlier epidemics and saw many people die despite the preventive measures he had helped put into place: "Indeed, the famous pestilence of the city of Crannon, or that written about by Thucydides or Galen or Avenzoar, does not seem comparable in wickedness to the

8. On Gentile da Foligno, see Campbell, *The Black Death and Men of Learning,* 9–13; Thorndike, *History of Magic and Experimental Science,* 3.233–52; French, "Gentile da Foligno and the *Via Medicorum*"; Arrizabalaga, "Facing the Black Death"; Ottosson, *Scholastic Medicine and Philosophy,* 50–52, 189–94; Bonora and Kern, "Does Anyone Really Know the Life of Gentile da Foligno?"; Ceccarelli, "Gentile da Foligno"; and Siraisi, *Arts and Sciences at Padua,* 149–70. See also Thorndike, "*Consilia* and More Works in Manuscript by Gentile da Foligno." It is still a matter of debate whether he died in Foligno or Perugia.

9. His writings are drawn from the 1964 reprint edition of Sudhoff, "Pestschriften aus den ersten 150 Jahren," 36–87 and 332–96, otherwise referred to as "Pestschriften" (repr.) in my text; and Gentile da Foligno, *Consilium contra pestilentiam*; and *Super prima fen quarti Canonis Avicennae.* The *consilia* are generally ordered as follows: I. *Consilium contra pestilentiam* (corresponding to "Pestschriften" (repr.), 336–37, which transcribes the beginning) addressed to city and university of Perugia; II. "Pestschriften" (repr.), 332–33, corresponding to the *consilium* to the College of Physicians of Genoa; III. "Pestschriften" (repr.), 333–35, corresponding to the *consilium* probably to Naples, which is mentioned in it; IV. "Pestschriften" (repr.), 83–86, corresponding to the *consilium* to the College of Physicians of Perugia.

10. Gentile, *Consilium,* a1r. See also as cited in Sudhoff, "Pestschriften" (repr.), 337. For an overview of treatises on the plague, see Castiglioni, "I libri italiani della pestilenza."

11. Thorndike, *History of Magic,* 243.

12. See Gentile, *Consilium,* a1r, where Gentile does not seem to feel that this pestilence is as grave as others written about before. I follow, and am greatly indebted to, Arrizabalaga, "Facing the Black Death," 247, for the development of Gentile's views in his *consilia:* "If we look at Gentile's four *consilia* together, it is evident that his perception of the *pestilentia* of 1348 changed as the course of time allowed him to become aware of the actual dimensions of the tragedy."

invading pestilence."[13] The plague for Gentile had become "fearful" and "of such malignancy," as he put it in his second *consilium,* that it escaped easy definition. The pestilence was what it was "by whatever name it be given." The plague was extraordinary, "neither heard of nor described in books before."[14] There was nothing like it in recorded history and medical literature. It was, Gentile asserted in the *consilium* written just before he died, a marvel: "Some pestilence, marvelous and stupendous [*ammirabilis et obstupenda*], as it were, now seems to have superseded the pestilence of past times, and it seems to have come to Italy from the northern and eastern parts, beginning from the west of Italy."[15]

Gentile was not alone in judging the pestilence as something new. As Amundsen observes, "when the Black Death struck, it was, to the physicians of the time, a new disease, and so also were the various other pestilences that beset Europe in the ensuing centuries. [The doctors] felt acutely the need to investigate such diseases, to seek ways both to prevent and to cure them. Although many authors of pest tractates tried desperately to find the answers in the writings of classical and Arabic medical authorities, some dismissed the ancient writings as useless in the existing circumstances and called for experimentation and experience."[16] The famous surgeon and papal physician Guy of Chauliac (ca. 1300–1368), writing his *Grande Chirurgie* in mid-century at Avignon, perceived the pestilence as new and unheard of before, and, as Richard Palmer points out, "in Ragusa too the term *infermita inaudita* was used to describe it."[17] Yet had Gentile survived the plague, he would have found himself somewhat alone among doctors in calling the plague a marvel, though chroniclers such as the Florentine historian Giovanni Villani (ca. 1275–1348), who likewise died of the pestilence in 1348, claimed that the plague was "wondrous as though incredible" as it struck and progressed from the Orient.[18] Most doctors, directly after the Black Death

13. Sudhoff, "Pestschriften" (repr.), 84.

14. Ibid., 332.

15. Ibid., 84. So Gentile, "Consilium in epidimia Perusii," *Consilia,* signat. gIv, as cited in Arrizabalaga, "Facing the Black Death," 247 n. 36: "marvelous [*mirabile*] indeed is the pestilence about us."

16. Amundsen, "Medical Deontology and Pestilential Disease," in *Medicine, Society, and Faith,* 299–300.

17. See Campbell, *The Black Death,* 3; and Palmer, *The Control of Plague in Venice and Northern Italy,* 2.

18. Giovanni Villani, *Historie universali dei suoi tempi,* 12.199: "maraviglia quasi incredibile," where Villani also describes the plague as a wonder that many have already spoken about: "E più maravigliosa cosa e quasi incredibile contarono."

and, it would seem, over the next two centuries, did not consider the plague a marvel, which makes Gentile's description of it as "marvelous" somewhat novel in itself.[19] When, for example, the illustrious Florentine humanist and physician Antonio Benivieni (1443–1502) wrote about the pestilence in *De peste,* he made no mention of *pestilentia* as a wonder.[20] But when plague was grouped with other diseases such as syphilis in his posthumously published *De abditis nonnullis ac mirandis morborum et sanationum causis* (1507), a study that contains the description of necropsies performed by Benivieni himself and represents an early contribution to the science of pathological anatomy, plague suddenly became one of the many diseases that originated from concealed "marvelous causes,"[21] as the title *On Some Hidden and Marvelous Causes of Disease and Recovery* declares from the outset. By this time, however, plague shared the field with other, perhaps even more wondrous, new diseases such as syphilis.

Now Gentile da Foligno, along with being the first northern Italian to compose a number of *consilia* on the plague, was one of the most important doctors of his time. A practicing physician with important patients and professional civic duties, he taught medicine at Siena (1322–1324) and Perugia (1325–1327) and probably lectured at the *Studium* of Padua from 1337 to 1345, where he had been called to work as the personal physician to the ruler of Padua, Ubertino da Carrara. Though Nancy Siraisi gives little credence to the claim that he had been a pupil of Taddeo Alderotti (d. 1295),[22] he probably received his training in Bologna, clearly worked within the guidelines of Alderotti's school, wrote numerous *consilia,* and, according to Roger French, "helped to give Italian medicine a new character in the years after it was accepted in the universities in its Aristotelianized form."[23] He valued highly the study of anatomy, considering it fundamental to the knowledge of medicine; perhaps conducted a public dissection in Padua in 1341; and claims himself to have performed autopsies on those who died from the plague. Eventually, Gentile gained a reputation as an "arch-scholastic" for his lengthy commentaries and his

19. In the numerous writings on plague contained in Sudhoff, "Pestschriften," one can occasionally locate instances when the plague, over the 150-year period covered by Sudhoff, is explicitly referred to as a marvel or associated with the marvelous and marveling—for example, "Pestschriften" 4 (1910–11), 209; 6 (1912–13), 344; 17 (1925), 44, 68, 78.

20. Nardi, "Antonio Benivieni," 124–33, 190–97.

21. Benivieni, *De abditis nonnullis.* On Benivieni, see Stefanutti, "Benivieni, Antonio"; Long, "Antonio Benivieni and His Contribution to Pathological Anatomy"; and Siraisi, *The Clock and the Mirror,* 153–58.

22. Siraisi, *Taddeo Alderotti and His Pupils,* xxi.

23. French, "Gentile da Foligno," 21.

quaestiones, and he was consequently dubbed both *doctor subtilissimus* and *speculator.*[24] A distinguished and respected physician, Gentile was indebted in his work not just to Aristotelian philosophy and Galenic medicine but also to Arabic medicine, in particular Avicenna. Well into the sixteenth century the medical community continued to consult his commentary—the first near complete commentary—on Avicenna's *Canon.* Yet nowhere in his commentary on *Canon* 4.1, which addresses fevers that affect the whole body,[25] does Gentile ever describe plague as an inexplicable wondrous disease. Gentile reminds us that certain signs may appear to indicate the imminent presence of plague—"a multitude of small frogs"[26] as a sign of excess humidity being one familiar portent among many—but the advice he gives as a cure for "pestilence" is by no means out of the ordinary. Plague in Gentile's commentary is largely conceived as one disease among many. There is nothing extraordinary about it. Far from being a marvel, *pestilentia* is a commonplace, a topos of medical literature in general and of Gentile's commentary in particular. It has yet to become the "marvelous and stupendous" disease that Gentile describes in his last *consilium.* Quite the contrary, as Gentile insists at one point in his commentary, it is in fact well known ("notum est") that pestilence kills people in a few hours, so one must not at all marvel at the possibility ("nec de hac possibilitate est mirandum").[27]

Like the reaction of so many of his contemporaries, Gentile's response to the effects of the plague was largely conservative when it first broke out, even as he became aware of its extraordinary, wondrous nature. He may have grown impatient, as Anna Campbell argues, with "subtleties and theorizing when practical measures [were] urgently demanded."[28] But his recommendations for preventing the spread of the disease, neatly compiled in the first and lengthiest of his *consilia,* reflected the accumulated wisdom of the scholarly community in Italy, which was then the most advanced academic medical community in Europe, thanks to

24. Ibid., 28.

25. On the uses of Avicenna's *Canon,* see Siraisi, *Avicenna in Renaissance Italy,* 43–76 for the medieval period, esp. 56 for the importance of *Canon* 4.1: "If the number of commentaries is any guide, the most highly valued of all the parts of the *Canon* used in teaching *practica* was Book 4, especially its first section on fevers." This section was the most widely disseminated of Foligno's commentary—the commentary on Book 4 composed between 1345 and 1346, shortly before the plague struck Italy. See Ceccarelli, "Gentile da Foligno," 165.

26. Gentile, *Super prima fen quarti Canonis Avicennae,* y3r, and x3v–y4v for his discussion of the causes and signs of *pestilentia,* and the cures for it.

27. Ibid., y2r.

28. Campbell, *The Black Death,* 11.

its highly developed university system and growing civic concern for public health. Following Galen, the prevailing medical explanation for the plague was that corruption of the air occurred during periods of pestilence. Physicians therefore agreed that one should flee from fetid places to avoid the disease. Though it was often recommended to wash one's hands with vinegar or rosewater, bathing was sternly discouraged because it opened the pores to the corrupt, putrescent air. Consequently, the medical community advocated preventive measures that were often centered around methods of personal and communal hygiene. Combating the plague meant, above all, combating smells. "To any Galenist physician the link between stink and putrefaction," as Jon Arrizabalaga has written, "was as obvious as that between putrefaction and pestilence. And in fact the lack of stink—and still better the presence of a pleasant smell in the environment—was a definitive sign that putrefaction had disappeared and that the air had become purified. Therefore, stink perceived through the sense of smell played a central role in the semiology of pestilence in the same way that a pleasant smell was a sign of health."[29] For this reason, Gentile, like virtually every other doctor both during and after the period, advised people to fumigate their houses with aromatic plants and logs. He counseled the poor to inhale the odor of aromatic herbs which were easily located (marjoram, sage, and mint); and he insisted that everyone build fires "in the streets with the refuse of all the fetid things of the houses and the city."[30] One should avoid contact with the infected, not merely because they putrefied the air with the miasma excreted from their bodies but because "communication of the evil disease happens principally from contagious conversation with other people who have been infected." Conversation itself [*conversatio*], in the sense of gathering together and speaking in groups, was potentially lethal.[31] It was best, in short, to avoid social intercourse.

Gentile recognized from the outset the unprecedented contagious nature of the disease and eventually envisioned it as a wonder before he died, but he elaborated no radically new theory to account for its effects.[32] Sim-

29. Arrizabalaga, "Facing the Black Death," 275. See as well Cipolla, *Miasmas and Disease,* 4–7, though all the studies on medicine in this chapter touch upon the subject. It can be sampled, for example, in the treatises published by Sudhoff.

30. Gentile, *Consilium,* 4r.

31. Sudhoff, "Pestschriften" (repr.), 338. I follow here the translation of Henderson, "Epidemics in Renaissance Florence," 170. See also Gentile, *Consilium,* 4v; and Sudhoff, "Pestschriften" (repr.), 83 and 84.

32. By contrast, there was little conflict, either in theory or in practice, regarding the way urban communities in northern Italy resorted to treating the disease. Park ("Medicine

ilarly, over the course of the next two centuries the observations of doctors sometimes even conflicted with theoretically informed practical advice.[33] Yet, despite the medical community's inability to combat the devastating effects of the plague, doctors suffered no great loss of social standing.[34] Even in Florence, where fewer illustrious citizens became doctors after the plague, the medical community continued to develop along the lines of what Katharine Park calls "nascent professionalism."[35] Profiting from the commercial revolution and urbanization of the Middle Ages, as well as from the sustained economic prosperity of the Renaissance and the growing and competitive demands of the medical marketplace, the profession of medicine, which had long been defining itself over and against law, was marked by guild-controlled processes of training; degree-conferring institutions of higher learning; a clearly articulated community of workers; a developed, specialized vocabulary; and an increased specialization, regulation, and division of labor. Consequently, however disillusioned people may have been in Italy after the initial onslaught of the plague and its subsequent outbreaks, doctors continued to benefit from the long-term gains made since the thirteenth century in establishing medicine as a discipline worthy of advanced intellectual pursuit, particularly in academic centers such as Bologna where, thanks to the work of Taddeo Alderotti and his school,[36] doctors were considered trained philosophers and sometimes rivaled lawyers in wealth and prestige. Long thought to have been one of Alderotti's pupils, Gentile da Foligno, like so many other civic-minded physicians, was therefore honored by the city he had

---

and Society in Medieval Europe," 87) speaks of the "novel means" employed. There is much discussion as to how conservative or innovative the health officials were in relation to the medical community. For those who argue for a large difference, see Cipolla, *Public Health and the Medical Profession in the Renaissance* and *Miasmas and Disease;* Carmichael, *Plague and the Poor in Renaissance Florence* and "Plague Legislation in the Italian Renaissance"; Palmer, *The Control of Plague in Venice and Northern Italy*. Conversely, for those who see less of a division, see Arrizabalaga, "Facing the Black Death"; Palazzotto, "The Black Death and Medicine"; Henderson, "The Black Death in Florence" and "Epidemics in Renaissance Florence."

33. As can be gleaned, for example, from Jacquart, "Theory, Everyday Practice, and Three Fifteenth-Century Physicians," 147–48.

34. On this see Siraisi, *Medieval & Early Renaissance Medicine,* esp. 42–43; and Siraisi, "The Physician's Task," 108–9.

35. Park, "Medicine and Society," 75. See also Park, *Doctors and Medicine in Early Renaissance Florence* and "Medical Profession and Medical Practice." More generally on medicine and professionalism, along with above-mentioned titles (in particular Siraisi, *Taddeo Alderotti*), see Bullough, *Development of Medicine as a Profession*. See also Alford, "Medicine in the Middle Ages"; Amundsen, "Medical Deontology and Pestilential Disease"; and Kristeller, "Philosophy and Medicine."

36. On which see the seminal study of Siraisi, *Taddeo Alderotti*.

assisted in combating the plague—the *pestilentia* to which he succumbed in 1348 and which he envisioned in his last *consilium* as indeed "marvelous and stupendous."

Death and Storytelling: Boccaccio, Pigs, and the Marvel of Plague

Not everyone shared a high opinion of doctors after or during the Black Death. Boccaccio in particular singled out the medical profession at the beginning of his *Decameron* as ineffective in treating the diseased and filled with all sorts of greedy quacks:

> Against these maladies, it seemed that all the advice of physicians and all the power of medicine were profitless and unavailing. Perhaps the nature of the illness was such that it allowed no remedy: or perhaps those people who were treating the illness (whose numbers had increased enormously because the ranks of the qualified were invaded by people, both men and women, who had never received any training in medicine), being ignorant of its causes, were not prescribing the appropriate cure. (1. intro. 13; 51)[37]

Boccaccio was not alone in chronicling the failures of physicians during the plague. His contemporary, the historian Matteo Villani (ca. 1285–1363), was another, among many.[38] But Boccaccio's negative characterization of physicians is striking given the degree to which he made use of medical concepts throughout the *Decameron,* both in matters of detail and large-scale emplotment.[39] In abandoning the city to entertain themselves in the *contado,* for example, the members of the noble *brigata* effectively adhere to the advice of doctors such as Gentile da Foligno, who counseled everyone to flee from the plague and to avoid solitude while exercising the curative powers of their "imagination" [ymaginatio] and seeking delight in the form of "melodies, songs, stories and other similar pleasures."[40] Yet, even if the medical community's ranks had suddenly swelled with charlatans during the plague, we may legitimately ask if this should be

37. All references to the *Decameron* in my text are from *Tutte le opere,* vol. 4, ed. Vittore Branca; translations, with slight modifications at times, are from *The Decameron,* trans. G. H. McWilliam. References in my text are first to the original and then by page number to the translation.

38. M. Villani, *Istorie,* 4–5.

39. Cottino-Jones, "Boccaccio e la scienza"; Mazzotta, *The World at Play in Boccaccio's "Decameron,"* 32–34; and Olson, *Literature as Recreation in the Later Middle Ages,* 164–83.

40. Gentile, *Consilium,* 9r.

viewed so negatively in the context of the *Decameron.* Are not confidence men prized in the *Decameron,* and is not tricking people for monetary gain the mark of so many innovative Boccaccian heroes and antiheroes? Is there not something perversely admirable in the *Decameron* narrator's vision of a charlatan profiting from the ill? If, in the very first novella of the *Decameron,* Ser Cepparello can elicit laughter by pretending to be a saint when he is deathly ill, why cannot a charlatan, who infiltrates the ranks of the medical profession and cunningly takes advantage of the ignorant during the plague, invite laughter too—a dark and infernal laughter admittedly, but laughter nonetheless?

When read in the light of prevailing plague *consilia,* a sort of dark, carnivalesque humor pervades the novella centered around Maestro Simone, the doctor who is hurled into fecal matter by Buffalmacco, the gay and affable painter to whom the *Trionfo della morte* in the *camposanto* of Pisa has been attributed.[41] In the ninth story of day eight, Maestro Simone, having just arrived in Florence from Bologna, where he studied and practiced medicine, cannot fathom how two of his neighbors, Bruno and Buffalmacco, can be so happy when they are so poor. The doctor assumes that these men, known for their intelligence, must be drawing enormous profits from some other, hidden source. Eager to learn more, he strikes up a friendship with Bruno, who is only too happy to confirm the doctor's impression. Bruno then tells Maestro Simone that he and Buffalmacco belong to a special group, the origins and strange rituals of which are soon explained. Michael Scott left behind two disciples, whom he ordered to fulfill the commands and desires of certain gentlemen. As time passed, the two wizards decided to remain in Florence, taken in by both the pleasures of the city and the "ways of its people" (8.9.18; 652). They made close friendships, Bruno claims, "without caring whether they were rich or poor, patrician or plebian, provided only that they were men whose interests coincided with their own" (8.9.18; 652). In an effort to please their friends, the wizards then organized a "brigata" that met twice a month, the purpose being to grant each of the twenty-five men the pleasure of his wishes for those two nights. Having been admitted into this secret male society, Bruno and Buffalmacco, regardless of their social backgrounds, subsequently enjoy all the riches and luxuries of the world in monthly feasts that were and are, as Bruno puts it, "a marvelous thing to see" [maravigliosa cosa a vedere, 8.9.20; 653].

41. Noted in Kirkham's splendid study of the novella, to which I am indebted, "Painters at Play on the Judgment Day," 258, 273–74. For other readings of this novella, see in particular Mazzotta, *World at Play,* 200–206.

Maestro Simone, who longs to be part of this secret society, never experiences the marvel of these make-believe feasts. Instead, in a parody of confraternal initiation rites, Maestro Simone is eventually hurled into a Florentine sewer, after having taken and then broken his vow of silence. This fecal dunking, which takes place at the very end of Lauretta's tale, elicits laughter from both Bruno and Buffalmacco, and it draws fits of laughter from the *brigata,* who have made of day eight an occasion for telling stories of pranks: "There is no need to inquire whether the ladies laughed heartily over certain of the passages from the queen's story: they laughed so much that the tears ran down their cheeks a dozen times at the very least" (8.10.2; 666). There is, to be sure, universal slapstick humor in this novella. But for an audience fleeing the plague, or for a readership that has recently experienced it, the novella of Doctor Simone tumbling into a privy is also grimly funny in the way Thomas Mann's carnivalesque, snub-nosed clown elicits fits of tearful laughter before he rips off his buffoon's mask in *Death in Venice* and sticks out an impudent tongue. It is a laughter that cannot escape, even as it finds a deeper resonance in, the presence of death, and not least because prior to this nocturnal dunking Maestro Simone walks among the tombs of Santa Maria Novella, the very church from which the *brigata* itself first set out to escape the plague. From the perspective provided by a reading of the *consilia* against the pestilence, the *brigata* members here laugh hysterically, even to the point of having tears in their eyes, at a doctor who in their own time would be as good as dead.[42] Maestro Simone is not only covered in the matter that Petrarch satirized as the principal objects analyzed by physicians (feces and urine);[43] he is also covered from head to toe with the medium universally thought to foster and mark the presence of the plague. The doctor's place is with corrupt, putrescent air—perhaps one more oblique reminder in the *Decameron* of the medical community's helplessness before the pestilence.

For Boccaccio, not a fabulous banquet in which social boundaries are violated, but the plague itself constituted a marvel. "It is a remarkable story that I have to relate" [Maravigliosa cosa è a udire quello che io debbo dire], the narrator insists toward the beginning of the *Decameron,*

> and were it not for the fact that I am one of many people who saw it with their own eyes, I would scarcely dare to believe it, let alone commit it to paper,

42. However curative humor might be for doctors, the laughter inspired by this tale also registers "the simultaneous closeness and distance of the plague," and hence, to adapt Bernardo's observations about the plague itself, it "provides a kind of death rattle in the laughter of the *brigata*." I cite from Bernardo, "The Plague as Key to Meaning," 49.

43. Kirkham, "Painters at Play," 260–61.

> even though I had heard it from a person whose word I could trust. The plague I have been describing was of so contagious a nature that very often it visibly did more than simply pass from one person to another. In other words, whenever an animal other than a human being touched anything belonging to a person who had been stricken or exterminated by the disease, it not only caught the sickness, but died from it almost at once. To all of this, as I have just said, my own eyes bore witness on more than one occasion. One day, for instance, the rags of a pauper who had died from the disease were thrown into the street, where they attracted the attention of two pigs. In their wonted fashion, the pigs first of all gave the rags a thorough mauling with their snouts after which they took them between their teeth and shook them against their cheeks. And within a short time they began to writhe as though they had been poisoned, then they both dropped dead to the ground, spreadeagled upon the rags that had brought about their undoing. (1 intro. 16–19; 51–52)

Echoing in many ways Dante's reaction to the sight of Geryon rising up from the pit of hell, Boccaccio here acknowledges that his own representation may appear to be an infernal lie (*Inf.* 16.124).[44] Yet rather than focusing on a demonic beast that blurs the boundaries between fiction and fact, Boccaccio exemplifies the power of the plague by focusing on pigs, and it is significant that he does. The pig, as Isidore of Seville (d. 636) had written, was an inherently filthy animal, named after mire ("Porcus quasi spurcus") because "it stuffs itself with mud, immerses itself in slime, and covers itself with dirt" (12.1.25).[45] The presence of the pig signaled the presence of filth and hence, in the minds of city officials, the threat of pestilence. Echoing earlier communal statutes, early plague legislation in Italy strictly forbade the presence of pigs in the city, limiting the number butchers could keep and slaughter and regulating how they disposed of their remains.[46]

But pigs were also akin to humans in medieval thought, and therein lay the ambivalence of their position, their "abominable quality," according to Fraser Harrison, in their "manifold resemblance to the human being."[47] In *De anatomia porci,* composed some time in twelfth-century Salerno and one of the earliest surviving treatises on anatomy, the pig is chosen for dissection because "although some animals, such as monkeys, are found to resemble ourselves in external form, there are none so like us internally as

44. On the literary models for the introduction, see Branca, *Boccaccio medievale e nuovi studi sul "Decameron,"* 381–87.

45. Isidore of Seville, *Etymologiarum sive originum libri XX.*

46. Though these measures were never entirely enforced. See for example Carmichael, *Plague and the Poor,* 96–97; and Cipolla, *Miasmas and Disease,* 18–20.

47. Harrison, *Strange Land, The Countryside,* 64.

the pig."[48] Throughout the Middle Ages and the Renaissance, the pig was further represented in churches with "jocular affection" playing musical instruments and dancing, unmistakably figured erect like a gay traveling minstrel.[49] A little more than a century after the writing of the *Decameron,* Marsilio Ficino—who stands as the conceptual endpoint of the period in intellectual history traced in this chapter—remarks in passing that humans can in fact infect pigs during the plague "because of a similarity not, I should say, of spirit but of skin-color."[50] Like, in other words, infects like. Humans may contaminate pigs because pigs occupy a similar yet transgressive position in Renaissance European culture. Pigs are at once reviled for filth and dissected because their organs are thought to resemble those of humans. They are vilified because they carry leprosy yet praised as the food of Christians rather than Jews. They are condemned for being gluttonous yet recommended for consumption because they bear "a certain similarity with our body."[51] Hence, as Peter Stallybrass and Allon White write, the pig's "mode of life was not different from, but alarmingly imbricated with, the forms of life which betokened civility. It is precisely 'creatures of the threshold' which become the object of fear and fascination."[52] Pigs, in short, occupied an ambivalent position in society, and this hybrid position in turn marked them as a privileged figure of the carnivalesque, of which the plague itself bears so many characteristic imprints. In the introduction to the *Decameron* we find, to be sure, many demonized features of carnival: the familiar focus on the lower parts of the human form (the groin where the plague so often strikes);[53] the grotesque, open body (swollen here with "gavoccioli" shaped like eggs or apples and covered with "dark blotches or bruises" [1. Intro. 11; 50]); gender indifferentiation, impurity, and pollution; a world turned upside down and leveled; the presumed presence of the marketplace and processes of exchange in the form of contagion or conversation; the transgression of the inside and outside; and a hilarity and gaiety sometimes provoked by the sight of a world whose hierarchies have thoroughly collapsed.

48. Corner, *Anatomical Texts of the Earlier Middle Ages,* 48 and 51.

49. Harrison, *Strange Land,* 50–51. See also Sillar and Meyler, *The Symbolic Pig,* 16–27.

50. Ficino, *Consilio,* 57.

51. Ficino, *Three Books on Life,* 181, and see 420 n. 5 (2.6) referring to previous works of Galen and Arnald of Villanova.

52. Stallybrass and White, *Politics and Poetics of Transgression,* 47, but see in particular the entire section "Thinking with Pigs," 44–59.

53. For a reading of the significance of the plague's effect on the reproductive systems as a Boccaccian critique of the Chartres school, see Mazzotta, *World at Play,* 24–28.

The ambivalence of the pig's position in medieval society further reflects the ambivalence of humans' position during and after the plague in Boccaccio's *Decameron.* If it was conventional in medical thought from antiquity to assume that animals could infect humans, the inverse was not traditionally the case.[54] Physicians, for that matter, generally assumed that animals themselves even remained immune to the plague because they had a fundamentally different constitution.[55] At most, animals infected humans, not the other way around. Along these lines, medieval doctors often assumed that the plague first infected plants, which, once consumed, passed the disease on to animals and then to humans. The disease, in the earliest of plague tractates composed during the Black Death, contaminated the "food chain," advancing progressively along the "three degrees of life." The pestilence wreaked havoc, but theoretically it did so in an ordered, logical way, with the disease first ingested and then later digested.[56] Boccaccio, however, claims to have witnessed the opposite. He has seen with his own eyes not a filthy pig infecting humans but a filthy impoverished man infecting healthy pigs. The marvel of the plague for Boccaccio, then, lies not just in its ubiquitous presence and peculiar mode of infection, nor in its capacity to pass from one person to another through the medium of inanimate objects, itself a concept initially foreign to medical theory, though early health ordinances during and after the Black Death suggested the possibility.[57] The marvel for Boccaccio lies in the way the plague transgressed and disrupted humans' secure place within the cosmos. As in Pico della Mirandola's *Oration on the Dignity of Man,* man is here a uniquely mobile creature. Yet in a carnivalesque version of this protean capacity, he has become the unwelcome carrier of a deadly disease. In the cosmic chain of being, man is no better than a pig, not changed but grotesquely deformed, not a marvel but the bearer of a wondrous, contagious plague.

54. For an overview of contagion in classical thought, see Grmek, "Les vicissitudes des notions d'infection."

55. Palmer, *The Control of Plague,* 7.

56. See Arrizabalaga, "Facing the Black Death," 248; and d'Agramont, "Regiment de Preservacio a Epidimia o Pestilencia e Mortaldats." See also, for the classical precedent on food poisoning, Liber, "Galen on Contaminated Cereals." In the same way, Johannes Jacobus claimed in his treatise (written sometime around 1364) that "a plague among animals will not pass to human beings, nor will the reverse occur. Thus we may see men dying while animals are immune, or the mortality may be among cattle and other animals, and sometimes among birds or among swine" (cited in Singer, "Some Plague Tractates," 180).

57. Henderson, "The Black Death in Florence," 142.

For Boccaccio, with man the agent of contamination itself, it is therefore fruitless to attempt to understand the plague according to current medical concepts, much less to treat it or prevent it. The retreat of the *brigata* to the countryside may consequently begin as an escape from the disease, but it finally ends up as a retreat into civility amid death. This marvelous disease is all too easily communicated, transmitted, as Gentile observed on more than one occasion, through conversation, the very act of gathering together in groups. Words, which in the *Decameron* sustain social order, comfort, and console, have now indirectly become agents of contamination. To tell stories is to put oneself in the setting through which the disease is passed on from one person to another in social gatherings. But it is also to come to terms with, and often creatively to celebrate, the contaminated world in which these same storytellers are bound to die. The *Decameron* in this way teaches us not so much how to survive such a pandemic—however much it engages in an overall therapeutics of recreative play[58]—as how to die properly while affirming life in the process. The art of the *Decameron* is, even from the first novella, very much about dying as an art that physicians, for all that they counseled us to engage in mirthful storytelling activities, never practiced in their aim to purify us of a novel pestilential disease.

Though doctors were unable to understand the true nature of the plague or to console and tell the curative stories that they would have other people tell, Boccaccio nevertheless reveals his admiration for at least one doctor in the *Decameron*. Maestro Alberto is not just "a brilliant physician of almost universal renown" (1.10.10; 108) but, Boccaccio observes, a highly refined, restrained, and educated man who knows how to live well, to love like a stilnovist poet with "the nobility of his spirit" (1.10.10; 108), and, most importantly, to tell a good brief story. Because of his ready wit, Boccaccio describes him as a "wise and excellent man" (1.10.19; 110). This is a man of great culture and elegance who can courteously put even the wittiest of women in her place with swift repartée. Inversely, Maestro Simone, the one male doctor who seeks to wax eloquent, proves comically bombastic and is known only as a fool as he goes parading about with all his regalia and robes (though it is important to note that Boccaccio does not explicitly mark him as incompetent). To Maestro Simone's credit, he does eventually learn how to participate in the pranks against Calandrino, the very pranks that render both Buffalmacco and Bruno so

58. See Olson, *Literature as Recreation*.

happy even though they are poor. Nevertheless, within Boccaccio's universe of professional types, which includes priests, lawyers, notaries, and scholars, Maestro Simone operates as the structural antipode to Maestro Alberto. Both men were trained at Bologna, one of the great centers of medical learning in the Middle Ages, but apart from that, Maestro Alberto and Maestro Simone could not be more different. As Victoria Kirkham points out, Maestro Simone recalls in his name, his faith in magic, his lust for money, and his final upside-down posture the simonists of *Inferno* 19; he further recalls, by virtue of his final destination in the sewer and his unctuous personality, the flatterers steeped in feces in *Inferno* 18.[59] Maestro Alberto, by contrast, is welcomed into a garden not unlike the one in which the members of the noble *brigata* dwell as they tell their stories and hone their telling (1.10.14; 109). Moreover, whereas the language used to describe Maestro Simone recalls the low style of the fabliaux so often employed in Dante's *Inferno,* the language of Maestro Alberto remains courteous and falls well within the tradition of "*stilnovo* diction."[60] Whereas the effeminate Maestro Simone ends up trembling "more than a frightened woman" (8.9.94; 663), Maestro Alberto is recognized as a "patently wise and excellent man" who, despite his old age, has proven himself to be a noble, virile lover. Whereas Maestro Simone would fall in love with "the countess of Cesspool" (8.9.73; 660) and is reprimanded by his own wife, Maestro Alberto, in Bakhtin's terms, adores the pure, classical body of his "fair lady's fine and delectable features" (1.10.11; 109) and departs from the gathering in the garden admired by the lady he has wooed. There is the doctor of carnival, who unwittingly loves a women of "feces," and there is the doctor of classical form, who admires Malgherida dei Ghisolieri, "a strikingly beautiful woman" (1.10.10; 108) from a refined Bolognese family.

Doctors thus hold an ambivalent position in the *Decameron.* They can be debunked and quite literally dunked in feces, but they can also effectively cure people of diseases, woo, eloquently instruct with words, and be rewarded and made famous for their work as professionals. Nor should it be difficult to imagine why Boccaccio holds such an ambivalent view of the profession of medicine. On the one hand, doctors could inform patients that they were going to die, but they could not and did not prepare patients for death, any more than they could or did console those who mourned the dying patients. The task of consoling and healing with

59. See Kirkham, "Painters at Play," esp. 261–65, for a full analysis of the Dantean echoes.
60. Branca, *Tutte le opere,* commentary, 1040, ad loc.

words belonged instead to the storyteller, whose authority, as Benjamin has it, comes from death itself.[61] The duties of the medical profession stopped, in this respect, where the storyteller's began. Hence, Boccaccio's own job, as he informs us from the outset, is not to counsel but to console men and women after a time of pestilence and massive loss of life (*proemio* 2). On the other hand, doctors held a liminal position in society. The *medicus* mediated between the inside and the outside, as well as between the particular (located in a single body) and the universal (construed to encompass even the entire cosmos). Doctors were concerned with the particular and the universal—the realm of the body, with all its fetid odors and excrescences, and the realm of spirit, the causes of things that animate the cosmos. They are at once grounded in the very gritty matter that we find so much of in Boccaccio's tales—feces, filth, and odors—and they are intimately concerned, as Boccaccio is, with diagnosing the signs of things to describe and uncover deeper patterns of meaning. Like Boccaccio, doctors diagnose—which in its literal sense means "to describe"—people from all walks of life, the poor and the rich, the merchants and the aristocrats, men, children, and women. Their world, like Boccaccio's, is untidy and impure, yet it is a distinctly rich and varied one. Bound to the world of commerce, lucre, and the market, doctors exercised a mechanical art, but in exercising a conjectural art, they, like Boccaccio, were engaged in the highest kind of intellectual pursuit.

Socrates and the Plague: Ficino, the Melancholic Humanist Physician

Unlike Boccaccio, for whom medicine could be used *in bono* and *in malo,* and for whom the impurities of the body could be the subject matter for serious though still playful prose, Petrarch was in his writings largely inflexible in his judgment of the medical profession. Though he recognized some of the merits of physicians, he did so rarely. In a remarkable letter to Boccaccio, Petrarch chides his friend for having desired to summon a doctor to his bedside in a moment when Boccaccio was gravely ill. In point of fact, if he had possessed the money, Boccaccio would surely have paid for the medical advice. Petrarch, cognizant of this fact, can only be grateful for his friend's penury in solitude: "if poverty, as you yourself say, gave a reason for not summoning a doctor from afar, there being none in

61. Benjamin, "The Storyteller," in *Illuminations,* 93–94.

your solitary location, I applaud your solitude and your poverty" (*Sen.* 5.3, 171). So fierce was Petrarch's disapproval of the medical profession that sometimes he refused to use physicians when he was seriously ill.[62] For in Petrarch's mind, doctors not only dealt solely with corporeal matters and false eloquence, disputing in the manner of scholastic—and hence false, loquacious—philosophers; they were also money-grubbing sycophants. Moreover, they employed Greek terms and relied on Arab authorities, using a kind of knowledge, Petrarch tells Boccaccio in a letter, that was oriental and consequently alien: "In fact, the patients' need and the deceivers' promise are Greek, as are the names of their herbs and leaves and roots: balaustium, reubarbarum, calamentum. Everything is done in Greek, and what is even more troubling, in Arabic, so that the more far-fetched the lie, the more it is credited, and the more foreign a remedy, the more it costs; the minute they gain admission, they give the Greek name of the disease or, if necessary, invent one" (*Sen.* 5.3, 176). Petrarch's charge against the medical profession in this respect constitutes a calculated charge against the opponents of the pure classical scholarship and the Roman models and authorities that he as a humanist avidly sought to imitate, foster, and disseminate. For that matter, Petrarch's charge against the medical profession relies on and largely rehearses the position of just one such classical authority: Pliny the Elder.

Yet the humanist project inaugurated by Petrarch also became an integral part of the medical profession. Already in Petrarch's own time, doctors had begun to assert that they should be lettered in the liberal arts, and "this Trecento participation of doctors in humanistic culture," as McClure observes, "burgeoned in the Quattrocento."[63] Even Coluccio Salutati (1331–1406), in responding to a physician's query regarding Petrarch's attack on the medical profession, justified the importance of humanist culture for doctors.[64] Finally, by the 1490s, as Jerome Bylebyl observes, there had been a complete revival of ancient medical sources, and this rebirth brought about a gradual glorification of Greek authors when humanists began attending to their works.[65] As a result, medicine could now actually claim its own "Petrarch" in the form of Nicolò Leoniceno (1428–1524), a pioneering humanist physician and professor

62. This does not mean, however, that Petrarch never called upon doctors—see Benedek, "The Medical Autobiography of Petrarch." He also counted a number of doctors his close friends.

63. McClure, "Healing Eloquence," 330.

64. Ibid., 340–44 for a synthetic discussion.

65. Bylebyl, "Medicine, Philosophy, and Humanism in Renaissance Italy," 38–39.

of philosophy at Ferrara and Bologna, "who recalled the medical art from the lower regions"[66] both by leading the effort to provide critical editions of Greek medical texts on the basis of close philological analysis and by offering accurate Latin translations of them. Now, thanks to the work of Leoniceno and other humanist physicians, medicine had its own exemplary models of imitation and authority in the form of Galen. Likewise medicine could boast its own full-fledged Renaissance, having rescued ancient medicine from the barbarity of the Arabs and the dark ages of intervening medieval commentators like Gentile da Foligno, the *doctor subtilissimus*. Now a doctor could be a humanist as well, operating at once at the level of theory and that of practice in a profession that had need of authoritative, philologically accurate texts.

Marsilio Ficino, translator of Greek texts and eloquent Platonic scholar, stands at the crossroads of humanism and the medical profession in late-fifteenth-century Italy.[67] This is certainly the case with regard to his influential *Consilio contro la pestilenzia,* a work that he composed as plague afflicted Florence in 1478 and that, after the original publication in 1481, eventually competed in number of printings with his subsequent *De vita,* which is so much more widely read today. Like many *consilia,* Ficino's *Consilio contro la pestilenzia* is a conservative text. It is a practical text too, written out of "charity toward [his] homeland" and in the vulgar tongue "so that every Tuscan can understand it and cure himself." A work consulted and considered a classic of pestilence *consilia* well into the eighteenth century, the *Consilio* eschews many "subtle and long disputations,"[68] just as Ficino claims it will. In this respect, Ficino is distancing his style from that of scholastic doctors, such as Gentile da Foligno, to whom Ficino still refers more than to any other doctor in his text. Yet in the process of writing this more readable and accessible *Consilio,* Ficino also introduces a novel element when he rehearses the familiar counsel that one of the best protective measures against the plague is to be happy, advice that appeared in virtually every treatise on the plague. "One must," Ficino here writes, "live happily, because happiness fortifies the vital spirit; and one must live in moderation and with sobriety, because sobriety and moderation in living is of such value that Socrates the philosopher kept himself alive through these means when many fierce

66. Ibid., 39. Bylebyl is citing none other than the anatomist Gabriele Fallopio (ca. 1523–1562).

67. On Ficino in this regard, see McClure, *Sorrow and Consolation;* Kristeller, "Philosophy and Medicine," 36; and Moraglia's introduction to Ficino, *Consilio,* 5–47.

68. Ficino, *Consilio,* 55.

pestilences plagued the city of Athens."[69] Ficino, fine humanist that he is, finds a classical model to exemplify this strategy of survival: we must behave like Socrates to live through the plague.

Ficino's vision of Socrates as a sober and moderate man is a strange one if we think of the Socrates in Plato's *Symposium.* In that particular text, which was so important to Ficino, Socrates proves to be a man prone to flights of ecstasy and acts of excess, whether in his process of dialectical argumentation, his desire to strain for an absolute, or his capacity to drink anyone under the table and get close to the youngest and most beautiful available male. Yet Ficino's vision of Socrates as a moderate and sober man is not at all strange if we turn to Ficino's own *Commentary on Plato's Symposium on Love,* otherwise entitled *On Love,* completed in 1469, a decade before the *Consilio.* There Ficino transforms Socrates into "a man melancholy by nature,"[70] a man concerned not with the body but with the spirit alone. Glossing the Alcibiades episode, Ficino uses the occasion to describe Socrates as a man who would rather die than change his nature: "In his own defense before the judges he told the judges that if they spared him from death on condition that he never afterwards philosophize, he preferred to die rather than give up philosophizing."[71] Significantly, the text of the *Symposium* here has been conflated with the text of the *Apology,* where Socrates is condemned to die for having corrupted the youths of Athens, and where we learn that to die is not just nothing to fear but the greatest good (40b–42). With the conflation of these two Platonic texts, however, Ficino's Socrates has also become a deadly serious thinker rather than the elusive, enigmatic character, the genius or quack by turns, that Plato makes him out to be in the *Symposium.* Socrates, the consummate ironist, has here been pinned down, we might say, as a version of Ficino himself: a sober, moderate, and melancholic man. In the same way, in his *Commentary on Plato's Symposium* Ficino transforms Eryximachus into a respectable physician whose crude materialistic theory of love is taken at face value and openly understood to harbor transcendent philosophical meaning. Evidently, Ficino cannot see the humor of Socrates as a "silenus-figure"—the oxymoronic Platonic hero who could be both comic and tragic, crass and enlightening, ugly and beautiful, common and elite, drunk and sober, sublime and ridiculous[72]—just as he cannot detect, through the figure of the pompous Eryximachus, Plato's implied agon

69. Ibid., 107.

70. Ficino, *Commentary on Plato's Symposium on Love,* 156.

71. Ibid., 157.

72. On this, see Clay, "The Tragic and Comic Poet of the *Symposium.*"

with the medical profession in the *Symposium*. This is because philosophy and medicine were equally serious domains of intellectual and practical pursuit for Ficino, and neither of them could be ironized.

The day Ficino and his companions actually gathered together at Careggi to talk of love, November 7, 1468, was not, as far as I can tell, a day that fell in a particularly severe period of plague.[73] Had it been, "flee fast and far and come back late" would no doubt have been Ficino's advice, just as it had been his advice to the general populace at the end of his *Consilio*.[74] Yet there were other ways to combat the plague. As Ficino knew, and as he sometimes repeated in his own *Consilio,* melancholics like Socrates were often thought to possess the best constitution to resist the noxious air of the plague. According to Ficino, the plague, which often appeared under the sign of Mars and Saturn, afflicted "least of all melancholics"[75] because their veins and pores were narrower and closer knit. If you had to combat the plague, then, your best bet was not to find happiness in humor—the gay and affable stories Gentile da Foligno advised people to tell in order to rid themselves of melancholy, and the stories Boccaccio's ten narrators often tell even as they periodically laugh in the face of death. Your best bet was to find happiness in philosophical thought, the elite stuff that one studied assiduously, the stuff that made one become in the process a melancholic professional, like Ficino a doctor and humanist writing a popular treatise for his fellow Tuscan citizens dying from the plague in the country and the streets. If you wanted to survive the plague, your best overall strategy would in fact be to concentrate on death itself and become, even if you were not one constitutionally, a melancholic like Ficino.

In 1494, just five years before Ficino died, Florence officially opened its first *lazzaretto* for plague victims, though the charitable hospital could hardly cope with the number of the diseased.[76] By this time, however, the plague was no longer envisioned as the marvel that Gentile and Boccaccio had witnessed. The plague, which ravaged the cities and the countryside on the average once every five years, was as commonplace as the

73. Del Panta, *Le epidemie nella storia demografica italiana,* 116–37. Late 1468 would seem to mark the end of a period of plague that had begun in 1463, though plague was certainly present and strong in Florence in August 1468, on which see Corradi, *Annali delle epidemie occorse in Italia,* 181. For the dating of "the actual banquet rather like it," see Ficino, *Commentary on Plato's Symposium on Love,* 27.

74. Ficino, *Consilio,* 108 and passim.

75. Ibid., 59, and for the confluence of Mars and Saturn, 56.

76. See Henderson, "Epidemics in Renaissance Florence," 173–74.

consilia that flourished from the late fourteenth century on. The far more interesting and privileged disease for Ficino was melancholy, the disease of intellectuals, the malady of the male elite, and, according to Andrea Corsini, a full-fledged professional disease.[77] But then syphilis, a new and even more wondrous disease,[78] suddenly appeared in Italy and ravaged all of Europe, eliciting wonder and fear from humanists and physicians alike. Now, for the first time in Renaissance Europe, the newness of a disease—or, more precisely, whether or not there actually could be a new disease—became a matter of serious intellectual debate among humanist physicians. Among those addressing the wonder of new diseases in the sixteenth century was Girolamo Fracastoro. Yet in doing so, Fracastoro conflated the marvels of this new disease with the emerging sixteenth-century aesthetic of the marvelous. With Fracastoro, one of the most renowned humanist doctors of his time, syphilis as a wondrous disease became not just a matter of epistemological and cultural concern but one of poetic concern, as he made it, in the process of mythopoetically naming it, the subject of a learned, epic song.

77. The novelty of Ficino's seminal approach to melancholy is stressed in Klibansky, Panofsky, and Saxl, *Saturn and Melancholy,* 254–74; the authors point out that Ficino, in the process of bringing together all the prior notions of the topic in his influential *Three Books on Life,* was "the first writer to identify what 'Aristotle' had called the melancholy of the intellectually outstanding men with Plato's 'divine frenzy'" (259), and that for Ficino not only was a melancholic predisposed to intellectual work but, inversely, intellectual work made a person melancholic (261). See Corsini, "Il 'De Vita' di Marsilio Ficino," 12–13, on *De vita* as the first book dedicated to "professional diseases."

78. See Foa, "The New and the Old," 42 n. 6. One can sample the debate, as it evolved soon after syphilis appeared, in Amundsen, "The Moral Stance of the Earliest Syphilographers, 1495–1505," in *Medicine, Society, and Faith,* 310–72; Sudhoff, ed., *Earliest Printed Literature on Syphilis;* and Arrizabalaga, Henderson, and French, *The Great Pox,* esp. 264–66.

Three

FRACASTORO AS POET AND PHYSICIAN

Syphilis, Epic, and the Wonder of Disease

A given scientific discipline represents a commitment to a "style" of representation, in the same way that a given genre represents a commitment to a structure of representation by which to figure the contents and relationships obtaining within a finite province of fictional occurrence. Sciences are created by the effort to reduce some area of cognitively problematical experience to comprehension in terms of some area of experience that is considered to be cognitively secured—either by established disciplines or by the ongoing "common sense" of the culture in which the creation is attempted. All systems of knowledge begin, in short, in a *metaphorical* characterization of something presumed to be unknown in terms of something presumed to be known, or at least familiar.

—HAYDEN WHITE

My subject is not physical illness itself but the uses of illness as a figure or metaphor. My point is that illness is *not* a metaphor, and that the most truthful way of regarding illness—and the healthiest way of being ill—is one most purified of, most resistant to, metaphoric thinking.

—SUSAN SONTAG

Girolamo Fracastoro (ca. 1478–1553) lived a full and prosperous life during the height of the Italian Renaissance and at a time when the discipline of medicine experienced a full-blown Renaissance of its own, fueled by the work of humanists like him.[1] A famous physician and a respected

1. The White epigraph is from "Foucault Decoded: Notes from Underground," in *Tropics of Discourse,* 252; the Sontag epigraph is from *Illness as Metaphors,* 3. In both quotations the

humanist, Fracastoro spent most of his life in Verona and in the surrounding regions, except when work and duties drew him elsewhere, as when he was called by Pope Paul III to attend the Council of Trent as the Church's official physician in 1545. Trained in the profession of medicine at the University of Padua, one of the oldest and most distinguished universities in Europe, he taught logic and anatomy there from 1501 to 1506. At Padua he also studied philosophy under the famous and controversial Pietro Pomponazzi (1462–1525), whose teaching undoubtedly influenced him. Through his studies, Fracastoro acquired a philosophical interest in trying to explain natural phenomena in terms of the then established laws of nature, and to derive additional laws of nature from the direct observation and study of it. But unlike Pomponazzi, Fracastoro was not a speculative philosopher, and he did not enter into controversial theological debate. By the same token, as a natural philosopher and a physician, Fracastoro was a thinker dutifully working within systems of knowledge, not the iconoclast some have made him out to be in his time and our own.

Though a physician by profession, Fracastoro's interests were wide and varied. They ranged from astronomy to astrology, medicine to philosophy, mathematics to theology, botany to cartography, geography to poetics. He was as at home reading Aristotle and Galen as he was reading Catullus, Lucretius, and Virgil, the three poets he imitated and emulated most, and according to the author of his life in the third edition of his *Opera omnia* (1584), he counted Plutarch and Polybius as his two favorite authors. In keeping with these varied interests, he maintained close ties with an array of extremely influential and diverse humanists, among them Andrea Navagero (1483–1529), Pietro Bembo (1470–1547), Julius

---

emphasis is from the original. There is a growing body of specialized studies on Fracastoro's contribution to medicine and science. I have found invaluable, and throughout my discussion rely on, Nutton, "The Seeds of Disease" and "The Reception of Fracastoro's Theory of Contagion." I have also found useful Peruzzi, "Antioccultismo e filosofia naturale"; and especially Pearce, "Intellect and Organism in Fracastoro's *Turrius*" and "Nature and Supernature in the Dialogues of Girolamo Fracastoro." For a balanced placement of Fracastoro in sixteenth-century medicine, see Wightman, *Science and the Renaissance,* 275–83. His works are collected in Fracastoro, *Opera omnia* (hereafter cited as *O.O.* with page number), to which should be appended, among the works I have consulted and from which I cite, Fracastoro, *Scritti inediti;* Pellegrini, *La dottrina fracastoriana del "contagium vivum";* and Fracastoro, *Trattato inedito in prosa.* Unless otherwise indicated, I rely on the following for the original text and translations, cited hereafter in my text by page number or, in the case of poetry, by line: *De contagione et contagiosis morbis,* hereafter cited as *DC;* and *Fracastoro's "Syphilis."* I also rely on Kelso's translation of *Naugerius, sive de poetica dialogus,* hereafter cited as *N.* Some of the translations have been slightly modified. All other translations are my own.

Caesar Scaliger (1484–1558), Gianbattista Ramusio (1485–1557), and the reformer Marcantonio Flaminio (1498–1550). Like many sixteenth-century Italian humanists, he knew both Latin and Greek, though he did not perfect the latter, and he wrote both poetry and prose. His works include several poems in Latin and the vernacular; an unfinished epic; a number of scientific and cosmographical studies, the most important being *Homocentricorum sive de stellis liber unus* (1538) and *De sympathia et antipathia rerum* (1546); and three dialogues on poetry, intellection, and the soul, respectively *Naugerius sive de poetica, Turrius sive de intellectione,* and the unfinished *Fracastorius sive de anima,* all published posthumously in his *Opera omnia* in 1555. But Fracastoro is most famous for his medical study, *De contagione et contagiosis morbis* (*On Contagion and Pestilent Fevers,* 1546), which he probably began in about 1533 and had largely completed by 1538, only to revise it in 1542; and his medical poem, *Syphilis sive morbus Gallicus* (*Syphilis or the French Disease,* 1530), which he began while sojourning along the Garda to escape an outbreak of plague at Verona in about 1510, and then radically revised over the course of a twenty-year period, submitting it once to Bembo for comments and corrections. "When I was younger," he tells us in the section devoted to the cure of syphilis in *De contagione,* "and owing to a dangerous plague in my city, I had retired to my country-place where I had abundant leisure for the task, and I wrote a poem on this disease. But the poetic form . . . does not admit everything or allow the discussion of all points; I was therefore obliged at that time to omit much. However, now that I am writing on the treatment of this disease, not in verse as a poet, but as a doctor, what I have to say will be more valuable, especially since this malady cannot be properly treated unless one has thoroughly grasped the nature of contagions" (*DC,* 267).

Like many humanists, Girolamo Fracastoro sought to build on, while revealing lacunae in, the scholarship of classical antiquity. By doing so, he aimed to add his name to the rolls of the truly great, a list that stretched far back into a past that Italian humanists had helped to restore and to understand better during the previous century. This was particularly true with regard to Fracastoro's work as a philosopher-physician, in which he counted himself an innovator working within an established medical tradition whose roots extended deep into ancient Greece. Galen may have written on sympathy and antipathy, as Fracastoro points out in his dedicatory letter to *De contagione,* yet nothing of it has survived, and Hippocrates may have touched on the subject of contagion, "but rather as an observer than as one who records [its] essential nature" (*DC,* b). "Little has been published on these two subjects in the works of our ancestors" (*DC,* b), he affirmed, and by "ancestors" Fracastoro here meant—as other humanist physicians did in early cinquecento Italy—Greek authorities, not the "barbaric" intervening medieval and Arabic commentators.

For Fracastoro, the revered ancient Greeks laid the foundation for knowledge, but there was much that they purposely left undiscovered so that others after them would have something to do. It was the job of the ancients to provide "general facts and the first principles of things" (*DC,* d), something true not merely in the discipline of medicine but "in all branches of learning" (*DC,* d). Consequently, much as his good friend Gianbattista Ramusio extended geographical knowledge as he wrote about new lands discovered beyond the confines of the Ptolemaic world—a knowledge Fracastoro would then employ in his own active interest in cartography and constructing globes—so Fracastoro would enlarge our understanding of medicine through a close examination of as yet uninvestigated subjects. He alone of the moderns would talk about contagion, a topic "full of wonder," he indicates in a letter.[2] In so doing, Fracastoro would coin new terms (*fomes*) and concepts (*seminaria*) to explain in natural terms the natural phenomena he observed. It would be an arduous task, a sort of heroic enterprise, he implies, as he sets out to investigate what physicians have erroneously ascribed to occult causes in his own time and what his ancestors left in the dark:

> You will perhaps be surprised that I have undertaken to write about these two subjects, one of which has been left almost untouched by our ancestors, while the other is admitted by all to be beyond the reach of human knowledge. Certainly, I too admit that the sympathies of things and the nature of contagions are very difficult and arduous themes to treat. I will even admit that he would be a foolish and presumptuous man who presumed to investigate their nearest and special causes. But I do not hesitate to affirm that one who should investigate the intermediate causes would discover much that might not only give pleasure but also be very useful. (*DC,* d)

There is a certain amount of professional posturing in this dedication. Cognizant that he writes on "an important subject and full of interest" (*DC,* b), Fracastoro was no doubt aware that the ancients had spoken of contagion and that it was a topic of keen modern concern.[3] But it was

2. Pellegrini, *La dottrina fracastoriana,* 35: "admiratione plena."

3. See in particular Nutton, "The Seeds of Disease," 23–30 (esp. 24 with reference to his posturing in this dedication and letter); and Nutton, "The Reception of Fracastoro's Theory of Contagion," passim.

important for Fracastoro to think of himself as an innovator, courageous in his enterprise, a first among physicians. In portraying himself as engaged in an arduous intellectual inquiry, Fracastoro speaks in large measure as a humanist, whose profession will not only allow him to benefit humankind and supplement the limited knowledge of classical antiquity, but will simultaneously win fame for himself by uncovering the deep hidden order of things. However, Fracastoro also thinks of himself, and here in part speaks, as a poet. In the course of defining his aims and winning fame for himself as a philosopher-physician, Fracastoro in his dedication appeals to the familiar definition of the rhetorical force of poetry, which often enough borrowed from medicine the image of the doctor to characterize the work of the poet as a physician of souls. Following the Horatian adage, medical knowledge, like poetry, is for Fracastoro both *dulce et utile,* pleasurable and useful. This is significant, for in his *De contagione* Fracastoro consciously distinguishes the poet from the physician. He claims that he now writes as a physician and that he can therefore treat his topic, which he had otherwise treated accurately enough in his poem, more comprehensively. Poets are constrained; physicians are not. Physicians can speak both discursively and in a presumably analytic mode, unburdened by the conventions of poetic discourse, which would limit their free reign over their material and demand that they always seek to delight their audience. "As for myself," he writes once more in *De contagione,* "in the poem which I dedicated to Pietro Bembo . . . I did, indeed, touch on all these questions [regarding the substance and principles of syphilis], but only so far as the poetic form allowed. But since verse does not admit of exhaustive treatment of a subject, I was obliged to pass over many points in regard to the whole subject, and if I now proceed to deal with these, I think it will prove worth while" (*DC,* 143).

My argument in this chapter is that the two discourses of poetry and medicine are nevertheless closely connected in Fracastoro's writings and that both are fundamentally rhetorical in nature. The metaphoric structure of poetic discourse influenced Fracastoro's medical writings just as medical thought—or, in Hayden White's terms, the metaphoric structure of all incipient systems of knowledge, such as we might characterize Renaissance medicine—determined in part the structure of his poetic masterpiece, *Syphilis,* which won Fracastoro fame in his own time. What linked poetic and medical discourses in Fracastoro's writings, and made them equally pleasurable and instructive, was not just their shared use of metaphor as a figure of speech and thought but their shared interest in the passion of wonder. Wonder in the early sixteenth century was as much a matter of epistemological as of aesthetic concern. Wonder could be pleasurable, the source of all poetic inspiration and its delightful effects, as Pontanus claimed in a treatise to which Fracastoro repeatedly refers in his *Naugerius* (*N,* 59–60). By the same token, as Fracastoro explains in a surviving fragment that records his inspiration to write the poem *Syphilis,* wonder could be the source of all great philosophical knowledge. Through wonder, there was in truth no great difference between the poet and the philosopher, and hence, in Fracastoro's mind, between a poet and a physician, both of whom sought to explain the hidden causes of things at times through the awe-inspiring, metaphoric structure of myth.[4]

De contagione: *Wonder, Metaphor, and the Seeds of Disease*

"If truly something new is presented to us as unknown," Girolamo Fracastoro writes in his scientific, medical study *De sympathia et antipathia rerum,* "and it does not have the appearance of some menacing evil, then not fear but wonder alone arises in us. Wonder, in fact, is nothing other than a suspension of the spirit, or rather, its fixed intent and direct application. . . . If therefore something unknown is presented as simply unknown, then curiosity alone results, that is, the application of the mind to that thing unknown and to its marginal features" (*O.O.,* 100r).[5] Sometimes, however, Fracastoro writes, strange things do inspire fear, while at other times they produce the contrary effect, in which case Fracastoro, good physician that he is, describes how the facial muscles operate, the heart dilates, and the mouth gradually changes position in response to a wonder that is not so much threatening as downright humorously odd: "Also there are those new things which customarily move us to laughter. In the first place this truth must be known that every happiness makes a dilation of the heart, the spirits, and the diaphragm, and the dilation of these dilates also the muscles at the sides of the mouth, and provokes that movement of the mouth called laughter, which has in its nature some result, by which internal happiness is manifested on the face. . . . Laughter is a movement composed of wonder and happiness" (*O.O.,*

4. Fracastoro, *Scritti inediti,* 25–34. For the centrality of wonder in Fracastoro's thought, see the excellent pages of Pellegrini, *La dottrina fracastoriana,* 3–5; and Eatough's "Introduction" to *Fracastoro's "Syphilis,"* 10, 18–19.

5. He then goes on to remind us that he has written on the psychology of admiration in *Turrius,* on which see *O.O.,* 183v.

100v). In the work to which *De sympathia et antipathia rerum* forms the introduction, Fracastoro then turns to address, amid so many things "full of incredible wonder," one such marvel in the world: "the nature of contagion" (*O.O.*, 79v).

To explain contagion, Fracastoro advocates for the first time that there are *seminaria* that occasionally emerge from objects where they have been stored, fly about in the air, again take root in our bodies, grow, blossom forth, infect people, and sometimes devastate humankind, at which point these *seminaria* continue to migrate from body to body, once more passing on the disease, sometimes after a lapse of centuries.[6] The term *seminaria,* which at one and the same time evokes the notion of "seed-bed" and "seedlets," synthetically contrasts the minuteness of infectious agents with their immense potential for reproductivity and diffusion. Yet this concept, which was Fracastoro's invention and his alone, was on occasion ridiculed by fellow sixteenth-century physicians. Their facial muscles no doubt tightened into a smirk as they laughed, according to Fracastoro's theory of the psychology of wonder, at the novel theory they sometimes found—as did Giovanni Battista Da Monte (1489–1551), an eminent rival physician from Verona—absolutely ridiculous. But the related notion of "seeds of disease," if not strictly *seminaria,* had been around for some time. Gentile da Foligno mentions it in his consilium on the plague, and it appeared in Tommaso del Garbo's commentary on Galen's *De differentiis febrium.*[7] Moreover, many physicians embraced Fracastoro's *seminaria* wholeheartedly, and some, such as Josephus Struthius (1510–1568), who wrote about the disease in his *De morbi Gallici pulsibus* (1555), found it a useful and beautifully phrased extension of Galen's ideas.[8]

6. I have retained the term *seminaria* throughout and made no attempt to translate it. Calling it either "germs" or "seedlets" narrows the concept.

7. Gentile, *Consilium contra pestilentiam,* 3v, where he refers to "pestilentie semina." Nutton, "The Seeds of Disease," 21, refers to Tommaso del Garbo's *In libros de differentiis febrium Galeni commentum.*

8. Struthius, *De morbi Gallici pulsibus,* in Luigini, *De morbo Gallico omnia quae extant apud omnes medicos cuiuscunque nationis,* appendix 3.96, hereafter cited as Luisinus: "The *seminaria,* through which this disease is contagious, are tiny little bodies, just like atoms (not however of the Epicurean type) which together evaporate and are carried about with vapors, and easily insert themselves into phlegmatic humor on account of their sympathetic nature, and other *seminaria* are born analogously by means of this humor. Which things Girolamo Fracastoro of Verona examined beautifully in his book *De sympathia et antipathia rerum* and here and there in the three books *De morbis contagiosis,* which Giovanni Battista Da Monte [1489–1551] laughed at . . . judging the tenets of Fracastoro ludicrous figments of the Epicureans and strange new inventions. As if these tenets were not truly old and indeed very true, which things Galen recalls where he treats pestilential diseases in his book *De differentiis febrium.* . . . Scholars of

Though a few physicians may have ridiculed Fracastoro's tenet of *seminaria contagionum,* the notion fit systematically into the cognitively secured understanding of humoral medicine, and soon enough it was absorbed into familiar models of Renaissance and early modern epidemiology.[9] Why did this happen? Why did a concept that Fracastoro considered a major contribution to a subject "full of wonder" soon lose its novelty and become just another "beautiful examined" issue? The answer advanced by Vivian Nutton, who has extensively written on and researched the subject, is that the notion of seeds of disease had a great metaphoric appeal at a time when physicians had begun to debate not just syphilis as a new disease but the very notion of whether there could be a new disease. Not long after the publication of *De contagione,* and in particular after the 1550s, "Fracastoro's contemporaries used his terminology interchangeably with what they had known from Galen, Hippocrates, and their medieval interpreters."[10] This indicates for Nutton that they held no strict, rigorous interpretation of his *seminaria* as "germs" but employed the word in a far looser, metaphoric sense, as many had indeed already done with Galen's reference to the "seeds of disease." Physicians adapted Fracastoro's concept to the growing, commonplace thought that air transmitted the disease through some sort of agency. It amounted, often enough, to the incorporation of Atomist theory into Galenic medicine. This incorporation bothered some physicians, who accused Fracastoro of being an Epicurean, but it satisfied most, who found in his terminology one more viable metaphor to describe the processes of transmission that all were seeking to better understand.[11]

The concept of *seminaria contagionum* was not taken literally but had a poetic appeal as a figure of thought.[12] This is important, for it goes to the heart of a fundamental difference between modern and Renaissance science. Modern historians came up with the Whiggish notion that Fracastoro had anticipated the concept of modern germ theory, but this view ignored the fundamental rhetorical structure of scientific knowledge during the Renaissance. In the nineteenth century, for example, medical discourse still used metaphors to describe reality. According to

the art of medicine have often asked me why the Morbus Gallicus was deemed new, since all the symptoms seen in it are familiar."

9. Nutton, "The Reception of Fracastoro's Theory of Contagion," passim.

10. Ibid., 232.

11. Nutton, "The Seeds of Disease," passim; and Nutton, "The Reception of Fracastoro's Theory of Contagion," 198 and 232–33.

12. See Singer and Singer, "The Scientific Position of Girolamo Fracastoro," 30.

Michel Foucault, metaphoric descriptions had perhaps even increased in some respects.[13] The difference, according to Foucault, was that in the Renaissance—and in Fracastoro's own time and in his own mental framework—poetry and scientific knowledge consciously availed themselves of the same metaphoric processes for understanding the world. "To think," as Fracastoro points out in his *Turrius,* "is nothing other than to move through that which is connected to another" (*O.O.,* 183v). We begin this movement toward thinking through wonder, yet there are risks involved. "Who does not want to be dragged into error," Fracastoro warns, "must be very wise and skilled in recognizing the connected elements, in what relationship they stand, and in knowing our own ways of understanding" (*O.O.,* 195r). On the one hand, the mind can bring together separate things in such a way as to know the invisible operations of nature. This is in many ways the work of the natural philosopher, and consequently (for Fracastoro) the physician, who understands even the most recondite aspects of Nature "through similitude or dissimilitude" (*O.O.,* 175r). On the other hand, the mind can take objects ordinarily disjoined and, by selectively bringing them together, can create things that are figments of the imagination, some true, some not. This is the work of poets, who find a "certain pleasure" in making connections "out of the similitude of things" (*O.O.,* 175v). Both the poet and the natural philosopher, and hence for Fracastoro the poet and the physician, think rhetorically through the figure of similitude. Their mode of understanding the world is essentially the same. "All things," as Fracastoro summarily states, "are therefore understood through the appearances of other things" (*O.O.,* 175r).

In *De contagione,* Fracastoro wonders at things, yet he renders the wondrous part of a cultural commonplace by situating it within a larger similitude of things, which Foucault has characterized as central to the episteme of the sixteenth century and which Hayden White has viewed, in his tropological "decoding" of Foucault, as fundamental to the metaphoric structure of scientific knowledge at its inception.[14] When, for example, he discusses contagions that infect by means of *fomes,* a term he coins to describe objects that function as vehicles for *seminaria,* Fracastoro turns

13. Foucault, *The Birth of the Clinic,* xi, for example: "From what moment, from what semantic or syntactical change, can one recognize that language has turned into rational discourse? What sharp line divides a description [in the eighteenth century] that depicts membranes as being like 'damp parchment' from that other equally qualitative, equally metaphoric description [in the nineteenth] of them laid out over the tunic of the brain, like a film of egg whites?"

14. Foucault, *The Order of Things;* and White, "Foucault Decoded," esp. 246 and 252.

to the structure of familiar experience to illustrate how a malady can be transmitted in such a manner to the amazement of all: "If one desires to be convinced and feel no surprise that they can last and preserve their power so long in *fomes,* he should consider similar cases of this sort. Do we not observe that in wood, clothes, etc., a strange smell may be preserved for a long time, and that not due to some definite quality in them without material basis, but rather to bodies so very small as to be invisible to us? Or take the case of soot and smoke when walls are covered with it; do not these too, by the admixture of very small particles, become a dye that lasts without alteration for a very long time? Surely there are countless examples of this sort" (*DC,* 13). "Even more wondrous and hard to explain," Fracastoro asserts, "are those diseases that cause contagion, not by direct contact, or by *fomes* only, but also at a distance" (*DC,* 19). Nevertheless, however much "many people marvel" at the transmission of diseases across immense distances and over vast expanses of time, "we should consider precisely similar instances," Fracastoro cautions, "that we may be less surprised. Who would imagine that tears could be drawn from us, even from a long distance, by onions and garlic; that pepper, iris or ptarmicum could make one sneeze . . . ?" (*DC,* 29).

Fracastoro relies from the outset on the similitude of lived experience to define contagion, and he uses a specific rhetorical term in his *De contagione.* "When someone has been heated or sullied by something," Fracastoro writes, "we do not say, except by a metalepsis [*nisi per transumptionem*], that he has suffered contagion; because contagion is a precisely similar infection of the actual substance" (*DC,* 3–5). Yet we can only begin to understand contagion, a subject "full of wonder," through metaphoric discourse, through a likeness that requires us constantly to attribute to it a host of foreign qualities. We can best understand contagion only by first comparing and contrasting it—in this case through *dissimilitudinem* rather than *similitudinem*—to houses burning:

> Now when a house catches fire from the burning of a neighboring house, are we to call that contagion? No, certainly not, nor in general when the whole thing is destroyed primarily as a whole. The term is more correctly used when infection originates in very small imperceptible particles, and begins with them, as the word "infection" implies; for we use the term "infected," not of a something that is destroyed as a whole, but of a certain kind of destruction that affects its imperceptible particles. By the whole, I mean the actual composite, and by very small, imperceptible particles, I mean the particles of which the composite and mixture (combination) are composed. Now burning acts on the thing as a whole, whereas contagion

acts on the component particles, though by them the whole thing itself may presently be corrupted and destroyed. (*DC,* 5)

Fracastoro's initial investigation of the notion of contagion emerges not so much from empirical experience as imaginatively from the meaning of a single word. To infect, *inficere,* is to "stain," "tinge," as when a drop of ink falls into water and disperses, changing eventually the color of it all.[15]

Through the opening example of the houses burning, Fracastoro makes it clear that he uses the word "contagion" in the widest possible sense. He is concerned not only with contagious diseases but with the natural process by which one object passes on to another some foreign quality, thereby "tainting" the other object. A house passing fire does not qualify because fire is not something that taints but something that destroys. Though fire is not a process of contagion, heat is. As Fracastoro indicates, "an especially good instance of the contagion that infects by contact only is that which occurs in fruits, as when grape infects grape, or apple infects apple" (*DC,* 9). This process of "contagion" occurs because excess heat, evaporating from one putrefied grape or apple, "has passed on to the second fruit" (*DC,* 9). Heat is nevertheless transmitted in different ways in these two exemplary cases. With the fruit, the heat is passed on invisibly; with the burning houses, the heat is passed on through the visible means of flames. For contagion to occur, it must take place by means of "imperceptible particles, which [in the case of the fruit] are hot and sharp when they evaporate, but are moist in combination" (*DC,* 11). Between the two images of neighboring houses in flames and heat transmitted from fruit to fruit, Fracastoro inserts his notion of *fomes,* which literally means "tinder."[16] The term *fomes* thus functions as an especially apt metaphor for the agent that allows heat, an element essential for processes of contagion, to be released in the form of those hidden, invisible *seminaria.* In the opening pages, then, we can readily trace a consistency of imagery governed by the trope of metonymy. From flames we move to *fomes,* the "tinder" that give rise to flames. From the two related images of tinder and flames we then turn to the heat generated from them. Beyond this, Fracastoro will later use the image of "smoke" to describe and render evident "in the manner that is easiest to see . . .

15. On the meaning of "infection," and its history as a term and its relationship to notions of contagion, see Temkin, "An Historical Analysis of the Concept of Infection," in *The Double Face of Janus,* 456–71, esp. 457.

16. *Fomes,* as Wright (*DC,* 301 n. 4) points out, is a term used by Fracastoro to describe the explosive force of gunpowder.

how the *seminaria contagionum* are carried to a distant object and in a circle" (*DC,* 28–31). If Renaissance rhetoric drew on medical concepts to define as contagion the process by which the passions of the orator could enter into and stimulate the passions of the auditor, so medicine in the Renaissance, as evidenced in Fracastoro's *De contagione,* occasionally structured its discourse rhetorically.[17]

Time and again, Fracastoro relies on similitude as a figure of thought to account for the seemingly marvelous effects of contagion and the existence of invisible particles, for all things, as he says in *Turrius,* are understood through the appearances of other things in a world that is organically closed, connected, and whole. This is not to say that Fracastoro does not use observation when conceptualizing in this manner. It is, however, to say much about the field of perception within which Fracastoro operated, about the nature of scientific observation of the time, and about how it differed fundamentally from our own. "The observing gaze," Foucault writes, "refrains from intervening: it is silent and gestureless. Observation leaves things as they are; there is nothing hidden to it in what is given. The correlative of observation is never the invisible, but always the immediately visible, once one has removed the obstacles erected to reason by theories and to the senses by the imagination. In the clinician's catalogue, the purity of the gaze is bound up with a certain silence that enables him to listen. The prolix discourses of systems must be interrupted."[18] It is precisely this pure clinical gaze that Fracastoro lacks. He aims to describe not the visible but the invisible—imperceptible particles. To do so he relies as much on existing theories and "cognitively secured" systems of thought as on his own imagination, in which he can take a certain pleasure, as Fracastoro's poet does, in making connections out of similarities and in constructing rich metaphors. Fracastoro's gaze therefore perceives contagious diseases in particular—and the entire uni-

17. The transmission of heat, we may note in passing, is as much a medical concept as a descriptive rhetorical one. Traditionally, rhetoricians turned to the image of fire to describe how they invoke in themselves heated emotions so that they can in turn evoke those same emotions in the public, but as Struever reminds us, "the mention of 'fire' invokes the Hippocratic elements, humors, temperaments." Later in the century, one Renaissance rhetorician, obviously taken in by the overlapping of medical and rhetorical discourses, likened this process of inflaming an audience to "contagion." Just as heat invisibly passes from one object to another, disturbing the humors of simple and complex living organisms, so the heat of passions analogously passes on from the rhetor to an audience disturbed and visibly transformed by the experience. See Struever, "Rhetoric and Medicine in Descartes' *Passions de l'âme,*" 198; and Rebhorn, *The Emperor of Men's Minds,* 88.

18. Foucault, *The Birth of the Clinic,* 107.

verse and its invisible workings more generally—through the operation of similitude. Similitude allows him to advance the notion that contagion is invisible, that it takes place by direct contact, that *fomes* preserve a disease over short distances, and that imperceptible particles transmit it over long ones. Taken together, all these instances point to the existence of *seminaria contagionum,* a concept that then becomes real in *De contagione* when Fracastoro likens it to some other process—the passage of smells, heat, and the like. In this respect, it is not just the reality of "imperceptible particles" that is here metaphorically described. It is metaphoric discourse—the constant likening of one thing to another through "similitude"—that reifies in its turn a rich metaphor for describing contagion, *seminaria,* and then transforms it into something putatively real. Fracastoro's *seminaria* may be compared to other things and thereby familiarized; but that only draws attention away from the fact that they originated as and remain metaphorical themselves. No one, after all, has seen these seeds, least of all Fracastoro, who may have been more influenced by Lucretius's *De rerum natura* than by Galen's *De differentiis febrium* when he came up with his novel notion of *seminaria contagionum*—a notion that made at least one physician laugh with mocking wonder.[19]

Syphilis: *Wonder, the Metaphors of Illness, and Naming a "New" Disease*

The work to which *De sympathia et antipathia rerum* forms the introduction—*De contagione*—addresses one source of wonder that perplexed Fracastoro's culture at the time in which he wrote. This wonder was syphilis, "a new disease," as Fracastoro describes it in his *De contagione,* "long unknown on our continent, but it has appeared in our time among other marvelous phenomena" (*DC,* 135). Fracastoro calls the disease "syphilis" here, using the title of a poem he composed a decade and a half earlier, rather than the popular appellations "Morbus Gallicus" or "Neapolitan disease," which he conveniently listed along with a host of other terms in his *De contagione* (*DC,* 135). Syphilis had been universally recognized throughout Europe as a new and wondrous disease from the moment it

19. On the importance of Lucretius, see Singer and Singer, "The Scientific Position of Girolamo Fracastoro," 30; Wright, *DC,* 302; and Nutton, "The Seeds of Disease," 9. His importance is recognized yet ultimately downplayed by Pellegrini, *La dottrina fracastoriana,* 8–14; and it is largely dismissed in Hendrickson, "The 'Syphilis' of Girolamo Fracastoro," 516–17.

appeared on the continent.[20] Chroniclers such as Ramusio, Fracastoro's good friend and informer on much about the New World, remarked in his *Delle navigationi e viaggi* (1550–1559) how the malady seemed "a great marvel" to all those who witnessed or had contact with it,[21] and how physicians simply did not know how to treat it.[22] "A horrible and contagious disease, seeing that so many died of it," syphilis was a "marvel" that inspired fear, not laughter, in Ramusio, as it passed quickly from Hispaniola to the rest of Europe, leaving scarcely a part of the inhabited world untouched.[23]

Ramusio, who dedicated his *Delle navigationi e viaggi* to Fracastoro and provided him with information about syphilis, was not alone in locating the origins of this new disease in the New World. At the same time, Ramusio's observation about syphilis as a "great marvel" in some respects conforms to a familiar mechanism in the narratives of the New World, which typically transform the wondrous into a latent and potent symbol of loss.[24] In the *Decades,* for example, Peter Martyr (1457–1526)—yet another chronicler who was a source for Fracastoro—briefly registers his astonishment at the rapidity with which all seeds ripen to maturity in the New World—"O marvelous fruitfulness" [O mira ubertas]—before he returns to the more sedate task of cataloguing "the best" that the "native trees and fruits of diverse kinds" have to offer. Yet all this "marvelous fruitfulness," composed of both common and exotic flora, could just as easily be threatening. "Our men," Peter Martyr writes, "found certain trees in this province, which bore great plenty of sweet apples, but hurtful, for they turn into worms when they are eaten. Especially the shadow of the tree is contagious, for such as sleep under it any time have their heads swollen and lose their sight."[25] As Europe's conquerors invaded a land that must have sometimes seemed—as it did to Columbus—like Eden, they could not help but encounter, in the ripeness of the moment that the marvelous initially seemed to proffer, the symbol of an original, distant pastoral bliss. With the image of a "sweet" ingested apple metamorphosed

20. See, in general, Foa, "The New and the Old"; and Arrizabalaga, Henderson, and French, *The Great Pox,* esp. 264–66.

21. Ramusio, *Delle navigationi e viaggi,* 92r.

22. Ibid., 92r.

23. Ibid., 92r and 65v.

24. For reflections on the function of wonder in the New World, see Greenblatt, *Marvelous Possessions.*

25. D'Anghiera, *De rebus oceanicis,* 25v and 39v. I draw the translation from Eden, *The First Three English Books on America,* 131 and 106–7; I have modernized the English. Peter Martyr did not associate syphilis with the new world, however.

into a worm, the wonder of discovery suddenly gives way to the wonder of recognition, and with that recognition the explorers rediscover the familiar haunting presence of Edenic loss. By contrast, syphilis never appeared so wonderfully attractive to chroniclers who linked its origin to the New World, but as a marvel it did often emerge in their narratives as a powerful symbol of loss. Not far beneath the surface of Ramusio's chronicle is the implication that syphilis spread primarily because of the lascivious, and hence sinful, nature of European men and women. For his part, Gonzalo Fernandez de Oviedo, the first chronicler to link the disease to the New World, viewed syphilis in his *Historia general y natural de las Indias* as payment in kind for the sin of greed, in this case the European greed for gold.[26]

But early syphilographers viewed the disease not so much as payment for a particular person's sin as a *flagellum dei* that indiscriminately struck the community at large. Long before the association between syphilis and the New World was ever broached, syphilographers interpreted the disease as God's visitation of anger upon all humankind for our sins, whether blasphemy, adultery, theft, pride, greed, religious torpor, schism, or licentiousness.[27] Initially, however, there was little personal shame in contracting the disease. It was only after 1520, according to most scholars, around the time in which both Fracastoro and his good friend Ramusio were writing, that syphilis was linked to the sin of a particular person. And it was only after 1520 that syphilis really began to be seen as a venereal disease,[28] a disease, as Fracastoro writes in *De contagione,* that first "appeared on the sexual organs, because it was in that locality and mainly from sexual intercourse that the contagion had its origin and beginning" (*DC,* 153). Soon enough, writers of imaginative literature seized on syphilis as an object of representation, with very different strategies in mind. Some found the wondrous disease good for grim, moralizing, satiric humor; others superimposed pox—eventually construed as the disease of prostitutes—onto a misogynistic image of feminine otherness and sexuality.[29] It would seem that in the European Renaissance, syphilis

26. Cited in Gerbi, *La natura delle Indie nove,* 520.

27. Amundsen, "The Moral Stance of the Earliest Syphilographers, 1495–1505," in *Medicine, Society, and Faith,* 310–72 passim.

28. This was first pointed out in Temkin, "On the History of Morality and Syphilis," in *The Double Face of Janus,* 472–84. For more on the moral attitudes toward syphilis, see Amundsen, "The Moral Stance of the Earliest Syphilographers"; and Schleiner, "Infection and Cure through Women" and "Moral Attitudes toward Syphilis."

29. Quétel, *History of Syphilis,* 11, 67–72.

could inspire both fear and hilarity in the popular and learned imagination of writers and readers. But syphilis, which Fracastoro in his medical study *De contagione* does not consider the product of evil or a sign of sin, instills neither fear nor pity in this physician. Neither does it inspire hilarity, because frankly syphilis is not ridiculous, though Fracastoro does acknowledge at one point that people do look perfectly ludicrous when, to the amazement of everyone, their hair falls out all over their bodies (*DC,* 139). Rather, syphilis elicits the passion of wonder, though a wonder that dissipates as philosophical inquiry produces knowledge. Syphilis may seem a marvel, but we must not marvel, Fracastoro claims in his *De contagione,* if marvels indeed appear from time to time:

> Now, in the first place, we ought not be surprised that novel and unusual diseases appear at certain times, diseases not conveyed from one country to another, but arising from their own peculiar causes. For instance, in the year 1482 there broke out a certain kind of pleurisy which affected almost the whole of Italy. And in our own times there have appeared in Italy those fevers never before observed there, which are called "lenticulae," and have been described above. Also, in bygone years, we have observed a contagious ophthalmia that attacked certain countries; again, we have seen that pest which is prevalent among cattle only and is recorded above. Hence it ought not to surprise us that the French Sickness also, though not previously known to our continent for many centuries, has now broken out for the first time. There will come yet other new and unusual ailments, as time brings them in its course; just as mentagra appeared among the ancients and has never since appeared again. And this disease of which I speak, this syphilis too will pass away and die out, but later it will be born again and be seen again by our grandchildren, just as in bygone ages we must believe it was observed by our ancestors. (*DC,* 145–47)

Like Fracastoro, other physicians recognized the novelty of the disease and regarded it with wonder. It was a "monstrous disease," the physician Jacopo Cattaneo (*fl.* 1510) of Geneva recorded in about 1504, "never before seen in any century, and unknown throughout the whole world"; another, Giorgio Vella of Brescia, deemed it "new and painful and indeed worthy of wonder."[30] Unlike most observers, however, physicians, bringing their professional expertise to bear on the topic, sometimes became highly self-conscious about the very discourse of novelty and wonder associated with the disease. Early syphilographers were largely in agreement that the disease was "unheard of before," as Bartholomaus Steber,

30. Cattaneo, *De morbo Gallico tractatus* (probably composed in 1504), in Luisinus, 1.123; and Vella, *De morbo Gallico,* in Luisinus 1.180.

professor of medicine and rector of the university of Vienna, phrased it in his *A malafranczos, morbo Gallorum, praeservatio ac cura* (ca. 1497).[31] But with the publication of Nicolò Leoniceno's *De morbo Gallico* in 1497, a debate soon developed as to whether the disease was in fact new.[32] Much of the "violent controversy," as Fracastoro himself put it (*DC,* 143), revolved around trying to establish a name for the disease. Had the ancients provided a full classification of diseases, Renaissance syphilographers asked? If so, we can rule syphilis out as a new disease; if not, how is it possible for a new disease to arise, and what are we to call it? For Leoniceno, a hellenist who refused to admit any supernatural explanations to account for natural phenomena, the answer was that there could be no completely new diseases. The disease had existed, but the ancients neglected to name it because it had never appeared in such a virulent way. To prove this, Leoniceno, who rigorously grounded his knowledge on Greek authorities, proceeded to demolish any possible connection between syphilis and prior diseases mentioned in classical texts.[33] Other syphilographers disagreed; some, such as Fracastoro, waffled.[34] Eventually one threw up his hands in disgust, having obviously grown weary of the entire debate. Giovanni Pascale (*fl.* 1534), a physician interested more in the essence than in the name of the malady, asked: "Why, concerning the novelty of this disease, is it elaborated on by garrulous, loquacious, villainous, and most inactive physicians, and especially with the greatest of all possible wonder?"[35] Yet another syphilographer, the German physician Wendelin Hock von Brackenau (*fl.* 1502–1514), who had been trained in medicine

31. Steber, *A malafranczos, morbo Gallorum, praeservatio ac cura,* in Sudhoff, ed., *The Earliest Printed Literature on Syphilis,* 265.

32. On Leoniceno and his school, see Carrara, "Fra causalità astrologica e causalità naturale"; the brief yet cogent observations of Foa, "The New and the Old," 28–29 and esp. 42–43 n. 9; and, above all, on Leoniceno and syphilis, see Arrizabalaga, Henderson, and French, *The Great Pox,* 56–87, discussing the debate at the court of Ferrara. More generally, see the excellent summary by Grafton, Shelford, and Siraisi, *New Worlds, Ancient Texts,* 176–93. For Renaissance medical treatises on syphilis, I rely on the material in Sudhoff, ed., *The Earliest Printed Literature on Syphilis;* and Luisinus.

33. On Leoniceno and syphilis, see Arrizabalaga, Henderson, and French, *The Great Pox,* 56–87 in general.

34. As there were completely new climates, the Ferrarese physician and professor of medicine Antonio Musa Brasavola (1500–1555) argued, so there could be completely new diseases: Brasavola, *De morbo Gallico* (1553), in Luisinus, 1.575ff, for example. Fracastoro in some ways sat on the fence. He agreed with Leoniceno—"a man of the greatest learning and authority" and "the first to clear up this difficulty"—that syphilis "was a disease never named by the ancients" (*DC,* 143), yet he maintained that new diseases could arise.

35. Pascale, *De morbo quodam composito qui vulgo apud nos Gallicus appellatur,* in Luisinus, 1.192. See Arrizabalaga, Henderson, and French, *The Great Pox,* 259–61.

at Bologna, argued for the absolute centrality of wonder in coming to terms with the disease: "our understanding," he wrote in his *De morbo Gallicus opus* (1514),

> begins through the path of the sense, and we must understand through those things which are previously known, and from the understanding of the unknown come to understanding through wonder—at any rate those things that are dealt with in parts of philosophy; and thus it is of the greatest necessity to wonder about the marvels of philosophy. For the Greeks and Egyptians began to philosophize by wondering, and from wonder they arrived at the known from the unknown. So also it happens in medicine, that through wonder about some disease unknown to us we can come to knowledge of it. So it has occurred at this time, namely from the year 1494 of our Lord to the present year of 1514, in which a certain contagion, which is called Gallicus. . . . Indeed, that disease has received many names, for, just as it has invaded the peoples of many climates, so diverse names have been placed on it.[36]

The wonder of syphilis initially compelled Fracastoro to compose a poem on the subject, although many Renaissance followers of Aristotle thought that writing a philosophical-medical poem simply meant putting philosophy into verse, and that this did not constitute "poetry," which should be the imitation of great and heroic exploits. According to Aristotle's *Poetics,* "people generally attach the word 'poet' to the name of a particular meter and speak, for example, of elegiac poets and epic poets, calling them poets, not on the basis of imitation, but indiscriminately according to the meter they use. This is customary even when what is produced is a versified treatise on medicine or natural science. But Homer and Empedocles have nothing in common except just their meter, and it is right, therefore, to call the one a poet and the other a physical philosopher rather than a poet" (1447b).[37] For Fracastoro, however, poetry taught, and one of the ways it taught was through wonder inspired by the beauty of eloquence. Fracastoro makes this claim most forcefully in his *Naugerius.* The poet "who wishes to arouse admiration in all" (*N,* 69) seeks to construct beauty, he writes, for "all falsification is ugly and precludes admiration" (*N,* 70). Once more, in his *Turrius*—the dialogue that follows directly upon the *Naugerius*—Fracastoro insists that poets "are used to wonder and are customarily conquered by the greatness and a beauty of things" (*O.O.,* 206r). For this reason, poets are like philosophers, who

36. Hock, *De morbo Gallico,* in Luisinus, 1.268. See Arrizabalaga, Henderson, and French, *The Great Pox,* 254, 259–61, 270.

37. Aristotle, *Aristotle's "Poetics,"* 45.

"are inclined to wonder" (*O.O.*, 205v), and, like philosophers, poets are propelled through wonder to understand and take pleasure in "the causes of things" (*O.O.*, 206r), just as Lucretius did in his *De rerum natura*. Poets may imitate to know, and by imitating they may come to know with pleasure the causes of things through wonder, which is the passion that stimulates inquiry in the philosopher and leads to the highest level of understanding:

> Hence, among poets many were also great philosophers, just as among philosophers many were great poets. They differ in this respect: those that by nature are more philosophers than poets insist more and find greater pleasure in uncovering the causes of things; those instead that are more poets than philosophers are captured by the beauty of things; they love to imitate and illustrate those things and cannot stand that there is something lacking in any degree of beauty or decorum. For this reason, in the event that some things happen to be missing, they add them and invent them and in a certain sense generate perfect things. Poets in a certain sense take pleasure in giving birth to that which is conceived, the philosophers instead take pleasure in keeping those things inside. So philosophers are born more to know and less to imitate, the poets more to imitate. If, however, some are inclined to both activities, they are both philosophers and poets. (*O.O.*, 206r)

For Fracastoro, for whom "there is practically only one sort of subject which is absolutely beautiful, the heroic" (*N*, 64), epic poetry moves readers most of all through wonder toward an understanding of the causes of things. Accordingly, Fracastoro, who aims to create both an epic poem and an edifying medical text that discloses the "vast work of Nature," privileges the passion of wonder from the outset. In an opening that borrows from the *Georgics* in style but from the *De rerum natura* in subject matter (1.1), Fracastoro calls upon the muses as "lovers of wonders" (1.14) to help him disclose the causes of this "novelty" (1.12).[38] Guided by these lovers of *mira*, Fracastoro then turns to discuss the wonder of the new disease that has struck the world in his own time:

> Therefore seeing that contagions vary so much in nature and type and that there are many seeds, with fascinating characteristics, contemplate this one too whose origin is heaven. It burst into the air, a disease as marvelous as it was strange. It did not infect the silent creatures of the deep, the swarms of those that swim, nor birds, nor dumb animals wandering in high forests, nor

38. As Eatough points out in Fracastoro, *Fracastoro's "Syphilis,"* 112 n. 12, the term is Lucretian. Lucretius, for example, also speaks of the "novelty" of his topic in *De rerum natura*, 1.139.

> herds of oxen or sheep or herds of horses, but out of all the species the one that is great through its mind, the human race, and it feeds, pasturing deep within our limbs. Moreover, from the whole of man this filthy disease seizes on that in the blood which is thick and dirty through its sluggishness, feeding on the rich slime. The disease and blood correspond in this particular way. Now I shall teach you all the conditions and symptoms of this sad contagion. (1.294–308)

In terms of *De contagione* and, more generally, *De sympathia et antipathia,* syphilis is here regulated by "analogy," the principle of "selective affinity," which regulates all things and determines that some diseases affect some things while others affect others.[39] In speaking of the variety of diseases and how they afflict and infect a multitude of animate things at different times, Fracastoro further invokes the classical idea of the harmony of nature, "above all a wondrous nature" (1.261–62), which maintains its balance not despite, but precisely because of, the discordant elements in it. Syphilis is marvelous in part because it affects people rather than animals or vegetation, thereby ensuring the harmony of things. Nature, according to the classical principle of *concordia discors,* needs our diseases, and there is beauty in this perfect balance if we only contemplate our diseases from the viewpoint of Lucretian serenity: "felix qui potuit rerum cognoscere causas" [Happy is he who has been able to win knowledge of the causes of things, *G.* 2.490].[40]

For Fracastoro, however, it is difficult to maintain a posture of Lucretian philosophical detachment and serenity. The philosophical poet, immersed in his own time, cannot retreat from the world in which he lives. As Fracastoro contemplates the disease, his poem consequently takes a turn toward epic heroism rooted not in philosophical detachment but in historical engagement. To mark this shift textually, Fracastoro alludes to the moment when Aeneas hopes to lift up the spirits of his weary companions by having them project themselves into a happier future in which all the trials of the past are but a pleasant memory. "Forsan," Aeneas says to his companions on the shores of Carthage, "et haec olim meminisse iuvabit" [perchance even this distress will some day be a joy to recall, 1.203]. "Forte," Fracastoro announces to his readers, "etenim nostros olim legisse nepotes, / Et signa, et faciem pestis novisse juvabit" [For perhaps in the future our descendants will find pleasure in reading them and in recognizing the plague's symptoms and shape, 1.312–13].

39. See in particular Fracastoro, *DC,* 38–39.
40. Virgil, *Eclogues, Georgics, Aeneid.*

Fracastoro nevertheless marks a significant change in temporal focus as he echoes the *Aeneid.* In the *Syphilis,* heroism takes place not in the past but in the present, and the trials Fracastoro's heroes must face seem greater by comparison. Aeneas had to face the passion of Juno, Dido, and Turnus. Europeans must face a greater passion in the form of the disease of syphilis, which many believed had come about from men lying with whores. As a sign of the deleterious effects of this disease, the origins of which according to popular conceptions were in lasciviousness, the disease first strikes men and women in the genitalia, literally "eating" away at the seat of desire: "Slowly a caries, born amid squalor in the body's shameful parts, became uncontrollable and began to eat the areas on either side and even the sexual organ" (1.330–31). One boy, Fracastoro recounts, is even wounded to the point of being unrecognizable, much as Virgil's Deiphobus was: "Ugly sores (ye gods have pity) began to devour his lovely eyes and his love of the holy light and to devour his nose, which was gnawed away, leaving a piercing wound" (1.405–7). Yet this disease not only engages people in a sort of war, attacking and leaving them savagely marred; it also moves with Mars, the god of war (1.413). Indeed, syphilis eventually becomes a metaphor for the inability of the Italians to liberate themselves from the foreigners who have invaded Italy and transformed Fracastoro's homeland into a place of death, war, and disease (1.416–20, 437–40).

Fracastoro was not alone in envisioning syphilis through the imagery of warfare, an image that in our own time is the most common and nefarious of metaphors of illness, according to Susan Sontag. Sixteenth-century syphilographers occasionally demonized syphilis as a ruthless enemy that engaged us in a battle at once personal and communal. "It declares war [*bellum*] on the physicians," the syphilitic Joseph Grünpeck (ca. 1473–ca. 1532) wrote in his *Libellus de mentulagra alias morbo Gallico* (1503), "unfurling on the outer surface of the skin its banner of hate and strife," while in response "doctors, provoked by this signal into offering combat and into attacking it with potent medicines, attempt to snatch it forth and destroy it."[41] Not only did soldiers spread the disease when they first invaded Italy; the disease left those soldiers pitiful victims. Grünpeck's description of Maximilian's soldiers strewn about the fields, stricken by the disease, not only makes them appear as defenseless, battle-weary victims; it transforms the disease into a victorious agent engaged in a merciless

41. Gruner, *Aphrodisiacus,* 67, 63–69 for the Latin text; I rely on the translation in Zimmerman, "Joseph Grünpeck's *Libellus,*" 379.

war against them.[42] These soldiers have lost the battle. Filthy, pus-ridden, and pathetic, picking at their scabs—one might recall—like the diseased sinners in canto 29 of Dante's *Inferno,* Maximilian's soldiers have been defeated by an enemy who not only savagely maims them but deprives them of even a remotely heroic appearance. About forty years later, one syphilographer, describing how the illness "eats up the cartilage," was taken in by this sort of imagery of warfare and went so far as to recall the Greek invasion of Troy as Virgil portrayed it in one of the most pathetic and tragic moments in the *Aeneid:* the illness, we are given to believe, affects the diseased "in the manner of the character of Deiphobus," who is described in book 6 of the *Aeneid* as "Mutilated from hand to foot, his face and both hands cruelly torn, ears shorn away."[43]

In the first medical poem describing the disease, *El somario de la medicina* (1498), Francisco Lopez de Villalobos (1473–1548), a young medical student at the University of Salamanca, proclaimed that syphilis—"So evil and perverse and cruel past control, / Exceedingly contagious, and in filth so prodigal"—was a vile disease "against which victory is not attained [*no se alcança vitoria*]."[44] Syphilis could therefore not be for Villalobos the subject of heroic verse. Grünpeck's description of the soldiers strewn about the battlefield, grotesquely laughing at themselves and picking at their ugly, filthy scabs, would leave little to recommend the notion that syphilis made for heroic epic. There is, after all, little glory, much less "victory" to be attained, in being portrayed as Deiphobus, whose vulnerable body records all the savagery of the Greeks and who, far from being portrayed as heroic, recognizes Aeneas instead as the one surviving hero from the Trojan war (*Aen.,* 6.546). Fracastoro's representation of disease, however, may be characterized as consistently heroic in his use of the metaphor of warfare, and this is true even where he warns against just such tendencies. "We must not say, as some do," Fracastoro writes in *De contagione,* "that poisons and contagions try above all to make for and attack the heart, like an enemy, as though they possessed cognition and will" (*DC,* 34–35). Yet contagious diseases occasionally take on a demonic character in

42. Ibid., 374.

43. Antonio Gallo [Antoine Lecoq], *De ligno sancto non permiscendo,* in Luisinus, 1.396: "Cartilagines quibusdam momento depascitur, ut Deiphobi personam sic affectos agere credas, lacerum crudeliter ora: Ora manusque, ambas, populataque tempora raptis / Auribus, & truncas inhonesto vulnere nares." The citation is from *Aen.,* 6.495–97.

44. Lopez de Villalobos, *Text and Concordance of the "Sumario de la medicina,"* 82; I use the translation, slightly modified for accuracy, from Gaskoin, *Medical Works of Francisco Lopez de Villalobos,* 94. See Riddell, "Sebastian Brandt," 63–74, esp. 72.

his medical treatise, appropriating human or animal-like qualities, as they "lurk, hostile and insidious" (*DC,* 49). As enemies of our bodies and, by extension, as enemies of our bodies politic once they become epidemics, contagious diseases must be remorselessly and heroically attacked and killed, "blotted out and, so to speak, slain, expelled, or broken and altered, or driven back" (*DC,* 191). Needless to say, Fracastoro capitalizes on just such heroic imagery in his *Syphilis,* where this new and highly contagious disease becomes, as it was for so many in the Italian Renaissance, a feared and privileged object of wonder against which we are engaged in a war. Thanks to the work of physicians, one could win the battle, and therein lay the value of the struggle. One could emerge, not unscarred, but a better person as a result. One could actually come out purified from the struggle. This was Fracastoro's strategy. Fracastoro transforms the disease into a living being that victimizes the subject it attacks; yet Deiphobus can be cured, his scars wiped away. There will be a time, in the Virgilian phrase, when one can look back happily on all this.

Engaged in a war from which we will emerge victorious (2.10), the second book addresses the pain the body must endure to survive. We must discipline our bodies and our desires; admit no leisure into our lives (2.87); refrain from sexual pleasure (2.113–14). We must combat this "savage plague" (2.256) as though engaged in a constant battle against an enemy. Much as Allecto changed shape and invaded Amata in book 7 of the *Aeneid,* syphilis surreptitiously winds its way into the bodies of men and women like a serpent, as it manages "to snake inside the body in wondrous ways" (2.197). As victims of the disease, we must even cut into ourselves at times, scarring the body with knives (2.165–68). Phlebotomy becomes the medical equivalent in Fracastoro's text to the epic convention of wounding, while the myth of the discovery of mercury, whose "marvelous structure" (2.276) yields a "miraculous power" (2.271), conforms to the epic topos of the descent.[45] Ilceus, who receives word in a dream of what he must do, is guided into the Underworld (2.369–74). Like Aeneas, Ilceus comes to a fork in the road, and, like Aeneas, he is ritually cleansed. The goal of the voyage, as it traditionally is for the epic hero, is purification and renewal. Yet mercury, which Ilceus discovers, is not the cure about which the poet of *Syphilis* finally sings; it is just one of the many "wondrous discoveries of men" (2.4). The true cure, guaiacum, Fracastoro anticipates instead at the beginning of book 2.

45. Some of these topoi, along with others, are noted in Ziolkowski, "Epic Conventions in Fracastoro's Poem *Syphilis.*"

There he reminds the reader that his age, despite all the hardships of disease and war and famine, distinguished itself by sailing across the oceans and making contact with the New World, which is a land full of wonders about which Fracastoro will only partly sing.

Toward the beginning of the third and last book of *Syphilis,* Fracastoro finally tells how Columbus and his men disembark at Hispaniola and discover the cure. Hispaniola is a second golden-age land, the Biblical Ophyre, a grand and beautiful place that inspires awe in the Spaniards, who marvel at its rich golden river: "some gazed in wonder at the river's deep yellow stream and sifted the gold-mingled sand" (3.149–50). Appropriating elements of the *Aeneid,* Fracastoro has the voyagers come to the New World as Aeneas voyaged to Arcadia, with nymphs of the sea—along with the inhabitants—wondering at the Europeans: "they marveled at the tall ships with their massive structure, at the men's garb and flashing arms" (3.203–4).[46] The world discovered in Fracastoro's poem is a world full of marvels, both familiar and new, just as it was for Fracastoro's friend Ramusio and a host of other chroniclers. Yet amid this beauty in a land full of extraordinary variety, the Spaniards hear the birds of Apollo prophesy in a story "wondrous to tell" (3.172) how their bodies will soon be "filthy with an unknown disease" (3.190). From health the Spaniards have come to sickness, from joy to fear, from purity to impurity, and from wonder at the richness of things in a place "fertile in gold" (3.34) to the anticipation of, and subsequent recognition of, Edenic loss. Hispaniola, which initially appeared as a *locus amoenus* of "happy groves" (3.1), a rich pastoral paradise, has suddenly become a place of woe as the Spaniards, marveling (3.248), gaze at a host of men, women, and children gathered together in a valley and covered with scabs overflowing with pus. Columbus, recognizing this to be the horrible illness that the birds of Apollo had prophesied, turns to the native king for an explanation.

The king recounts the origins of the unknown disease and the strange accompanying rite. A long time ago, he explains, a young shepherd named Syphilus, who tended the flock of king Alcithous of Hispaniola, pitied the sheep and oxen languishing beneath the scorching heat of the sun during the summer solstice. Defiant, Syphilus looked up to the sky and hurled insults at the sun. He declared that he would now worship king Alcithous, who had the power to provide both Syphilus and his weary flock with relief. The country folk and shepherds soon followed Syphilus, emboldened by his arrogance. So too king Alcithous, flattered by the adoration,

46. On wonders and wondering in epic, see Biow, *Mirabile Dictu.*

ordered his subjects to worship only him as a god. But the sun god, Apollo, responded with anger to this rebellion. He sent a devastating illness to plague the land. This disease, which horribly disfigured bodies with "vile sores" (3.329), attacked Syphilus first of all. Syphilus first disregarded the power of the gods who govern the cosmos and the laws of men. But he also turned his back on Apollo, and thereby on all that Apollo represents. His crime, so viewed, was a rejection of not just the god of philosophy, poetry, and medicine but the god whom Fracastoro, as a poet-physician, counted as his own muse,[47] and the god whom Fracastoro indeed invokes in the opening of *Syphilis* as the one who first dignified the subject he treats:

> Do not disdain my undertaking, this labor of medicine [*medicumque laborem*], such as it is. The god Apollo once dignified these matters: small things, also, often have within them their own particular delights. Be certain that beneath the slender appearance of this topic there lies concealed a vast work of Nature and of fate and a grand origin. (19–23)

A philosophical poem, which brings together poetry and medicine to disclose a "vast work of Nature," thus closes with a myth of a shepherd who, laboring so close to Nature in all its wonder-inspiring grandeur and beauty, rejects the god who inspired the making of the poem in the first place as a *medicum laborem*. Syphilus, who symbolically turns away from the god of medicine, must therefore be dealt with harshly within a medical poem. He must suffer terribly so that others, like the Spaniards (3.402), may wonder at his disease and its cure. And by that wondering, readers may come to understand the true nature of the disease and its cure in guaiacum, which astonishingly heals all the sores (3.86).

In locating the guaiacum in the New World and in showing us how we may win this heroic battle against syphilis, Fracastoro still had to adapt the structure of pagan epic to the theological structure of the Christian universe. He needed to bring his reader from one conception to another of the causes of things in history, from seeds that kill to seeds that literally cure in the form of the guaiac tree that has sprouted from just such a seed. "The seeds of things" [*semina rerum*], about which Lucretius spoke in his *De rerum natura* but which did not make him wonder, therefore become in Augustinian terms the *rationes seminales* that created the miracles that men could marvel over as signs of God's unfolding power and presence in history. Those miracles would be found not in Europe but in the Arcadia

47. See, for example, Wright, *DC,* vii–viii, esp. notes 2 and 3; see also Eatough in *Fracastoro's Syphilis,* 112 n. 19.

of the New World, where nymphs spoke to the sailors on their ships and where one finds not greed, lust, or syphilis but the cure. Trees, as in Peter Martyr's description of the New World, may hold the figurative fruit of Adam's sin, but they may also contain, as Fracastoro's Columbus discovers, the seeds of redemption. Hence, the overall structure of Fracastoro's philosophical and heroic epic is made to conform to a familiar threefold Christian pattern. The land discovered must operate as a healthy corrective to the errors of the past. The first book consequently tells the story of sin, and it has its epic antihero: the disease that "has raged" [saeviit, 1.5, 67, 196] and has transformed the scarred sick into vulnerable, tragic figures like Deiphobus. The second book tells the story of purgation, and it involves the epic descent and the punishment that the body must endure, with "the torture of mercury" envisioned as "the atonement of sin."[48] The third book tells the story of redemption, in which the holy wood becomes the pagan version of the holy cross; its "holy seed" [semine sacro, 3.405] compensates for the "seeds of disease." History thus falls into a providential plan, and the wonder of epic leads to joyful admiration in the final verses of the poem.

Yet there is a problem in all this for a humanist poet and physician such as Fracastoro in search of fame (1.294–311). Lucretius, enlightened by philosophy, requires that we read through his poem to become enlightened even in the face of plague at the end. In theory, however, it hardly matters if we remember his poem or not, only that we reach a state of happy Epicurean understanding beyond history, at which point we are supposed no longer to wonder at the causes of things but to contemplate them with serenity: "mirari mitte" (6.1056).[49] Unlike Lucretius, who sang in his epic of philosophical detachment, Virgil sang of empire and history through the heroic exploits of a man and arms. Hence, so long as Rome remains, so too Virgil's name will stay with us all, and Rome, for Virgil, will survive as an empire without end. Things, however, are different for Fracastoro. Fracastoro sings of a disease that will come and go just as empires and civilizations come and go. Fracastoro's humanist desire to win fame for himself through poetic form is thus potentially undermined by his profession. On the one hand, his profession provides him with the material and knowledge to write a *medicum laborem*. On the

48. Temkin, "On the History of Morality and Syphilis," 475.

49. See Clay, *Lucretius and Epicurus,* 260; and Gage, *Myth and Poetry in Lucretius,* esp. 224–25. Lucretius, *De rerum natura,* enforces this connection between wonder and ignorance in the last book, no doubt to remind us that wonder is precisely not the emotion we should experience in the face of the plague (6.489, 608, 655, 850, 910).

other hand, his profession provides him with the inescapable foresight that the very same medical knowledge, which dominates so much of the poem and is integral to its *materia,* will one day no longer be needed. As Fracastoro announces in *De contagione,* that day has already come. The disease, having "now entered on its old age," has already begun to disappear, and soon enough "it will come to pass, at length, that it will be unable to propagate itself and will cease to be" (*DC,* 157; see also *DC,* 145). In writing about syphilis, Fracastoro has thus linked his name not to the fiction of philosophical detachment or to an empire's permanence in history but to the current medical belief that contagious diseases operate in cycles:

> For a time will come again, by permission of the fates, as the years slip by, when the plague will pass away and lie sleeping deeply in black night: in turn after long centuries that same disease will rise again, and once more visit the heavens and air, and again some age to come will regard it with wonder. (1.315–18)

Future ages will wonder at this disease. As a result they may regard Fracastoro's poem with wonder, admiring it and consulting it for its beauty and its cure. In remembering Fracastoro's poem, perhaps they may remember him. Perhaps, for that matter, we can one day look back happily on all this.

Coming upon syphilis, then, was not like discovering the New World, which the ancients, as Fracastoro reminds us in his poem, had simply never seen (2.35–36). Coming upon syphilis meant facing a marvel that had existed all along but to which no one had yet given a name that had adhered. The ultimate problem for Fracastoro consequently becomes one of naming a wondrous illness that must be classified under the rubric of a "new disease" (*DC,* 147), even though Fracastoro is sure, as his esteemed predecessor Leoniceno was, that the disease had been around for a long time. Not even the ancients, who must have witnessed syphilis, had given it a name. The ancients had given names to other marvels. The voyagers had given names to lands discovered in their heroic exploits of wonder (3.22). The "Indians" had given the name to the tree that cures the disease. Now it was Fracastoro's turn. As a humanist poet and professional physician in search of *fama,* Fracastoro aims to name a marvel that the ancients had no doubt witnessed but never sufficiently recognized for what it was. He will do what they never did—fix for future generations the disease in epic form, create an enduring medical myth by which he can be remembered. And yet what we remember today is not the details of the myth he created but simply the name he gave to the disease, a name that may etymologically mean—in all its curious ambiguity—either "lover of swine" (*sus-philos*) or "one who makes love" (*sym-philos*).[50] The humanist physician and poet, hailed in his own time as a second Virgil and much admired by Bembo, has gained immortality not so much through poetry, through the cure he offered, or through his supposed contribution to modern contagion theory. He has instead gained immortality by giving a name to a disease that marks the syphilitic person through literary myth, whether he or she knows it, as both a lover of carnal knowledge and a lowly lover of swine. As Giambattista Vico knew, there are far stranger things to be found and to wonder at in the original metaphoric meanings of words.

50. Eatough in *Fracastoro's "Syphilis,"* 25 and n. 170 for a bibliography on the debated etymology of the name.

Ambassadors

Four

EXEMPLARY WORK

Two Venetian Humanists Writing on the Resident Ambassador

"I would consider myself most fortunate if you were to teach me all about the ambassador, his office and aim, in much the same way as these very same things are discussed by others with regard to the orator. It is likely indeed that the orator, who shares in part the name of ambassador, is similar to the ambassador, and perhaps in ancient times they were the same, doing the same thing." "With great pleasure I will try to please you," responded the spirit, "and touching on only the universal notion [of the ambassador], I will try to be brief, in such a manner that you will neither feel that I have obscured things nor desire more information on the truth of the matter." "That," I said, "would be pleasing. And in just such a manner, I understand, Ermolao Barbaro treated the art of being an ambassador. . . ."

—TORQUATO TASSO

Andrea Navagero, Fracastoro's close friend and a revered Venetian humanist, came into contact with many marvels of "America" when he was ambassador to Spain. On more than one occasion he wrote back to Gianbattista Ramusio about some of the "new things" his acquaintance Peter Martyr had spoken of, as well as some of the things that he had even seen for himself and tasted, such as the remarkable "potato."[1] But for Navagero, who cared more for the old than for the new world, the true marvel rarely consisted of something so alien or exotic. In his diary, Navagero occasionally praised the botany, palaces, people, and customs of

1. Navagero, *Opera omnia,* 265, 277–78. The epigraph is taken from Tasso, *Il messaggiero,* in *Prose,* 58; my translation.

Spain. He admired the water in particular.[2] And as if it were jogging his memory and bringing to mind Venice with its lovely canals, he praised—as one might expect an amateur botanist would have praised—the irrigation systems and aqueducts, which for the most part kept the market districts in the cities clean. But by and large, Navagero's diary, like most ambassadorial diaries or reports, is filled with bland impersonal facts. The office of the resident ambassador was not created so that humanists like Navagero could go about the world admiring the things they had seen, nor to allow its occupants to marvel (as Navagero did on occasion in his letters) at things or people borne from a strange and foreign land, gripped by the kind of wonder we more often associate with such Renaissance travel writers as Gianbattista Ramusio or Peter Martyr. "As a matter of fact," Ottaviano Maggi admonished some forty years later in his treatise on the ambassador, "it must be recognized first by the ambassador that he should never seem to be struck by wonder or to stand in awe; for wonder is born from the ignorance of things, in which state of wonderment it is disgraceful for a man, who in his entire life has undertaken matters of great weight, to be deeply engaged."[3] The resident ambassador, entrusted with grave matters, should never appear in the least bit puzzled. The business of the resident ambassador was not to wonder about the things he saw, nonplussed as he traveled to a foreign power. The business of the resident ambassador was to represent his government abroad and collect reliable and useful facts. Therein lay his *dignitas,* his worth and place in society. Any deviation from that behavioral norm signaled a fall from accepted diplomatic decorum. At the very least, it made the ambassador appear, both to the host power and to his own, as less than exemplary.

Venice, the government for which Navagero was gathering news, traditionally looms large in the historiography of diplomacy and ambassadorial service in the Italian Renaissance for a number of reasons. As a maritime republic with a wide network of commercial interests overseas, Venice was one of the first Italian states to send ambassadors on lengthy and somewhat regular missions throughout Europe and even the Orient. Venice's ties with other states far and wide consequently contributed to the development in Italy of the novel institution of the resident ambassador, an institution Garrett Mattingly in his magisterial study considers to be the "distinguishing feature" of Renaissance diplomacy as a whole.[4] In addition, from the thirteenth century on, Venice

2. Navagero, *Opera omnia,* 329, 334; see also 279–80.

3. Maggi, *De legato libri duo,* 64v, hereafter cited by page number; all translations are my own. My thanks throughout to Timothy Moore for all his help with the Latin.

4. Mattingly, *Renaissance Diplomacy,* 10. See also his "First Resident Embassies."

required its ambassadors to deliver a report as soon as they returned home from missions. Those reports—eagerly sought after in their own time and now considered rich, useful, and at times colorful documents of the age—gradually crystallized into a distinct literary form during the Renaissance: the *relazione*.[5] Venice thus stands at the origins of Italian Renaissance diplomacy, its sovereignty and right to send resident ambassadors having stood unchallenged. Likewise, Venice contributed to the creation of the resident ambassador, which in its turn brought about a "revolutionary change" in diplomatic practice by shifting the focus from the medieval view of a single Christian society to a Renaissance European view of a more fragmented society composed of separate sovereign territorial powers.[6] Furthermore, Venice produced a unique body of diplomatic writings, thereby further distinguishing the Venetian ambassador from his contemporaries. According to Ludwig Dehio, moreover, Venice has a unique place in the development of modern diplomatic practices, not because it was a "balanced" or "mixed" government but because Venice, out of geographical necessity, occupied an extended intermediary role between disparate cultures and, as a result, learned how to adjust flexibly and rapidly to different, difficult, and unexpected diplomatic conditions as they periodically arose.[7]

But Venice also has pride of place in studies of Renaissance diplomacy because of some longstanding assumptions on the part of historians regarding the civic commitment and high ethical standards of the patriciate.[8] Scholars have done much to expose the Venetian patriciate as a far from ideal group, some having gone so far as to portray them as downright greedy and violent. In the process, scholars have dispelled the image of the Venetian patriciate ambassador as part of a serene and responsible caste unperturbed by conflicts of interest. In point of fact, a large majority of the patriciate, Donald E. Queller argues, avoided being elected as ambassadors, many made every effort to keep from serving or repeatedly arrived late to their posts, and some scandalously leaked secrets.[9] The image of the

5. On the uniqueness of the Venetian *relazioni,* their importance in their own time, and their value for modern historians, see Queller, "The Development of Ambassadorial Relazioni."

6. Mattingly, *Renaissance Diplomacy,* 44; see the entire discussion in part 1, "Medieval Diplomacy, Fifteenth Century," 15–44.

7. Dehio, *The Precarious Balance,* 22–28, 37.

8. Mattingly voices this commonplace view when he turns to discuss the birth of Italian diplomacy during the formative period of 1455–1494 (*Renaissance Diplomacy,* 81).

9. Queller (in *The Venetian Patriciate*) provides an overview of the scholars who, along with himself, have demystified the longstanding ideal vision of the Venetian patriciate. See also Queller, "The Civic Irresponsibility of the Venetian Nobility," and *Early Venetian Legislation on Ambassadors,* 56–58.

Venetian ambassador as a tireless and selfless agent of the state, however, is not just a modern historiographical construct fashioned principally from the end of the nineteenth to the middle of the twentieth century. It is also an integral part of the larger, more comprehensive "myth of Venice"—a myth constructed primarily during the Renaissance, in part as an ideological response to a series of diplomatic failures in Venetian policy toward the turn of the fifteenth century.[10] Venetian humanism, which was always patrician humanism during the quattrocento and early cinquecento, helped perpetuate and fashion in unified form the myth of Venice as a politically serene republic with a socially responsible, devoted, and protective patriciate in charge. By extension, Venetian humanism, with its focus on *unanimitas* and the absolute subordination of the individual to the community, helped create the image of the patriotic and selfless Venetian patriciate ambassador.[11] For a long time—indeed, ever since the Renaissance—Venetian ambassadorial work was perceived and presented as exemplary diplomatic work.

This chapter focuses on the treatises of two Venetian humanists, Ermolao Barbaro (ca. 1454–1493) and Ottaviano Maggi (d. 1586). Much is known about both the diplomatic service and the scholarly work of Barbaro.[12] Perhaps best remembered for his polemic with Giovanni Pico della Mirandola, in which he advanced the virtues of rhetoric over Scholasticism in a manner at once serious and tongue-in-cheek (1486), Barbaro studied at Padua in the 1470s. He began interpreting and studying Aristotle during those years, presenting the *Ethics* (1474–75) and

10. On the myth of Venice, see the synthesis and bibliography in the first chapter of Muir, *Civic Ritual in Renaissance Venice,* 13–61.

11. As King points out (*Venetian Humanism in an Age of Patrician Dominance,* 190), patrician humanism in Venice did not privilege, as it did in Florence, a search for self-expression in a shifting and mutable world or, as it did in Rome, an interest in curial matters; rather, its focus was on "a set of ideas that encourages self-control and self-sacrifice, acquiescence to the will of the whole community, faith in the timeless stability of the city, unquestioning loyalty to traditional values." On Venetian humanism see (in addition to the synthetic study of King, which provides a full bibliography) the seminal works of Branca, "Ermolao Barbaro and Late Quattrocento Venetian Humanism" and "L'Umanesimo veneziano alla fine del Quattrocento."

12. On Ermolao Barbaro, I am indebted to Mattingly, *Renaissance Diplomacy,* esp. 94–102; Bigi, "Barbaro, Ermolao," 96–99; Branca, "Ermolao Barbaro"; King, *Venetian Humanism,* 197–205, and "Caldiera and the Barbaros on Marriage and the Family"; Doglio, "Ambasciatore e principe"; Paschini, *Tre illustri prelati del Rinascimento,* 11–42; Ferriguto, *Almorò Barbaro;* Figliuolo, *Il diplomatico e il trattatista,* which provides the most extensive sequential overview of Barbaro's diplomatic duties in Milan, from March 23, 1488 to April 11, 1489, and then in Rome, from May 21, 1490 to March 11, 1491; Fubini, "L'ambasciatore nel XV secolo"; and now the studies contained in *Una famiglia veneziana nella storia.* I cite from the editions of Barbaro's *Epistolae* and *De coelibatu* listed in the references. All translations are my own.

Politics (1475–76), as well as later translating the *Rhetoric* (1478–79) and eventually providing in 1481 an edition of the works of Themistius, a Greek rhetor and commentator on Aristotle. In 1462 he accompanied his father, Zaccaria Barbaro (1422/23–1492), on his diplomatic mission to Rome, and there the younger Barbaro may have attended the lessons of Pomponio Leto (1428–1498) and Theodore Gaza (ca. 1400–1475). Later, from 1471 to 1473, he was with his father in Naples, where he met the great humanist Giovanni Pontano (1426–1503). There he wrote an elegant little treatise in praise of celibacy, *De coelibatu liber,* which echoed yet ideologically revised *De re uxoria liber* (1415–16), a treatise about the virtues of marriage composed a little more than half a century earlier by his illustrious grandfather, the celebrated Venetian humanist and statesman Francesco Barbaro (1390–1454). The year 1480 marks the beginning of an important friendship with the Florentine humanist Angelo Poliziano (1454–1494), whom he met in Venice and with whom he later kept in contact. Barbaro stayed with his father in Rome once again from 1480 to 1481, not just accompanying but this time assisting him in his diplomatic duties; then he aided his father in Milan in 1485, at the court of Ludovico Sforza. Three years later, in March 1488, the Venetian senate sent the younger Barbaro, who had been elected to the senate in 1483, as ambassador to the court of Sforza in Milan, and there he established contacts with important Milanese humanists. In the meantime, Barbaro continued to maintain close working ties with a number of humanists, in particular Giorgio Merula (1431–1494), Giorgio Valla (d. 1499), and Girolamo Donato (1454–1511). In April 1489, Barbaro returned to Venice, but he was soon sent as ambassador to Rome. It was probably during this pause in his diplomatic duties, after returning from Milan and before departing for Rome in May 1490, that Barbaro reflected on his varied experiences and composed his treatise on the ambassador, *De officio legati,* perhaps in defense of his own diplomatic activities at the court of Sforza.[13] On March 6, 1491, Pope Innocent VIII nominated Barbaro to the patriarchate of Aquileia, a post he eventually accepted after much reflection and without the approval of the Venetian senate. Before dying of the plague in Rome in July 1493, he completed his major work, *Castigationes Plinianae et in Pomponium Melam.*

13. In his edition of Barbaro's *De coelibatu,* 17–19, Branca makes the argument for this dating, sustained by Figliuolo (*Il diplomatico,* 78), who reads the entire treatise as an attempt on Barbaro's part to excuse himself on his return from Milan for his diplomatic handling of the events surrounding Sforza's interests in Forlì (see Figliuolo, esp. 78–81).

By contrast, little is known about Maggi's life and studies. Unlike Barbaro, he did not belong to the ruling elite of the Venetian patriciate, and it is not clear where he came from. Perhaps originally from a Florentine family line that eventually made its way to Venice via Brescia and Milan, Maggi, who may well have studied at Padua,[14] not only wrote a treatise on the ambassador, *De legato libri duo* (1566), but also translated into the vulgate two Platonic dialogues and Cicero's letters to Brutus. In the presentation to this second translation, *L'Epistole di M. Tullio Cicerone scritte a Marco Bruto* (1556), Maggi informs us that he applied himself to the study of ancient letters and languages from an early age. In particular he focused on classical Latin, for, as he observes in a characteristically humanist manner, the writings of classical antiquity can be adapted to present circumstances, especially to teach the kind of eloquence that flourishes in Venice and, he asserts, in Venetian embassies.[15] For Maggi, as for so many humanists, the *translatio studii* required a full-scale translation of ancient works into the modern tongue, so as to make classical literature both available to a wide audience and useful for contemporary practice. Maggi likewise informs us in his *De legato libri duo* that he has extensive diplomatic experience. He served as secretary to Alvise Mocenigo (1507–1577), the Venetian ambassador to the Holy See from 1558 to 1560, a two-year period in which the papacy shifted from the guidance of Paul IV to Pius IV. Upon his return to Venice in 1560, Maggi was nominated to be secretary of the senate. A year later he was sent abroad to France, this time with the Venetian senator Marcantonio Barbaro (1518–1595), ambassador to the court of Charles IX, a court fundamentally governed by

14. According to Girolamo Ruscelli (d. ca. 1566), who provided the introductory words to *De legato libri duo,* a1v–a2r, Maggi "expresses his thoughts most elegantly and eloquently in a Ciceronian style, and he writes exceptionally in Latin and Italian; he understands Greek, and has easily won the highest praise in philosophy and other forms of knowledge from the Paduan Academy and this state. Rightly, therefore, time and again this state has benefited from the service of the man in great things. As a matter of fact he was sent as a young man to Rome and France with most illustrious senators on ambassadorial missions, during turbulent times, in which places he easily showed prudence and usefulness in dealing with things. He opened up for himself an entrance to all offices available to one of his rank, and for this reason many honors were bestowed on him also in his absence. For that reason Ottaviano seems to have introduced fresh honor into his most noble family, which in every age once produced men of warlike virtue but continues to produce scholars with knowledge of letters, first in Florence, where the house got its start, then in Brescia, Milan, and Venice, into which cities the family had migrated so many centuries ago because of internal wars, as the histories bear witness."

15. Maggi, *L'Epistole di M. Tullio Cicerone,* 5, on applying himself to *buone lettere* from an early age, and 5–7, on the importance of translation and eloquence in Venice. For Maggi, I have used Tiraboschi, *Storia della letteratura italiana,* vol. 7, pt. 3, 1114–15, and the brief entry in *La piccola Treccani.*

Catherine de Medici, who had been declared regent and who dominated her son's policies. Maggi remained at the service of Marcantonio Barbaro from 1561 to 1564, during extremely turbulent times for France, with the nation now torn apart by both political and religious conflicts. Maggi's treatise on the ambassador, dedicated to the future doge Alvise Mocenigo, is the fruit not only of his diplomatic experience, which he periodically mentions throughout, but also of his vast learning as a humanist.

Both Barbaro and Maggi actively constructed the myth of the Venetian humanist ambassador as a selfless and tireless agent of the community in their treatises. But in a larger sense, Barbaro and Maggi wrote in the context of an existing body of literature on ambassadorial work, which they revised both in light of their different visions as humanists and in an effort to seek self-expression within the fluid genre of the Renaissance institute.[16] Barbaro's treatise, composed at the end of the fifteenth century and widely circulated in manuscript form, is extraordinarily significant in this context. A humanist with a strong Aristotelian bent, Barbaro is among the first Italians to write on the subject of ambassadorial work. His *De officio legati* is also the first such treatise written by a humanist; the first to address exclusively the functions of specifically the resident ambassador; the first to present the ambassador working for a sovereign, territorial power rather than for the public good of the larger, presumably unified society of Christendom; and the first to turn away completely from the medieval topoi that structure preceding treatises. Barbaro is an innovator within the traditional, existing discourse on ambassadors. He prefers brevity to discursivity, ethical to legal concerns, the personal example to the impersonal precept, the immediate present to the remote past, unified and focused discourse to the technical information provided in often extended *quaestiones.*

Barbaro's method of fashioning the ambassador, however, failed to be taken up by those who followed him, excepting possibly its influence on Étienne Dolet (1509–1546),[17] the great French humanist, who may have read Barbaro's treatise when he composed his own brief *De officio legati,* probably as a young diplomat serving Bishop de Langeac in Venice from

16. The texts are available, some of them abridged and/or summarized, transcribed in Hrabar, ed., *De legatis et legationibus tractatus varii.* For an overview of these treatises, see Behrens, "Treatises on the Ambassador"; and Mattingly, *Renaissance Diplomacy,* esp. the discussion of the treatises of the sixteenth century in the chapter "The Perfect Ambassador," 181–91. For a thorough study of ambassadors, see Queller, *The Office of Ambassador in the Middle Ages.*

17. Behrens ("Treatises on the Ambassador") draws out similarities between Barbaro's and Dolet's treatises.

1529 to 1530, or shortly thereafter. For the most part, humanists writing on ambassadorial work—and the great majority wrote from the mid-sixteenth century on—adopted a radically different rhetorical strategy. Unlike Barbaro, they piled up instances and exempla, they focused on classical antiquity rather than on the present, and they wrote lengthy treatises filled with all kinds of detailed information regarding the relevant qualities, education, and moral virtues required of an ambassador. Maggi's treatise is somewhat representative of these highly discursive writings composed in the second half of the sixteenth century. Maggi, to borrow Dolet's pejorative term, is something of a dull yet "ambitious compiler of examples" [exemplorum . . . ambitiosi congestores, c4r],[18] and his treatise, when compared to Barbaro's or Dolet's, is decidedly long. But given the generic constraints within which he operated in writing his treatise, Maggi is something of an innovator seeking self-expression as he mediates his identity, at least on one occasion, through the classical literary figure of Odysseus. Maggi also constructs specifically a Platonized image of the "perfect ambassador,"[19] and he certainly seeks to balance—although whether he achieves this balance is an open question—ancient with contemporary examples of ambassadorial work. Both Barbaro's and Maggi's treatises, the one fundamentally Aristotelian and the other Platonic in conception, are not only representative of the way two Venetian humanists helped construct the myth of the responsible Venetian ambassador; they are representative of two distinct and distinctive humanist approaches to writing on ambassadorial work during the height of the Italian Renaissance.

Fathers and Sons: Ermolao Barbaro's Trattato *as the* Ritratto *of the Resident Ambassador*

Though ambassadors had been around for a long time, the office of resident ambassador evolved out of the diplomatic needs and pressures of fifteenth-century Italy. This event occurred gradually at a time when the new study of humanism strongly advocated public debate and the perfection of oratorical skills based on a careful study of classical rhetoric;

18. Dolet, *De officio legati,* cited by page number in my text when the Latin is cited. For the translation I rely on "Étienne Dolet on the Functions of the Ambassador, 1541," hereafter cited by page number in my text. The reference here is to 91.

19. Though Juan Antonio de Vera would gain the reputation of having done so. See Mattingly, *Renaissance Diplomacy,* 181–91.

when the temporal powers of northern Italy vied for territorial control yet still managed to maintain a precarious unity among themselves based on an understood policy of "continuous tension";[20] and when the rest of Europe, then dominated by monarchies rather than small princedoms, dukedoms, or republics, did not feel the need to negotiate or maintain ties with foreign powers on a continual basis.[21] A number of gifted Italian humanists occupied the office of the resident ambassador, and some made good use of it to travel about the world, meet other humanists, and enhance connections among themselves. Not until the end of the fifteenth century, though, some fifty years after the French jurist Bernard de Rosier (1400–1475) composed one of the first extended treatises on the ambassador in the Renaissance,[22] did a humanist—and a humanist of extraordinary repute—address the work of the resident ambassador in treatise form. Ermolao Barbaro, trained at Padua, author and translator of multiple influential writings, philologist, and respected scholar of Aristotle, had all the attributes of the complete humanist. Not surprisingly, his treatise, *De officio legati,* is both elegantly written and elegantly conceived. No less surprisingly, his treatise breaks "decisively with the traditional technical and juridical treatises on ambassadors and embassies," as Vittore Branca put it.[23] Whereas the scholastic-minded Rosier, like everyone else before Barbaro, recognizes the ambassador's need for oratorical skills, his Latin reveals him to be no humanist, and his treatise contains a hodgepodge of information about every type of ambassador under the sun. By contrast, Barbaro is exclusive rather than inclusive in his choice of information, he writes for the most part with a Ciceronian Latin and in complex periodic prose, and he has organized his subjects thematically rather than schematically.

Though incomplete, Barbaro's *De officio legati* is still in its form a deceptively unified treatise, which we can loosely break down into three interconnected sections. In the first section (1–6), Barbaro provides a general definition of the ambassador, narrows down the main virtue to prudence, and provides an immediate focus by isolating the resident ambassador as the only one worthy of extended consideration. In the central and main portion of the treatise (7–46), Barbaro turns to discuss the work of resident ambassadors, whom he describes as those ambassadors "who

20. Ibid., 82.

21. Ibid., part 2, "The Italian Beginnings of Modern Diplomacy," 47–102 for a discussion of the resident ambassador and his importance in changing the face of modern diplomacy.

22. On Rosier's treatise, see now Fubini, "L'ambasciatore," 647–53.

23. Branca, "Ermolao Barbaro," 233.

KING ALFRED'S COLLEGE LIBRARY

are sent to and fro with simple general credentials, for the sake of guarding alliance and goodwill, so that they may take care to make and keep the one to whom they have been sent as eager and friendly as possible to their own citizens or princes" (4). Resident ambassadors, who noticeably work for a state rather than for the larger good of Christendom, must execute the commands given them absolutely and without question; they must never consider themselves more prudent than their superiors; they must see to it that they are held in favor and behave in an honorable manner; they must gather information and report it accurately; they must write down all the particulars of what they have heard but must never embellish or lie; they must be brief in their addresses and dignified in their behavior; they must not seek favor for themselves or others; and they must never compromise the reputation of incoming or outgoing ambassadors. More or less, these are the official duties of the resident ambassador. In the third and final section (47–57), Barbaro shifts his attention to the legal obligations and rights of ambassadors, their character in its more intimate aspects, their background and household. He ends by providing a picture of the ambassador's family with all its members leisurely engaged in the pursuit of an "art," whether that art be "painting or writing or singing or even playing at chess" (57). There is, then, a general, unifying movement in Barbaro's treatise, a movement that draws us from the outside in. We pass from the duties of a public official to his inner private household, from the state to the family, from civic work to domestic play. This gradual, uninterrupted movement from the public to the private and from *negotium* to *otium* enforces a natural and ordered connection between all areas of the ambassador's life.[24] The interests of the state and the interests of the individual, though hierarchically arranged, are one and the same. Just as the state oversees the work of the ambassador, scrutinizing every word he writes and ferreting out any possible embellishment or lie, so Barbaro's ambassador must oversee his household, ensuring that it is a place of peace and appropriate domestic activity. The ambassador organically stands in relation to his family precisely as the government, composed of the ruling patriciate, stands in relation to the state. The ambassador must preserve a good name and "privatam existimationem" not only for his own sake but, as Barbaro makes clear, because he works for the "publicam dignitatem" (30).

24. It is also accompanied by a shift in narrative voice. In moving from the topic of duty to play, from the state to the family, from business (*negotium*) to leisure (*otium*), Barbaro more and more addresses the reader directly, and even now and then breaks out into emotional interjections toward the end: "Hercule!" (42, 48), "proh scelus, proh monstrum, inusitato poenarum genere luendum" (53).

At first glance, much of what Barbaro has to say characterizes the ambassador in an ideal light. The ambassador, Barbaro insists, must even be like a priest to the state, at work on almost divine things (51), and hence immaculate in every way. Behavior that might possibly be excused in some administrators is entirely unacceptable in the resident ambassador, who must be beyond reproach. But Barbaro's treatise, which influenced such Italian humanists as Torquato Tasso, is not at all about constructing an abstract Platonic "Idea" of the ambassador. Rather, it is about Venetian ambassadors and, more specifically, the ambassadorial work of Barbaro's father and himself. True, Barbaro's treatise, once cut off from its roots in Venetian ambassadorial service, would eventually be read, as Maria Luisa Doglio notes, "in a Platonic key, centered on the absolute and universal value of the 'idea of the perfect ambassador,' in a manner homologous to the Ciceronian 'perfect orator.' "[25] But this was a philosophically skewed reading of a treatise that not only eschewed speaking of the perfect ambassador but, in keeping with its author's overall outlook, was fundamentally Aristotelian in its mode of thinking. When, for example, Barbaro mentions that the ambassador should be a man "mediocri ingenio" (18), he does not mean to say that the ambassador should be "of middling intellect."[26] Employing the word *mediocri* to designate the Aristotelian concept of *mediocritas,* Barbaro instead implies that the ambassador should avoid the extremes of being too shrewd, lest he come off as a spy, or too naïve, lest he end up being duped. Locating the proper balance between the two, Barbaro's ambassador finds his perfection not in the Platonic sense of "Ideal" but in the Aristotelian sense of "completed," which is best understood in the Latin term *perficio.* Barbaro's ambassador finds this "perfection" not in abstract dialectical thought but in real, worldly experience. Tasso and others may have occasionally read Barbaro's treatise in a Platonic light, but it was a light that they retrospectively shed on a text illumined by a different kind of thinking. Barbaro offers a vision of an ambassador that emerges from lived—rather than transcendent, as in Tasso's dialogue—experience. No spirit comes to illumine Barbaro, as one does to discuss ambassadorial work in Tasso's *Il messaggiero.* As a Venetian humanist ambassador, Barbaro has instead come to illumine us, by exemplifying the resident ambassador in his own and his father's work and by solidly rooting that work in Venetian diplomatic practice.

Though Barbaro initially announces that his treatise is about offering

25. Doglio, "Ambasciatore e principe," 298; my translation.

26. This is the rendering of King, *Venetian Humanism,* 203, whose reading of Barbaro, I hasten to add, is excellent and has powerfully shaped my own.

dispassionate "precepts" about ambassadorial service, his *De officio legati* is also in large measure an encomium to Venetian ambassadorial work. "It is one thing to act as an ambassador of a republic," Barbaro has Ludovico Sforza, the "prince" of Milan, say, "another to act as the ambassador of a tyrant" (12). Barbaro, as an ambassador to the longest-standing republic in Italy, is committed to articulating this difference in praise of Venetian ambassadorial service. From beginning to end, Barbaro's *De officio legati* is therefore punctuated at regular intervals with patriotic asides. Early on, Barbaro refers to Venetian custom to explain how long an ambassador should stay abroad (5). He admires the Venetian habit of scrupulously examining and taking seriously the word and deed of the ambassadors ("praesertim in nostra civitate," 15). "Nowhere," he remarks of Venetian ambassadors, "is there less delinquency, but nowhere is delinquency more hated" (15). He praises the Venetian practice of privileging and choosing cultivated and learned ambassadors ("praesertim in veneto," 25). Barbaro even defends Venetian snobbery as not a defect but an attitude that is earned. Venetian ambassadors, he writes in his longest patriotic aside,

> either because they enjoy separate laws, both in way of life and in dress, or because they punish the guilty more severely, or because they take pride in the antiquity of their race and the long time during which they have had freedom and power, are called haughty by enemies and the envious, severe by those who respect them. Accordingly, it is proper that we strive with the greatest zeal to disprove conclusively this ancient hostility to our name, not only by disputation or speech but by work and deed, though in a way that we seem to never have forgotten our public dignity. (25–26)

Ambassadors, according to Barbaro, must also be easygoing and good-natured, and this is "the special habit," he notes, "among Venetians and it is greatly recommended to and approved in all of them" (30).[27] Barbaro further praises the Venetian law of absolutely prohibiting ambassadors from accepting offers of any kind from foreign powers when in the service of the state ("Laus haec veneto," 38–39). "Give this to the fatherland," he declares in his last and most conspicuous patriotic aside, "not the man; the Venetian owes this more to the Venetian than anybody else owes it to another since this worth of the empire has not taken root, grown, and endured as much as by the harmony of the citizens among themselves. Who hates this harmony hates not those men whom he hates but clearly he hates the republic itself" (46).

27. It could also read: "This habit is peculiar to the Venetians and is especially recognized in them by everyone."

Along with being patriotic, Barbaro's treatise, in keeping with the patriarchal structure of Venetian society, is deeply patrilineal in conception. Three times Barbaro praises the paternal presence and authority of the Venetian senate: the "fathers" of the senate confer honor (12), the "fathers" demand absolute respect in their judgments (14), and the "fathers" must be obeyed at all costs (31–32).[28] Just exactly as many times Barbaro's own "father" is mentioned, though the references are, by comparison, more conspicuous and involved: there are three visions of Barbaro's father at work, which are then balanced by three longer pictures of Barbaro himself as an ambassador.[29] All these threefold references—to the fathers of the senate, Barbaro's father, and Barbaro himself—work together structurally

28. The references to specifically the "fathers" of the senate appear as follows: "laudatus sum a Patribus" (12); "Legatus, nisi se multo inferiorem et iudicio et usu rerum quam Patres existimet, protinus legati fine decidit" (15); "Ante omnia cavere debet legatus ne pro se neu pro aliquo aut de aliqua re cum Principe unquam loquatur, nisi Patres mandaverint" (31–32).

29. About his father, first: "My father stayed in Rome more than a year, in Naples two years, not because he did not wish to return home but because he could hardly find a successor that was considered adequate to those princes with authority and favor" (6). Second: "Ambassadors ought to see to it that they are held in favor and authority by those to whom they are sent; they will pursue it by the reputation of all virtues, but especially in the virtues of goodness and integrity and, as my father discussing with me about the office of the ambassador carefully expressed it, of a certain free and refined simplicity; for servility and rusticity yield contempt not authority. He also considers it of greater usefulness than a shrewd ingenuity and a desire to appear eager or showy" (16–17). Third: "My father Zaccaria sometimes used to question and interrupt the person who at the moment was speaking precisely about things he wished to know, so that he might not disclose his eagerness to know and so that he might be held in greater faith by the person if he wanted to question further" (21).

About himself, first: "I was once ambassador to Milan. The senate ordered that I announce to the princes that they put down their arms, which they had moved into the territory of Forlì. In the nick of time the news of their victory, and all the things that had taken place, came suddenly. I took my counsel from this change of events. I congratulated the prince. I pretended that I had come to ask the Milanese both to provide and look out for the tranquillity of Italy, and to allow the war to be settled not by arms but by legal right. I did not wish to change the substance of my commission, but because of the new situation that had suddenly arose, I gathered together new words. I was praised by the senators at home. The prince of Milan—although he hardly knew why I had come, had nevertheless certainly guessed why I had come—also admired me, I know, because I had related such things to him when things got arranged in that way all of a sudden. And I know that he then turned to his people and said that it is one thing to act as an ambassador of a republic, another to act as the ambassador of a tyrant. And that is true" (10–12). Second: "I was an ambassador to Milan. All types of lettered men came to me usually, as happens customarily to new ambassadors, though in my case, I believe, not to honor me as much as to check out what sort of man I was. Prince Ludovico also used to frequent my house. Word got around that I was held in his favor. Then those lettered men, who had attended my lectures at my house and were now lecturing themselves, wanted me to recommend them to their prince. Privately I denied that I would have recommended anyone to the prince. I pleaded as an excuse the regulations of my commission, according to which, much grave information left unsaid, it is not permitted any type of patronage on

and thematically. The Venetian senate is mentioned as "fathers" only in passing, yet we feel their presence everywhere: in the scattered asides praising Venetian custom and law, in an occasional oblique echo of a Venetian statute, and in the power of a seemingly ubiquitous governing body that can ferret out any lie.[30] The three brief insets of Zaccaria Barbaro, placed toward the beginning of the treatise, then prepare for the much longer threefold self-portraits of Ermolao Barbaro as an ambassador in Milan. These three self-portraits of Barbaro are set at regular intervals in the central section of the treatise, and each of them provides us with the most detailed and complex picture of ambassadorial work in action. In pictorial terms, we are provided with a background, middle ground, and foreground; the Venetian "fathers," Barbaro's father, Barbaro himself. The work, constructed at its core around the fatherland of Venice and paternity, spirals out from the *patres,* to the *pater,* to the son. And so too the "word" professing what it means to be an ambassador unfolds from the *patres* of the senate, who provide ambassadors with their orders and oversee their work; to Barbaro's father, who spoke to Ermolao "about the office of the ambassador" (16); finally to Barbaro himself, who now in fact provides us with a written treatise on "the office of the ambassador." The fathers of the senate divulge information to Barbaro's father, the father then verbally informs his son how to behave, and the son now informs us in his treatise.

By structuring his treatise in this way, by composing, in short, not just a *trattato* but a *ritratto,* Barbaro at once insists that his knowledge is grounded in practice, his "theory" of being an ambassador always based

the part of the ambassador. Nevertheless, I promised that I would have praised all the lettered men to the prince. And that I did. So the prince, hearing those men praised by me, approved my candor and modesty, even though I had asked for no privilege for anyone in particular" (34–37). Third: "As God is my witness, at first those people who met me coming to Milan did not ask me about the life and customs of my predecessor; nor did they think poorly about that man, but they spoke in such a way that they suggested a danger and suggested how I should be prudent. Truly he did not stop about his opinion of those men; so I responded that he should punish those men for their inquiring and curiosity. Truly, with my modesty I not only stopped and shamed in their tracks those men who were inviting me to jeer at and criticize my predecessors, but I also deeply humbled and crushed them" (43–44).

30. Barbaro comments: "Ambassadors ought to bear in mind this further point, that they learn and execute the command given them, nor should they ever judge themselves more prudent than their superiors. . . . It is extreme madness, and nearer to wickedness than the sin of madness, not, I say, to pass over or to disobey the commands of the government, but even to obey them grudgingly or negligently" (8, 13–14). Barbaro echoes and confirms in even harsher terms an act of July 13, 1478. See Queller, *Early Venetian Legislation,* 116.

on the praxis of having been one.[31] By focusing on himself and his father, however, Barbaro also foregrounds a deep familial connection between the two Venetian men. Nowhere is this family resemblance so powerfully delineated as in their shared capacity to dissimulate. "Remember," Barbaro warns at the center of his treatise,

> that as an ambassador you are not a spy; besides, it is easier to ascertain what is being done by those who seem to be unconcerned than by those who can hardly cover up [*dissimulare*] such concern. They ought to look through all things not furtively, not in the manner of thieves, but now simply and openly, now by degrees and with a certain discretion, as it were, not loudly but silently. (19–20)

Barbaro cautions us here against lying or spying, but he clearly values dissimulation, exemplifying it specifically in the cunning diplomatic art of his father. According to Barbaro's father, one must avoid acquiring the reputation of being shrewd, but that does not mean one should not be shrewd, just as one must avoid appearing eager while still being, as Barbaro's father unmistakably was, eager to pick up news. Feigning indifference, one must hide one's interests, disguise true motives. One must, in short, dissimulate. Barbaro's father does this brilliantly as an information gatherer. Barbaro does it equally well as a negotiator. In the very first example that we have of Barbaro at work as an ambassador, we are provided with a privileged glimpse into the double-game of irony that takes place between him and Ludovico Sforza, "the prince" of Milan. Sforza knows why Barbaro has come, yet he refuses to let on. Similarly, Barbaro knows that Sforza knows why he has come; indeed, Barbaro even makes a point of showing us that he knows that Sforza knows that he knows. Yet Barbaro persists in pretending that he has come for a different reason. He "feigns": "venisse me ad eos finxi" (11). If Barbaro is praised by Sforza, it is in part because he has the discretion to conceal the obvious. A flash of recognition effectively passes between Barbaro and "the prince,"

31. Branca ("Ermolao Barbaro," 233) discusses Barbaro's "portraits of inner life" in this treatise, which he compares to the Venetian painting of the period. Appropriately, Burke ("The Renaissance, Individualism, and the Portrait," 395) discusses how Renaissance portraits, far from expressing the concerns of isolated individuals, "are more often institutional than individualistic. The portrait usually represents social roles rather than individuals." Such is the case here. If this treatise is "autobiographical," as Figliuolo asserts (*Il diplomatico,* 77–90), then it is autobiography as collectivity; Barbaro as ambassador is an extension of his father and the state. Moreover, if part of this treatise, as Figliuolo asserts (*Il diplomatico,* 81), has a "forte aspetto di *excusatio,*" then Barbaro strategically defends himself by linking his activity in every way to the activity and expectations of the collectivity he represented as an ambassador.

binding the two in a tacit accord of mutually dissimulating behavior. In the complex and duplicitous world of Renaissance diplomacy, in which it was not always clear what one's own dissimulating government wanted of one (9), the truly successful ambassador needed to master the art of dissimulation. In this respect, Barbaro and his father were distinctly similar. For that matter, as masters of dissimulation, they were not at all unlike the dissimulating fathers of the senate: "And what if something should be such that the state did not want to know, or pretended it did not know [*aut scire dissimulaverit*], or no less, even if it had known, it would have made the same decision" (9).

Much of Barbaro's treatise, moreover, makes it performative of what it seeks to teach, with the son, praised by the fathers of Venice, putting into practice in writing the diplomatic tactics and advice of his father as an ambassador. If the ambassador should act with "a certain free and refined simplicity" (16), as Barbaro's father advises, the treatise—composed by the son—formally exhibits that simplicity from the outset. The son as *scriptor* exemplifies in his own prose the advice given to him by his father as *orator.* "The duty of the ambassador," Barbaro writes in the opening sentence,

> is to take on diligently the commands of the republic or of the prince according to the practice of which he got the name "legate" from "to be sent." Although the precepts of this office can be set down, nevertheless a certain *je ne sais quoi* depends more on the prudence of man than what can ever be committed to this treatise. Occasion will give [him] many counsels, as will daring; these counsels can in no way be fully comprehended in their entirety, just as all things cannot be predicted that are in [his] future. (2)

Barbaro knows the etymological meaning of *legatus* and he has no intention of investigating—as writers did before—the various terms used to designate the occupant of the office and the way those terms changed over time. Nor does Barbaro ever seek to cover in his treatise, as was previously the custom, every conceivable reason for sending a legate on a mission of any kind. Emblematic of Barbaro's refined simplicity is his brevity, for brevity, we learn, is pleasing to the busy prince.[32] Ermolao Barbaro learned how to be concise from his father, and we in turn are meant to learn from him. By the same token, if the ambassador must often talk around a subject to get where he wants to go, as Barbaro's father cunningly does by interrupting his interlocutor precisely when the most important topic is being divulged, then Barbaro employs a similar strategy

32. "Brevissima esse debet cum Principibus oratio; occupati enim sunt" (29).

of calculated indirection in his treatise by digressing precisely when he is really getting to the point. Twice Barbaro casually interrupts the narrative flow of his discussion with the adversative *sed;* he does this to bring us back to what we presume is the main topic of his treatise: ambassadorial work in general ("Sed ad praecepta veniamus"; "Sed haec alterius loci sunt"; 7, 28). But these calculated interruptions, placed in an "ingenious" but by no means "showy" way and thus in a manner that would seem to follow the advice of the father preparing his son for diplomatic service,[33] only draw us away from what is the true topic of discussion: Venetian ambassadorial work in particular and, more specifically, the work of Barbaro's father and himself. The digressions contain the true, innovative subject matter of Barbaro's treatise. They provide us with the exempla, and it is from these that we learn, for, as Barbaro says, "never is enough contained in a precept" (14).[34] The examples of Barbaro and his father function not at the service of the precepts, as illustrations to illumine a concept; instead they provide us with the minimal conceptual structure required to construct a treatise in praise of Venetian society and paternity, with Barbaro and his father as the shining examples of what it means to be good, wise, and prudent Venetian ambassadors.

Zaccaria Barbaro is viewed as exemplary because he stayed at his post even beyond the general allotted time, because he knew how to "diligently express himself" (16) and provide advice, and because he knew how to locate information without being recognized or appearing in any way indiscreet, exactly as a duty-bound, eloquent, and decorous Venetian patrician should behave. Above all, the son is exemplary, who consistently presented himself staged in the most dangerous, complex, and compromising situations. "Sometimes indeed reasons occur," Barbaro warns, "that require that certain types of commands must be softened and, as it were, cleaned up, as often plainly something happens unexpectedly [*supervenit*] that the senate did not know of at the time when it made its decision. In that case, multiple [kinds of] prudence must be employed" (9). Directly afterward, Barbaro employs the key word *supervenire* twice as he describes how, with great prudence, he carried out in a different way the will of the superiors when an unexpected circumstance suddenly arose. "Above all things," Barbaro then warns in the second self-portrait,[35]

33. As his father advises—Barbaro, *De officio legati,* 17–18.

34. On examples teaching more than precepts as a commonplace, see the synthetic remarks of Pigman, "Living Examples," 281.

35. Figliuolo points out that this took place in Pavia, where the Sforza court had moved for a brief period (*Il diplomatico,* 37–38).

"the ambassador must be on guard never to speak with the prince in favor of himself or for another or about anything except what the senators have sent him to speak about" (31). Having announced this, Barbaro then describes how he interceded on behalf of the courtiers of Ludovico Sforza and consequently emerged as the external unifying force between the two parties. Finally, Barbaro cautions:

> Generally princes question ambassadors about their successors and predecessors, and there can be many reasons why they may ask. It must not be undertaken that in responding ambassadors seem to have spoken not, I say, with a speech in any way suspicious, let alone with a desire to gaining something. Never is it proper, never is there a moment, when anyone should answer negatively about a citizen among foreigners. Pretend that that man, about whom someone questions you now, had first been questioned about you before. Would that man not be thankless and wicked if you should speak honorably about someone that he had spoken badly of before? or would you not be thankless and wicked if it were the other way around? And, by gosh, successors can drag down and criticize the behavior of their predecessors and condemn their actions, and conversely predecessors can do the same to their successors. Great and upright would be that man who would be able to avoid common and ordinary disgraces. (40–42)

No sooner has Barbaro made this observation than he reveals how he was questioned upon arriving in Milan yet responded to the "danger" by shunning and shaming his interlocutors. In these examples, Barbaro addresses the risks he faced in being an ambassador and explains how and why he succeeds. First, Barbaro shows that he is careful not to find himself caught between Sforza and the senate; he exercises his prudence; and he is praised by both the senate and Sforza. Second, Barbaro is careful not to be caught between Sforza and his courtiers; he acts wisely and discreetly; and he is praised by Sforza for his candor and modesty. Third, Barbaro is not caught saying anything compromising about the incoming and outgoing ambassadors; he exhibits the requisite *pudor,* and, even if he is never explicitly praised in this example, he nevertheless emerges as the model of the "great and upright" man who has unmistakably avoided the most commonplace disgrace. In passing from one example to another, Barbaro is praised less and less for his success, but this is because we, as the indoctrinated and admiring readers, are supposed to praise him more and more.

By focusing on himself and his father, then, Barbaro draws the reader into the actual experience of what it means to have been an ambassador, offering us a view of Venetian ambassadorial work that is concrete rather than abstract, deeply personal rather than detached, lived rather than bookish. We learn from experience—the praxis of being an ambassador is what teaches us how to be one—and accordingly Barbaro provides us with examples of that real experience drawn directly from his own life. In this context, it is significant that Barbaro eschews even mentioning one classical precedent to the office of the ambassador, preferring instead to single out only himself and his father as examples. He does this not because he could not recall those classical precedents but because he believed, like so many humanists and patricians of his and especially the next generation, that Venice was the ideal city not only of the present but of the past, unmatched and unsurpassed by even Greece or Rome.[36] Venice was a far more "perfect" state. "The Venetian is not arrogant," Barbaro records a senator as saying,

> but even if he were, there are nevertheless many reasons why he should become so: the immense wealth of Venice, its glories in war and peace, its empire so powerful on land and the sea that it yields only to the Roman empire in power, to no one in length. Ponder the customs of other states, imagine that the things which are in ours were in those: what, I implore, would they do, or what do we do, that they would not do? (27–28)

Barbaro advances this opinion through the voice of a third person. He discreetly claims that he is disinterested ("I neither approve nor disapprove," 27), yet we may rest assured that Barbaro shared the opinion of the senator whom he has taken the time to cite at length. After all, one does not need to look to classical literature to find an example of a prudent, candid, honest, refined, cultured, dissimulating ambassador. One need only look to Barbaro, who embodies all these virtues and capacities in his treatise, and who even translates many of the requisite virtues discussed in his treatise into a prose that prudently stages what it preaches—by being deceptively simple, by dissimulating, by concealing its own shrewdness, by not being showy.[37] There is no point in turning to antiquity, then. In Barbaro's Venetian ambassador, one finds not so much the Renaissance "rebirth" of the classical orator as his superior avatar, with the father having taught the son—and therefore having successfully brought him to "perfection," in Aristotelian terms, as an ambassador in a most perfect state.

36. Logan, *Culture and Society in Venice,* 5: "With Contarini came the perfection of the myth; Venice was the ideal state of justice, superior even to ancient Athens and Rome."

37. More generally, for a fine study on how humanists made their writings (often in complex and contradictory ways) performative of what they intended to teach, see Kahn, *Rhetoric, Prudence, and Skepticism.*

Nevertheless, this image that Barbaro fashions of himself as an ambassador contrasts sharply with the one forged in his letters. In point of fact, Barbaro proved to be the very opposite of the exemplary Venetian ambassador he portrays and praises in his treatise. Not long after composing *De officio legati,* Barbaro departed for Rome to take on the office of ambassador to the Holy See, the post reserved for the greatest of the Venetian diplomats. Unexpectedly, a circumstance occurred; it suddenly "popped up," to borrow the privileged term *supervenire* from Barbaro's treatise. The Patriarch of Aquileia died and Pope Innocent VIII, without consulting the Venetian senate, abruptly elected Barbaro to the position. This was a great, though unexpected, honor. "Not all things can be foreseen which are in the future," Barbaro had noted in his treatise, and so one must rely as a resident ambassador on prudence. Once more engaged away from home in diplomatic service, it was precisely the future that Barbaro did not see. This grave and previously unforeseen matter would require great prudence, for now, rather than confronting just "the prince" of Milan, Barbaro found himself caught between two competing and irreconcilable paternal authorities, the one temporal, the other atemporal: the supreme father of the church and the fathers of Venice. "Which of the commands was I to follow?" Barbaro reflected in a letter of January 7, 1492. Barbaro accepted the pope's offer, hoping that he could now devote himself completely to letters and pious study. But in accepting the offer, Barbaro also necessarily betrayed what every Venetian—and indeed every good ambassador—should uphold according to the precepts of the treatise he had composed just a year before. Not long after his election as the Patriarch of Aquileia, Barbaro was severely reprimanded by the fathers of the senate, and when he refused to obey their order to return home, he was declared a traitor to his homeland and roundly condemned.[38]

Odysseus Redux: Ottaviano Maggi's Perfect Ambassador

At the turn of the sixteenth century, a few treatises on the office of the ambassador appeared, but none of them were as elegantly fashioned as Barbaro's *De officio legati.* A notable shift took place in 1541, when the French humanist Étienne Dolet published his *De officio legati.* He

38. Paschini, *Tre illustri prelati,* 23–32; and Figliuolo, *Il diplomatico,* 133–42, discuss in detail the entire episode; see also King, *Venetian Humanism,* which integrates Barbaro's repudiation of public duty into a deeper understanding of his life (197–205) and how he emerges as a "tragic figure" (197). I cite from Branca, *Epistolae,* 74.

composed this treatise probably not long after completing his service as secretary to the French ambassador in Venice from 1528 to 1529. Like Barbaro, Dolet indicates that he is not out to provide every precept or examine every branch of learning required to make a good ambassador. Privileging brevity over distended discussion, he aims to set out a number of topics so that a fledgling or interested ambassador can add to them as they wish, "for it is an easy thing," he claims, "to add to another man's advice" (90). Brevity has the virtue of expansiveness, of creating possibilities for eventual extensions of thought. When Dolet therefore turns to discuss the office of the ambassador, he writes: "I am not unaware how brevity becomes a man who seeks to describe or explain a matter, and I am by nature fond of it. For what is the advantage of empty talk [*inanis loquacitas*], or what is the use of idle display in writing [*supervacanea scribendi ostentatio,* b2v]? And so I shall describe briefly the office of an ambassador" (85). This position is entirely consistent with Dolet's overall attack against the false eloquence that has crippled his age:

> I grant you that our age has such great good fortune, such well cultivated arts, such widespread knowledge of all the languages, that you see many a person who, from his earliest youth, has been splendidly trained in letters. What of it? If they spout eloquence, if they rattle out citations of many authors, if they make a display of the numerous branches of learning, are you convinced that they are therefore endowed with practical experience, which is the sole strength of a really suitable and acceptable ambassador. (83)

Yet Dolet is not entirely brief in his own treatise, and much of his treatise is not in any way grounded in experience. He does, after all, provide us with an extended list of statements regarding the immunity of ambassadors, and all those statements, he points out, do not "refer to our times (except in the slightest degree), but to the laws of the Greeks and Romans, that is, to the age of our ancestors, not of their descendants" (91). Dolet has drawn his information not from recent or current diplomatic praxis but from an attentive and dutiful reading of classical literature, and the list he compiles is comparatively long, occupying approximately a third of his treatise. By the same token, there are stretches of Dolet's treatise that are arguably full of "empty talk" and represent an "idle display in writing." It is unlikely that Dolet held the blanket view that "young men possess no experience in affairs, no prudence, nor any sagacity, no restraint and no self-control, but unbridled passions, arrogance, audacity—in short, every kind of rash and headlong impulse rules them" (82), since he probably wrote this treatise as a young man.

The inclusion of this kind of "empty talk," to the near exclusion of any reference to contemporary or medieval diplomatic practices, led Garrett Mattingly to criticize the writings of humanists on the duties of ambassadors.[39] Humanists' knowledge about ambassadorial work, Mattingly argues, became increasingly bookish, less concerned with the praxis of being an ambassador and more involved with what it meant to construct rhetorically the "perfect ambassador." Such is the case with Ottaviano Maggi's treatise, *De legato libri duo,* which appeared about seventy years after Barbaro's *De officio legati.* In this far more ample treatment of the subject by a Venetian humanist, Maggi makes a point of indicating time and again that he aims to create not a real but an ideal ambassador, a "perfect ambassador" who, even though he has never existed, may serve as an "example" to all when "grasped by the mind" (b1v). Maggi makes this point often enough, as when he discusses the demands placed on the "perfect ambassador," but never so strenuously as at the beginning of his treatise, where he places himself, in his address to his patron, Alvise Mocenigo, in a tradition that begins with Plato and extends on to Xenophon and Cicero (b1v). Imitating others, Maggi will do what the ancients did, but he will go one step further and provide us with "precepts never handed over in Greek or Latin literature" (1r). Needless to say, this task, which requires of Maggi great humility, is a heroic endeavor, an intellectual adventure of the highest caliber. Maggi conceives of himself as a pathbreaker, pushing classical models to their limit.

Maggi's intellectual adventure also has a patriotic purpose. In fashioning the perfect ambassador, Maggi writes for his fatherland, and in particular for the youths of Venice, so that he may provide them with rules of behavior, because "it seems indeed that the young of Venice especially abound in the precepts of all things that have to do with the working of the Republic" (1v). This concern for his fatherland, which is "dearer" to him "than anything else" (a3v), leads Maggi on a number of occasions to turn to and privilege Venice. He highlights the virtues of the Venetian practice of having the Republic's ambassadors present a full and accurate report to the Senate upon their return home (25r–v), and at another point, like those who created the myth of Venice, he speaks of his "most flourishing" city as having "a noble and exceptional sort" of political body because of its mixed form of government (44r), which perfectly combines (according to the ideal classical model) monarchic, oligarchic, and democratic elements into a harmonious, functioning whole. He fur-

39. Mattingly, *Renaissance Diplomacy,* 248.

ther praises the Venetian custom of welcoming foreign ambassadors to their republic, where the "greatest honors" are bestowed on them (8r), and he observes that in Venice it is forbidden to prove unwilling to take on the public office of the ambassador, though he acknowledges that some ambassadors are permitted to come up with a "legitimate excuse" (10r). Echoing and reinforcing the longstanding myth of the Venetian patriciate as a responsible diplomat, he writes that "we have seen that the most grave and patriotic senators most freely have taken on the burden of ambassadors, although they were overwhelmed by many obligations and were toiling under many domestic difficulties. And I do not think that one should marvel at that; for what attitude should they have, when they have been set afire with love for a fatherland of this type, which is the home of virtue, of the greatest power, and of dignity?" (10r). Venice, for Maggi as for Barbaro before him, epitomizes the perfect state where the ambassador is the perfect citizen. But Maggi does not, and cannot, rely on his own father as an exemplum, any more than he can rely on himself as an exemplum for what it means to be a good ambassador. Maggi cannot do this because he was not, nor would he ever become, an ambassador. He therefore turns to his patrons, Marcantonio Barbaro and Alvise Mocenigo, to locate the exemplary work required to become a "perfect ambassador."

In his *De legato libri duo,* Maggi seeks to paint for the first time ever the portrait of the perfect ambassador, using his Venetian patrons as privileged models. In the process, he attempts generally to balance past with contemporary examples. "Truly those things," he declares, "which pertain to undertaking a legation, must be absorbed from the old monuments of things done as from the histories of our own times" (1v). Thus, at the outset, Maggi discusses the ancient tradition of using ambassadors, the laws governing their conduct and protecting them, their immunity and elevated status as the sacred representatives of the state. Maggi also describes the dangers they have passed for their fatherlands. From the things "we read in histories" (3v) we then pass to the things of the present, a present closely linked to Maggi's personal experience of accompanying his patron, Marcantonio Barbaro, as an ambassador in France. Yet for the most part, while Maggi glances at present circumstances, his gaze, which is typical of the gaze of humanists of his time, tends to be fixed on the past to which he quickly and eagerly returns. This is the pattern throughout his treatise, and especially in the second section. There, relying on the writings of antiquity, he discusses the various disciplines the ambassador must master in his education, which includes all branches of the "liberal arts" (31r). The ambassador must have a thorough knowledge of sacred letters to ensure that he is a good Christian (31v–33v), but he must also undertake a rigorous program of study in dialectic, to learn how to separate truth from falsehood (34r–35r). Afterward he passes on to philosophy (35v–37r). First, the would-be ambassador must study contemplative philosophy: physics (37v–39r), metaphysics (39v), and mathematics (39v–40r), the last of which includes music (41r–v), geometry (41v), and astrology (42r–v). Then he must study active philosophy: economics (42v), ethics (42v–43r), and all aspects of civil administration (43r–46r). In addition, to be a persuasive orator the ambassador must learn classical rhetoric (46r–49v), but he must also study ancient history (50r–v), geography (54r–55r), and military matters (55r). He must even, for that matter, read classical poetry (50r–v), and especially the poetry of Homer, whom Maggi enlists as the greatest of them all and the one most worthy to read. Homer teaches about not just private but public things, kings and kingdoms, the customs and habits of men, the workings of republics. Plato preferred Homer above all poets, and Alexander the Great kept his poetry with him "in all places and at all times" [omni loco, & omni tempore, 50v].

The perfect ambassador that Maggi fashions acquires most of his education through extensive reading. His knowledge is bookish, and it requires elaborate training. When the ambassador leaves home, he should go with a fine library that would rival the greatest of humanist collections. However, in the midst of all this bookish knowledge he requires in an ambassador, Maggi suddenly turns to discuss experience. The ambassador, Maggi asserts, must also travel and live abroad. *Peregrinatio* makes for "prudence," which is the virtue—as every author on the subject pretty much agreed—that lies at the heart of ambassadorial work.

> But since prudence itself is a certain state of mind by which, by means of a certain reasoning, we have the choice of good and bad things; or rather it is a refined knowledge of those things that must be sought or fled, and which pertain to public workings and the life of men, it seems that it is acquired foremost from experience of affairs. For no one could be called prudent except those who, instructed by many years of experience, accustomed to the practice of many tasks, taught through spending time with the most prudent men, polished through knowledge of various peoples, states, and institutions, have become thoroughly conversant in the practice of the most important affairs. . . . Before all others truly this most outstanding virtue prudence is necessary altogether for all who take on the charge of being an ambassador. . . . Therefore, we make our ambassador above all prudent, so

> that he may know the proper moment of doing things, that he may have an understanding of the times and of the nature of the potentate to whom he has been sent; so that he may see far in advance future things; finally so that he may know how to taste the minds of men, perceive their will, and even penetrate their innermost senses. And since especially by the example of others, men in time become prudent, we want our ambassador to have obtained that example from travel, in which he has spent much time; and we want him to have traveled enough, to have observed most diligently various states and types of governments. Let him therefore have traveled through many regions, many provinces on land and on the sea; wisdom does not get enough help from reading, unless practice in handling affairs comes to it in addition. That practice is not acquired in any other way more easily than from long travels. He who has seen, read, and heard with his ears many things, who has traveled about all Italy, Spain, France, Germany, Greece, finally all parts of Europe and a good many parts of Asia, who has noted carefully the institutions, cities, laws, and commands in those same regions, and who has spoken to the most noble people in each place, must by necessity have extracted prudence from these experiences, as if from a spring. It was because of that that Homer's Odysseus was considered most wise, a man whom wandering, the experience of others, and the practice of affairs itself instructed. (59r–60r)

Even here, though, as Maggi shifts to discuss the prudence that is acquired from experience and not "a litteris" (60r), his treatise noticeably takes a turn back to classical literature and in particular to Homer, which is the kind of poetry the perfect ambassador should occasionally read. And the reason to read Homer, it would seem, is to follow the practice of Odysseus. We are expected here not to rob classical literature of its wisdom, as one might do in a more traditional allegorical reading, but to identify with its protagonist and to look to him as a model for behavior. A character in literature has in fact become a model to imitate. Browsing through Homer, as it turns out, is not such a bad idea, for in reading about Odysseus's travels, ambassadors are reading about, and no doubt glorifying in, an earlier version of themselves.

Now as a model of comportment, Odysseus is far from perfect:[40] he is a pagan, he conspicuously lies, he dissimulates, he is a trickster, he is a spy. Yet some of Odysseus's qualities would make him a first-rate ambassador. Odysseus is eloquent, a master rhetor, learned, dignified, and observant. But Maggi seizes on Odysseus, as many in the Renaissance

40. On Renaissance views of Odysseus, which are more ambiguous than Stanford indicates in *The Ulysses Theme,* see Defaux, *Le curieux, le glorieux et la sagesse du monde,* 35–38, 57–68, 131–32.

did, for a different reason. Maggi seizes on Odysseus as the multifaceted, resourceful *polytropos* hero because he had wandered so much in his years of exile, and through that wandering he had learned about the world. Strikingly, early instances of the term *peregrinatio* [wandering] occur when Maggi describes his own activity as a diplomat accompanying his patrons on various ambassadorial missions. "And since my fatherland itself has used my work," Maggi patriotically remarks in one such instance,

> and perhaps, as I hope, it will use it more, I thought it befitted my duty to be involved for a long time in public business, for I understood that I would do something very useful for myself and for the state, if to this teaching, which I had drawn from the sources of the philosophers, the practice of affairs were added, which is superior to the precepts of all the wise men, and if also travel [*peregrinatio*] were added, from which prudence is especially acquired, both on account of one's being around and living with many men, and because one's seeing various races, states, customs, and institutions. (a3v–r; see also b1r)

This humanist, who writes about the ambassador in imitation of Plato, Cicero, and Xenophon, thus writes about himself as well. He inscribes himself into the text as a figure who has wandered just as Odysseus did, and who, by virtue of that wandering, has acquired the practical experience and prudence that would make him, if only he were chosen, an exemplary ambassador too.

Like Barbaro before him, then, Maggi relies on exemplarity as the privileged mode of moral instruction and persuasion, but he does so in different ways and with markedly different results. Barbaro focuses on himself and his father to discuss the work of the ambassador. He looks not to Roman or Greek models and values but to peculiarly Venetian ones and, above all, to the examples of his father and himself. If humanist education in Venice distinguishes itself by becoming in the fifteenth century, as Margaret King argues, "the vehicle by which patrician culture can reproduce itself,"[41] the education required of an ambassador in Barbaro's humanist treatise literally reproduces patriciate culture by passing it on from father to son, with the son here fulfilling—in the Aristotelian sense of teleologically bringing to completion—the exemplary work of the father. Yet while Barbaro fosters the myth of the Venetian ambassador as the selfless servant and dutiful son subservient to and praised by the fathers of the state, he also foregrounds himself to such an extent that the treatise appears on close examination to be not only a discourse about

41. King, *Venetian Humanism*, 25.

ambassadorial work in general but also a congratulatory self-portrait of Barbaro as an ambassador. Maggi, by contrast, looks to a whole set of models other than himself—or at least this initially seems to be the case. Maggi is not an ambassador but a diplomat who has read and traveled widely. His Venetian contemporary models are consequently his patrons, whose favor he presumably seeks. Yet typical of a humanist, his models are also bookish and ancient. And when Maggi turns to discuss the prudence derived from practical experience, which is the prudence required of all ambassadors, he models the ambassador on Homer's Odysseus, the proto-romance hero who travels about the world and in the process learns about the nature of humans and their institutions. If Barbaro directly places himself as a "real" exemplary figure to teach us "prudence," Maggi can only inscribe himself into his text as an example to be followed by figuring himself as a "wanderer" and hence as an Odysseus figure. The shift from Barbaro to Maggi marks a shift in authorial strategy and modes of self-expression. We pass from the foregrounded self-portraiture of one of the greatest humanists of the time, who composes not just a *trattato* but a *ritratto,* to the self-inscription into his own treatise of a mid-level diplomat, who indirectly connects himself through the faintest verbal echo to the experience of being the perfect ambassador about which, as a widely traveled humanist, he writes.

Five

THE IMPORTANCE AND TRAGEDY OF BEING AN AMBASSADOR

The Performance of Francesco Guicciardini

> Tragedy, by means of legends and emotions, creates a deception in which the deceiver is more honest than the non-deceiver, and the deceived is wiser than the non-deceived.
>
> —GORGIAS

> In a comedy or a tragedy we do not have higher respect for the actor who plays the part of the master or the king than for the one who plays the servant. Instead, we pay attention only to the quality of the performance.
>
> —FRANCESCO GUICCIARDINI

The Ambassador Sets Forth

In his *Report* on Spain, written while he was resident ambassador to the court of King Ferdinand of Aragon from 1512 to 1513, Guicciardini reveals the humanist education he received through the age of fifteen,[1] as he goes about explaining the character of the Spaniards by superimposing their culture on his knowledge of ancient history, in particular his readings of Livy. At the same time, Guicciardini betrays his sense of superiority

1. On Guicciardini's early humanist education, see Ridolfi, *Life of Francesco Guicciardini,* 5–6. Guicciardini wrote in his "Ricordanze," transcribed in Guicciardini, *Scritti autobiografici e rari,* 53–54: "Attesi nella etá tenera secondo la voluntá di mio padre Piero, che diligentissimamente allevava e' figliuoli, a studiare in cose di umanitá, ed oltre alle lettere latine imparai qualche cosa di greco"—a Greek that Guicciardini nevertheless soon forgot. The epigraphs at the beginning of this chapter are drawn from Freeman, *Ancilla to the Pre-Socratic Philosphers,* 138; and Guicciardini, *Maxims and Reflections,* 97.

as a Florentine patriciate and cultured Italian. Unlike the Florentines or the Italians, who had long proven themselves great merchants and artisans in Europe, the Spaniards not only fail miserably at commerce and skilled labor but spend and distribute money poorly. Moreover, they are undisciplined, lazy, arrogant. All share the universal characteristic trait of simulation (75).[2] Hence, when Guicciardini describes their love of ceremony he speaks with the disdain of an elite, urbane Italian who scoffs at the failed Spanish attempt to be cultured. At almost every level, theirs is a confused society marked by *discordia,* which is their natural state, being "a clever but restless nation; poor, therefore tending toward thievery, and without any civilization whatsoever in ancient times" (80–81). Of all the European nations, the Spanish were conceptually the slaves, a nation historically placed in servitude (77). They belonged to a predominantly uncivilized nation with people "black of color and small in stature" (68–69), many of whom live in filthy quarters like pigs (73). Guicciardini therefore often speaks of the Spanish in his ambassadorial *Report* as though he were confronting not Europeans but boorish, dirty aliens, many of whom have a false sense of pride and are good at fighting only in exceptional circumstances. To their credit, the Spaniards have for the time being a good, wise, and prudent king, who has finally begun to lead them out of "darkness" (81) and their "natural obscurity" (89) into light.

Though in time Guicciardini would learn much from observing the statecraft of King Ferdinand, he had never wanted to leave for Spain, preferring instead to remain at home where he enjoyed a flourishing legal practice. Early in his life, he wrote the following in his *Ricordanze,* revealing his obvious pride in himself and his family regarding his election as ambassador to Spain on October 17, 1511, when he was only twenty-eight years old:

> And although I was uncertain whether to accept, seeming to me a trip not to undertake so as to disturb my work, which at the time, with respect to my age, was at a good point; and although it seemed to me that staying in Florence another two or three years would help assure the success of my legal practice, yet on the advice of my father Piero, to whom I had written, and who was then working at Montepulciano as commissioner, I accepted the

2. All translations, cited by page number in my text, are from Guicciardini, *Report from Spain.* On Guicciardini's work as an ambassador, see the fundamental studies by Otetea, "Guichardin ambassadeur en Espagne," in his *François Guichardin,* 40–73; Palmarocchi, "L'ambasceria del Guicciardini in Spagna"; Luciani, "Il Guicciardini e la Spagna," esp. on the *Relazione;* and the essential pages by Ridolfi, *Life of Francesco Guicciardini,* 23–46.

> offer. It seemed to him in fact that I had been greatly honored, since the legation to such an important king was extremely honorable, and the honor was all the greater because of my age. In the history of Florence no one had yet been elected to such a similar ambassadorial post when so young. And so only with great difficulty could I turn down the offer; also, being young, it shouldn't disturb me too much to go to a place so far away. Moreover, because my father considered that I would behave in a successful manner, it seemed to him that I would acquire honor and reputation [*riputazione*] from taking on the ambassadorial post.[3]

Even in his later self-deprecating *Oratio accusatoria,* a confessional work written in 1527, Guicciardini, dejected and held in poor favor at home, once more celebrates the moment when he was elected as the Florentine ambassador to Spain.[4] In an unprecedented decision, the Florentine government not only overlooked the fact that Guicciardini was by age ineligible for the post; they further honored Guicciardini by choosing him to guide the republic through an extremely difficult political moment. At the time, the Florentine government was uncertain whether it should align itself with the Spanish (the stronger pro-papal force) or the French (their traditional ally). In 1511, then, the Florentine government chose a young man, with no prior practical diplomatic training, to fulfill an important ambassadorial function at a politically vulnerable moment.

Guicciardini went to Spain not because he was flattered by the honor of being elected ambassador. Nor did he go because his father, who had decided so many other matters, insisted that he go. In all likelihood, Guicciardini went to Spain because he was in all things both highly ambitious and motivated by self-interest, his own *particulare.* Public service, Guicciardini points out in a maxim in an early version of his *Ricordi,* can prove beneficial if you use it to build a reputation, and ambassadorial service is just the kind of public service he had in mind.[5] In point of fact, advantages accrued to Guicciardini's favor not long after his return home

3. Guicciardini, *Scritti autobiografici e rari,* 69–70; my translation.

4. Ibid., 213–15.

5. All citations of Guicciardini's *Ricordi* in Italian are from the Sansoni publication edited by Raffaele Spongano; all translations are from *Maxims and Reflections.* The whole *ricordo* (B 167) reads: "Surely, services rendered to a people or to society at large are accounted less than those done to a particular person. Since they are done for the community, no one feels he has been personally served. Therefore, if you labor on behalf of a people or a community, you must not believe they will go to any trouble when you are in danger or need; nor should you believe that the memory of your services will cause them to forgo their personal interests. Still, you must not think so ill of public services that you neglect an opportunity to render them. For such services gain you reputation and favor, and that is fruit enough for your troubles. Moreover, in some cases the memory will be useful to you; those affected by it may be moved to act in

from Spain.[6] However, even if he benefited from his performance as an ambassador, and even if he acquired fame in the long term (he would one day be held up as the exception that proves the rule that young men should not be sent on embassies of great importance),[7] Guicciardini's experience at the court of Spain turned out to be a profoundly disappointing one, and not merely because he was constrained to live in a filthy, disordered nation. It was disappointing because, rather than operating at the center of things, Guicciardini found himself marginalized at the court of King Ferdinand, left in the dark about the policies of his own government if not completely forgotten. Fearful that he was falling into complete neglect, Guicciardini on one occasion wrote to his brother: "I would like you to write me often, and particularly about all the things that are going on all around, both inside and outside, because the Ten of War keeps me as high and dry as possible. And to understand the things that are happening there, it is necessary for me to manage here, for without a knowledge of those things I'm a fish out of water."[8] Yet a fish out of water Guicciardini largely remained during his residency as an ambassador to Spain. Long stretches of time passed without a word from the Ten of War. At one point, in fact, Guicciardini's brother informed him that the Florentine government rarely talked about his legation. He had been forgotten, "as if," his brother candidly remarked, he "were not even in the world."[9]

This profound shift in ambassadorial experience—from that of the young man sent with great honor to that of the man left in the dark about matters of diplomacy—affected Guicciardini and influenced the way he viewed and wrote about the world.[10] The earliest two versions of the *Ricordi,* the so-called Q^1 and Q^2 collections compiled while he was in Spain, bear the mark of Guicciardini's ambassadorial experience. The memory of his experience also remained crucial to him as he reflected on the work of ambassadors with increased detachment and skepticism

---

your favor. And if they are not moved as deeply as those who have benefited personally, they will at least act in your favor in those cases where not too much effort is required. Moreover, there will be so many people who feel this mild sentiment, that the sum of their gratitude may be quite considerable."

6. See Ridolfi, *Life of Francesco Guicciardini,* 48.

7. Gentili, *De legationibus libri tres,* 171: "I should make an exception in the case of Guicciardini, ambassador to the King of Aragon."

8. Guicciardini, *Le lettere,* 1.278. My translation from a letter dated 3–10 November 1512, to Luigi Guicciardini.

9. Ibid., 1.104. Letter from Iacopo Guicciardini, 23–30 April 1512.

10. A number of scholars have already emphasized this: Luciani, "Il Guicciardini," 992 and 994; Otetea, "Guichardin ambassadeur," 73; and Ridolfi, *Life of Francesco Guicciardini,* 44.

in the three consecutive enlarged versions of the *Ricordi*.[11] By the final version of the *Ricordi* (1530), Guicciardini in truth no longer adhered to Quintilian's dictum that the good orator—and hence, by extension, the good ambassador—is a good man, a *vir bonus* in the classical sense of the morally upright man and the man of distinguished social standing. Rather, in speaking about the ambassador, Guicciardini now tacitly adhered to Gorgias's dictum about tragedy: that the deceiver is more honest than the nondeceiver, and that the deceived is wiser than the nondeceived.[12] The ambassador, Guicciardini had come to believe by the time he wrote the last version of his *Ricordi,* is often the most persuasive and effective when he has been deliberately deceived by his own government regarding the mission for which he has been sent. Yet, so important for Guicciardini was his ambassadorial experience that he introduced himself into his *History of Italy* (ca. 1536–1540; printed posthumously in 1561) by referring back to the moment when he had been sent abroad with such honor as the Florentine representative to the king of Spain. In casting his gaze back on that moment from a vantage point a quarter of a century later, Guicciardini envisioned himself as the young man who would acquire the experience to become the storyteller who would write the tragic history we read. In that history, which relies on Florentine ambassadorial records throughout for character sketches and information about diplomatic practices,[13] ambassadors have an important role to play as the indefatigable executors of high policy.

Reading the Ricordi *in Light of Ambassadorial Work*

In his *Discorso di Logrogno* (1512),[14] composed while he was resident ambassador to the court in Spain, Guicciardini reconceptualizes the popular

11. The A, B, and C versions were composed respectively in or about 1525, 1528, and 1530. The designations Q^1, Q^2, A, B, and C refer to the five different versions of the *Ricordi* as they evolved in various stages, from the first notebook of collected fragments composed in 1512 to the final collection composed in 1530. See Fubini, "Le quattro redazioni dei *Ricordi*"; Scarano, "Le redazioni dei *Ricordi*"; and Gagneux, "Reflets et jalons."

12. For the general relevance of Gorgias for an understanding of humanist rhetoric and historical narratives of the Renaissance, see Struever, *The Language of History in the Renaissance,* esp. 10–17.

13. On Guicciardini's use of Florentine ambassadorial reports, see in particular Gilbert, *Machiavelli and Guicciardini,* 297 and, for some of the sketches that Guicciardini might have used, 123–28.

14. The *Discorso di Logrogno* is dated 27 August 1512. Gilbert (*Machiavelli and Guicciardini,* 83–104) discusses the importance of the *Discorso di Logrogno,* placing it solidly in the context of

Florentine government along the lines of a Venetian-styled state with a senate of "wise men" in control. In this new government, every former ambassador would be eligible to have a secure place in the senate, and every member of the senate would further oversee foreign policy by choosing new ambassadors. All these new ambassadors would then potentially become part of the elite governing body and would select other ambassadors, thus guaranteeing their future as a dominant force in the branch of government that would control, in Guicciardini's political plan, "all things of any importance."[15] The ambassadors sent out to represent the Florentine government would consequently be men of true insight as well as men of the *ottimati* class. They would be men like Guicciardini, who was indeed representative of these wise men with his elevated social station, humanist education, and concern for constitutional reform. At the same time, the ambassadors sent out to represent Florence would be at the helm of a well-run government, a balanced and socially mixed government that followed the wisdom of classical political theory by combining monarchical, oligarchic, and democratic elements. This is important, for as Guicciardini recognized later in life, you can generally tell a government by the ambassadors sent to represent it: "Duke Ludovico Sforza used to say that princes and crossbows could be tried by the same rule. Whether the crossbow is good is judged by the arrows it shoots. So too, the value of princes is judged by the quality of the men they send forth. We can guess, therefore, what sort of government there was in Florence when it employed as ambassadors simultaneously Carducci in France, Gualterotti in Venice, Bardi in Siena, and Galeotto Giugni in Ferrara" (C 171). Good governments send out good ambassadors; bad governments send bad ones. Yet if this is the case, if the relationship between an ambassador and his government is synecdochical, with the former viewed as an always accurate representative part of the whole, what if you are a good ambassador representing a bad government? How do you behave if you are a socially responsible ambassador working for a politically irresponsible government? How do you secure a view of yourself as "wise" if the government for which you work is not?

Like many humanists, Guicciardini believed that people prove their

---

the then current constitutional debates, humanist literature, and the Florentine political crisis of the period. Pocock has discussed the political importance of the *Discorso* in the context of Guicciardinian thought and Renaissance and early modern conceptions of political bodies in *The Machiavellian Moment*. On this treatise, see also the observations in Palumbo, *Francesco Guicciardini*, 36–46.

15. Guicciardini, *Opere*, 276; my translation.

worth in the course of occupying an office, by rising or failing to rise to the occasion. "The office brings forth the worth of the person exercising it," Guicciardini declares at the very end of his *History of Italy,* there echoing in even more synthetic form a maxim from his *Ricordi:*[16]

> How apt was that saying of the ancients: *Magistratus virum ostendit* [the office reveals the man]. Nothing reveals the quality of a man more than to give him authority and responsibility. So many speak well but do not know how to do so; so many on the benches or in the market place seem excellent men, but when employed, show themselves to be mere shadows [*ombre*]. (C 163; revised from B 36)

People occupying positions of responsibility distinguish themselves in their work, proving themselves and their character in the process. Inevitably, we judge people—to borrow from the maxim cited in the epigraph above—by the "quality of the performance," much as we judge actors on the stage. Guicciardini makes this point even more explicitly in his *Consolatoria* (1527), where he draws once again on the familiar Renaissance topos of the theater as a metaphor for life: "Some wise men say that life is similar to a play, and we praise people who perform in it not so much according to the role [*persona*] that they play but according to how well they play the role: because each of us has a role assigned to play in life, and what distinguishes us is the way in which we play it."[17] Yet when a person acts out the role of the ambassador, political affiliation and group identity matter deeply. The performance of an ambassador is directly linked to the character of his own government in that the former is considered an always reliable reflection of the latter. Hence, ambassadors cannot entirely disassociate themselves from the nature of the government for which they work, and this fact weighed heavily on Guicciardini in Spain. In a letter to his brothers, Guicciardini cries out with extreme embarrassment on one occasion that he cannot show his face in court unless he receives explicit instructions as to why he should be there, or unless he is at least informed of the events taking place at home. Otherwise, he fears, it might seem that he was just sent to stand

16. Where possible, translations (with only slight and occasional modifications) of the *History of Italy* (hereafter cited as *HI* and by page number in my text) are from Sidney Alexander's translation of Guicciardini, *History of Italy.* The following quotation is from *HI,* 442. All citations and references to the corresponding original Italian are from Guicciardini, *Storia d'Italia,* hereafter referred to as *SdI* and by page number in my text.

17. Guicciardini, *Scritti autobiografici e rari,* 186; my translation.

around the king's court like a "shadow" [ombra],[18] and to be viewed as a mere "ombra," Guicciardini judged later in his life, is indeed the worst fate for anyone engaged in a position of "authority and responsibility" (C 163). If the "quality of the performance" of Guicciardini as an ambassador is not up to snuff, if he appears—as he fears—a mere "ombra" at the court of Spain, his government is to blame, not him. As Guicciardini makes abundantly clear, he is doing, and has done, his best. He should therefore be judged a wise man, even if he is working for a less than wise government.

As an ambassador and a wise man, Guicciardini strove to be a good citizen, but he still worked, he believed, for a poorly constructed and generally mismanaged government. In the early Q^I version of the *Ricordi,* which were in all likelihood fragments from or preparatory notes for his *Discorso di Logrogno,*[19] Guicciardini observes that "a wise man is also a good citizen" (Q^I 6) and that "if a man is not really a good citizen, he will not long be thought one. Therefore, if he wants to give that impression, he must first strive to be good" (Q^I 3). Goodness for Guicciardini is, as it was for so many humanists of his generation, at once an authentic state ("chi non è buono cittadino") and an appearance ("parere"), an extension of a desire ("chi vuole") and a matter of public perspective ("non può essere lungamente tenuto"). You must be good, but you must also persuade people—by giving everyone a convincing and lasting impression—that you are, will be, and always have been good. The quality of the performance of the good man consequently reveals his true character at all times and in all places. In terms made familiar to the Renaissance in Quintilian's dictum "vir bonus dicendi peritus," the constructed *ethos* of the good man must perfectly mirror the inherent goodness of his *logos.*[20] Rhetorically, you can only move public opinion if what you say matches what you feel, the guiding precept here being that you can only move

18. Guicciardini, *Le lettere,* 1.121. Letter to Luigi and Iacopo Guicciardini, 13 May 1512.

19. Scarano, "Le redazioni," has demonstrated the close connections between the Q^I version of thirteen "ricordi" and the issues discussed in the *Discorso del Logrogno,* both of which Guicciardini composed before the fall of the Florentine Republic in 1512. She also points out that the term "il savio" does not just designate "cittadino da bene" from the class of "ottimati," as in Guicciardini's earlier *Storie Fiorentine,* but "l'*individuo* saggio, dotato di qualità valide anche al di fuori dell'ambito politico e, in quanto tali, suscettibili di essere considerate in se stesse e nelle loro varie implicazioni" (191; emphasis in original).

20. Quintilian, *Institutio Oratoria,* 12.1.1; the formulation, as Quintilian points out, was Cato the Censor's. For the debate over the *vir bonus* in the Renaissance, see Monfasani, "Episodes of Anti-Quintilianism."

others to action if you yourself are moved to do the same. The wise man must presumably do the same if he is to appear a good man, a *vir bonus.* And he will do so all the better if he works for a well-fashioned government, such as the balanced republic Guicciardini constructs in his *Discorso,* rather than the dysfunctional one for which, as an orator and *vir bonus,* he currently works. "Men," Guicciardini writes,

> are naturally inclined towards the good. Few, in fact, perhaps none, will do evil unless they expected some advantage or pleasure from it. True, the opportunities for drawing advantage from evil are many, so that men are easily deviated from their natural inclination. To keep them on it, the spur and the bridle were discovered, that is to say, rewards and punishments. When these are not used in a republic, you will very rarely find good citizens. In Florence, we see it proved every day. (Q^I 4)

There is an almost tragic quality to Guicciardini's vision in this early maxim, the sense, as he will express it more explicitly two decades later, that the wise men of his generation were born into a culture and society in decline.[21] This typically humanist sentiment of historical belatedness underlies, if only dimly, other maxims from the early Q^I version of the *Ricordi.* "Citizens who seek reputation in their city are praiseworthy and useful," Guicciardini writes; but then he demolishes this ideal vision with the following qualification: "provided they seek it not by faction or usurpation but by striving to be considered good and prudent and by doing some good works for the public. Would to God that republics were full of such ambition!" (Q^I 2). Would to God, Guicciardini implies, the citizens of Florence took on positions of responsibility and authority for the sake of the larger community and acted with ambition for the public good. But Florence, we are given to understand, is not a republic that fosters "good works for the republic"; it is a city of "faction" and "usurpation." "Oh, God!" Guicciardini exclaims in another maxim he composed while an ambassador in Spain, "how many more reasons there are to believe our republic will soon fail, than to think it will last a long time" (Q^I 11). For Guicciardini, Florence is bound to fail because it lacks a stable and responsible government. It is a city in decline, and Guicciardini cannot envision a comic resolution to this tragic state of

21. "All cities, all states, all reigns are mortal," Guicciardini observes. "Everything, either by nature or by accident, ends at some time. And so a citizen who is living in the final stage of his country's existence should not feel as sorry for his country as he should for himself. What happened to his country was inevitable; but to be born at a time when such a disaster had to happen was his misfortune" (C 189). Bondanella (*Francesco Guicciardini,* 83–85) best emphasizes the tragic character of Guicciardini's thought in the *Ricordi.*

political affairs. He refuses to look, as Dante looked two centuries earlier, to religion for a solution. Quite the contrary—in writing his *Discorso di Logrogno,* Guicciardini aims to locate a solution in a practical reconstruction of Florence as a different city, in worldly rather than otherworldly restoration.[22]

The Q² version of the *Ricordi* consists of the original thirteen *ricordi* of the Q¹ version and an additional sixteen that Guicciardini composed while still ambassador to Spain but some time after his *Discorso di Logrogno.* Taken together, these sixteen new *ricordi,* like the earlier thirteen that still make up almost half of the Q² version, focus on municipal concerns related directly or indirectly to the city of Florence. For the most part, however, they entertain a decidedly more negative vision of things. The sixteen *ricordi* added in the Q² version have grown even more tragic in tone.[23] They reflect not so much on wisdom and good citizenship as pessimistically on what it means to live in a world in which the Florentine popular government is not just bound to fail, as Guicciardini had predicted in the earlier *ricordi* (Q¹ 11), but has already failed, thanks in large measure to its flawed policy of neutrality: "Unless your safety is completely guaranteed by treaty or by such strength that no matter what happens, you have nothing to fear, you are mad to stay neutral when others are at war. For you do not satisfy the vanquished, and you remain prey to the victor. If you are not convinced by reason, look at the example of our city and what happened to it by remaining neutral in the war that Pope Julius and the Catholic King waged against Louis, king of France" (Q² 18). Speaking as an agent rather than a maker of policy, an actor improvising in the dark rather than a director governing the performance, Guicciardini all but announces that the Florentine Republic has fallen. And with the fall of the Florentine Republic, the young ambassador—so often kept in the dark by his own government and deceived by the king of Spain—no longer implicitly advocates rhetorical-ethical views espoused by Quintilian and evoked by humanists in the Renaissance with a resuscitated interest in the rhetor as *vir bonus.* Indeed, such humanist views seem to have little value now. Rather, now that "men are very false" (Q² 19)—and indeed Guicciardini had come to understand in his dealings with the king of Spain just how false they were[24]—the underlying rhetorical

22. *Discorso di Logrogno,* 250: "These reasons give me little hope for us but do not make me despair, because I believe that a great part can possibly be cured and that, even if the cure may well be very difficult, it is not impossible." My translation.

23. Gagneux ("Reflets et jalons," 75) emphasizes as well the shift to a more negative vision.

24. Scarano, "Le redazioni," 200.

strategy in the diplomatic game must change. Deception, not inherent goodness, breeds confidence. "It is very wise," he writes, "to manage your affairs secretly. But it is even more praiseworthy and more advantageous if you try as hard as you can not to appear secretive. For many men will become indignant when they see that you refuse to confide in them" (Q^2 16). The wise man has become the secretive man in Guicciardini's scheme of things, and to be secretive one must never let others even know that you have a secret (Q^2 27).[25] The good ambassador, working before a great, dissimulating king,[26] would be well advised to do the same.

Along with emphasizing the value of secrecy in a world of deception, the early Q^2 *ricordi* foreground "discretion," a virtue that was certainly commended to Florentine ambassadors when they were sent out to a foreign power,[27] and one associated early on with ambassadorial work in treatises on the subject. In Rosier's *Ambaxiatorum brevilogus* (1436), for example, which is among the earliest treatises composed on the subject in the Renaissance, the ambassador must have—as virtually everyone writing on the subject after Rosier maintained—prudence, but also "discretion," a term used so often in Rosier's treatise that it emerges as a dominant characteristic of ambassadorial virtue: "discrecio," he writes, "summe necessaria est" (15).[28] Rosier's addition of the term *discrecio* to his list of ambassadorial virtues ("De qualitate et moribus ambacxiatorum," 5) is not entirely a redundancy on his part, even though discretion was often taken as a synonym for prudence in medieval and Renaissance Italy.[29] The basis of prudence as a virtue is vision, hindsight and foresight, especially as one seeks to judge proper action in the present. For this reason Titian represented prudence as a threefold face with the accompanying inscription "[Instructed] by the past, the present acts prudently lest the

25. "Do not reveal your secrets to anyone unless forced by necessity, for you become the slave of those who know them. Furthermore, their being known may cause you harm. And even when necessity forces you to tell them, you should do so as late as possible. For when men have lots of time, they will think a thousand and one evil thoughts" (Q^2 27)

26. Gagneux, "Reflets et jalons," 75.

27. On discretion as a virtue expected of ambassadors, see Marzi, *La cancelleria,* 623, 632, 645, 665, 678, 696–97.

28. I cite from Rosier's *Ambaxiatorum brevilogus,* transcribed in Hrabar, ed., *De legatis et legationibus tractatus varii,* 3–28. References are by page number in my text. On ambassadorial discretion in Rosier's treatise and as a "tema ampiamente controverso nella diplomazia italiana dell'epoca," see Fubini, "L'ambasciatore," 652.

29. Consider, for example, Battaglia, *Grande dizionario della lingua italiana,* 639, ad loc., Cecco d'Ascoli (1269–1326): "Prudenzia, dico, ovver discrezione / altro non è, secondo il nostro stile, / che il ben dal mal discerner per ragione."

future spoil [its] action."[30] By contrast, discretion, which derives from the verb *discerno,* to distinguish, to sort out, to sift through, emphasizes not so much temporal as spatial relations, the delineation of boundaries, and, above all, differences.

For Guicciardini, discretion was necessary precisely because differences could rarely be broken down into binary oppositions but continually formed an untidy and often unpredictable set of possibilities in a world of flux. "Rules are found written in books," Guicciardini announces in the first of the new maxims he composed while an ambassador in Spain, "exceptional cases are written in your discretion" (Q^2 12). According to Guicciardini, one needs discretion because experience from time to time yields exceptional cases that books with rules have never entertained as possibilities. Discretion, which is a polyvalent term in all versions of the *Ricordi,* generally signals a capacity to know how to recognize and expediently adapt to different circumstances once they have been singled out in all their minute particularities.[31] As Guicciardini writes in the C version of his *Ricordi,* in a maxim derived from the one about secrecy cited above:

> You cannot always abide by an absolute and fixed rule of conduct. Often it is unwise to be open in your conversations, even with your friends—I mean, on those matters that should be kept secret. On the other hand, to act with your friends in such a manner that they notice you are being reserved is to assure that they will do the same with you. For the only thing that makes others confide in you is the assumption that you confide in them. Thus, if you reveal nothing to others, you lose the possibility of knowing anything from them. In this, as in other matters, you must be able to distinguish the character of the person, of the case, and of the occasion; and for that, discretion is necessary. If discretion is not given by nature, it can rarely be learned adequately from experience. It can never be learned from books. (C 186; revised from B 13 and, originally, Q^2 16)

Discretion is an innate capacity for Guicciardini, a flexible mode of operating in a world that does not conform in practice to any overriding master

30. For Titian's representation of prudence, and for the inscription from which I draw, see Panofsky, *Problems in Titian,* 103. See Gagneux, "Reflets et jalons," 78–79, on the relationship between prudence and discretion in Guicciardini's thought. For prudence in general in the Renaissance, see Kahn, *Rhetoric, Prudence, and Skepticism;* and Martin, "Inventing Sincerity."

31. See also the definition in Barelli's edition of Guicciardini, *Ricordi,* 255; Sasso, *Per Francesco Guicciardini,* 3 and 13–14; Gagneux, "Reflets et jalons," 78–79; Bondanella, *Francesco Guicciardini,* esp. 86. See also the fine observations of Palumbo, "Guicciardini, Gramsci e la forma-ricordo."

theory. Yet, along with being a faculty for distinguishing and discriminating, discretion for Guicciardini is an object of knowledge constructed textually. "Exceptional cases," Guicciardini writes in the Q^2 version of his *ricordi,* "are written *in* your discretion" [e casi eccettuati sono scritti *in* sulla discrezione]. Discretion thus not only allows us to sift through exceptional cases, but records them. As Guicciardini announces in the B version of his *Ricordi, discrezione* may even be conceived as a "book," though by no means a book like the one that contains his maxims:

> These *ricordi* are rules that can be written in books. But particular cases have different circumstances and must be treated differently. Such cases can hardly be written anywhere but in the book of discretion. (B 35, also 121; revised from Q^2 12 and later as C 6)

In the course of writing a book that can be read rather than a book that remains hidden from view, a book that relies on flexible yet limited strategies for coping with particulars rather than a book that seeks to contain the boundless particulars of extraordinary experiences as they unexpectedly arise, a book that is composed with discretion rather than a book that is made of discretion, and a book that cannot teach discretion yet should be read with discretion as one sifts through various maxims to form multiple, overlapping patterns of thought,[32] Guicciardini returned to reflect often enough on his work as an ambassador at the court of Spain. In one maxim, he enriched his thoughts about the example of his city in following a flawed policy of neutrality (C 68). In another maxim he recalled the observation of the king of Spain's powerful secretary, who noted, in the proverbial form that Guicciardini admired and employed himself, the inherent selfishness of all men, as well as the way the powerful always victimize the weak (C 144).[33] In three other maxims Guicciardini

32. For a fine reading of the C version of the *Ricordi* as a "book" that strategically structures its message of contingency in its own formal discontinuity, see Markulin, "Guicciardini's *Ricordi* and the Idea of a Book." Asor Rosa, "*Ricordi* di Francesco Guicciardini," 15 (but see also 24–25, 33, 78), speaks of the *Ricordi* as a type of book one must read with discretion insofar as the multiple maxims can always be arranged and rearranged into a seemingly endless variety of patterns of thought: "non c'è una linea, dunque, nella raccolta, che discenda da una premessa per arrivare ad una conclusione, ma una costellazione di punti, da ognuno dei quali s'irraggia la linea di un ragionamento possibile."

33. "I was in Spain when the news came that the Venetians had made an alliance with the king of France against His Catholic Majesty. Upon hearing it, Almazano, his Secretary, told me a Castilian proverb which says in effect that the thread breaks where it is weakest. What it means is that the weakest always get it in the neck; for men do not act according to reason or consideration for others. Rather each seeks his own advantage, and all agree to make the weakest suffer because he is the one they least fear. If you have to deal with those stronger

reflected on the diplomatic skill and good fortune of the king of Spain, who always got what he wanted, even when the public knew he was lying.[34] In these three maxims, the king of Spain emerges as the master-performer, the great manipulator of diplomatic mummery, if he is to be judged, as men are supposed to be judged, by "the quality of the performance." People may know that the king of Spain is dissimulating but that does not keep them from forgetting that he is acting, either because people are simple-minded or because they fall prey to their own self-deceptions. Deception, as Guicciardini remarks at one point, "is not a pleasant thing" and "odious," yet practically speaking, it is also "very useful" (C 104), and the king of Spain has made good use of deception, eliciting not just complicity, as actors do on the stage, but belief. At once the director and the actor of his own performance, the king of Spain draws applause, the "clamor" of the aroused and enthused public. He even becomes an object of admiration for Guicciardini, who was not immune to the deceptions of the king. Guicciardini, to be sure, recognizes the king's performance as a performance, but that does not keep him from enjoying and commending the spectacle much as informed spectators do in the theater.

Guicciardini, who was always an attentive observer of diplomacy and of human behavior in general, did not write, as an anonymous Venetian patrician did in the sixteenth century, a book of *Ricordi* devoted exclusively to ambassadorial work.[35] Yet Guicciardini did repeatedly and increasingly

than you, always remember this proverb, for it is a matter of everyday reality" (C 144; this *ricordo* was revised from B 129).

34. "When I was ambassador to Spain, I observed that whenever His Catholic Majesty Ferdinand of Aragon, most powerful and wise prince, was about to embark on some new enterprise, or make a decision of great importance, he went about it in such a way that before his intentions were known, the whole court and the people were already insisting and exclaiming: the king must do such and so. Then he would announce his decision just when all hoped and clamored for it, and it is incredible what justification and favor it found among his subjects and in his dominions" (C 77; this *ricordo* was revised from B 51). "Even though a man be a known dissimulator and deceiver, his deceptions will nevertheless, on occasion, find believers. It seems strange, but it is very true. I remember that His Catholic Majesty, more than any other man, had such a reputation; and yet there was never any lack of people who believed him more than they should. This stems necessarily either from the simplicity or from the greed of men. The latter believe too easily what they wish were true; the former simply do not know what is happening" (C 105). "One of the greatest pieces of good fortune a man can have is the chance to make something he has done in his own interest appear to have been done for the common good. That was what made the enterprises of His Catholic Majesty so glorious. They were always undertaken for his own security or power, but often they would appear to be done either to strengthen the Christian faith or to defend the Church" (C 142).

35. See Queller, "How to Succeed as an Ambassador."

draw on his experience as an ambassador to transform anecdotal information into proverbial and practical wisdom. Nor should Guicciardini's sustained interest in this period of his life as an ambassador strike us as surprising. Discretion, which Guicciardini viewed as an inborn capacity rather than a learned ability (C 186), might be necessary if one wished to succeed in all aspects of life. But like many skeptical humanists, Guicciardini fundamentally believed that knowledge came from practice not books, experience not reading, direct observation not inborn insight. "Let no one trust so much in native intelligence," Guicciardini warns, "that he believes it to be sufficient without the help of experience. No matter what his natural endowments, any man who has been in a position of responsibility will admit that experience attains many things which natural gifts alone could never attain" (C 10). Discretion is necessary—one needs a "good and perspicacious eye" in order to "discern" [discernere] the slightest variation in cases and thus to sort out "tiny differences" that nevertheless make for great changes in effect (C 117). But discretion, Guicciardini warns, is not enough. So too, Guicciardini's legal training and early schooling in the *studia humanitatis* may have prepared him for political life, but it did not constitute the ground for his practical knowledge as a citizen, wise or otherwise. Guicciardini's insight into human affairs instead began when he set out in political life, and that great moment occurred, as Guicciardini never fails to remind us, when he was elected ambassador to Spain from the Florentine Republic. As ambassador to Spain, Guicciardini first discovered the marginality of Florence to European political events and the limited utility of a humanist education to guide him reliably through a politically difficult moment, caught as he was between a powerful king's court and an indecisive Florentine Republic that sometimes kept him uninformed about the state of things at home. As ambassador to Spain, Guicciardini came into contact with a king who was the supreme master of dissimulation and knew how to manipulate everyone with whom he came into contact, including, to be sure, Guicciardini himself. As ambassador to Spain, Guicciardini came to learn that the position of the ambassador was symbolically central but politically powerless within the larger scheme of diplomatic relations among states. And as ambassador to Spain, Guicciardini first painfully became aware of the vulnerability of ambassadors and the inherent risks involved in conducting diplomatic relations.

This last lesson was certainly in Guicciardini's mind when, once again, in the late versions of the *Ricordi,* he turned to reflect on ambassadorial work. In one maxim, he includes advice to those who will come after him about what it means to be a good ambassador, a man who is drawn into the intimacy of power and lives in a world of mutual distrust and suspicion:

> It seems that ambassadors often take the side of the prince at whose court they are. That makes them suspected either of corruption or of seeking rewards, or at least of having been bedazzled by the endearments and kindnesses shown them. But the reason may also be that the ambassador has the affairs of that prince constantly before his eyes, and since he sees no others in as much detail, they assume greater importance than they really have. But the same is not true of the ambassador's own prince, whose distance allows him to see everything equally well. He quickly detects the mistakes of his minister and will often attribute to evil design what is more probably caused by bad judgment. If you are to become an ambassador, heed this well, for it is a matter of great importance. (C 153)

To protect himself and to perform his duty, Guicciardini's ambassador must develop a double vision. He must observe, take note, gather information, and send it back home, having obviously been sent to do so. To this effect, he must be attendant to the affairs of the foreign power to which he has been sent and he must see things as an ambassador is expected to see things: up close. Yet while "the ambassador has the affairs of that prince constantly before his eyes," he must recognize the decorous distance he needs to maintain. Intimacy creates distortion, fosters suspicion, even if it is only by being intimate with a foreign power that an ambassador can ever elicit trust, adequately gather information, potentially influence policy, examine details, and make fine distinctions. To this end, the ambassador must learn to see things as his prince sees things: at a distance. He must learn to envision himself through the vision of another. How, he must constantly ask himself, would the prince view this action that I have taken? How close is close? In the highly theatrical staging of diplomatic relations in the Renaissance, in which kings like Ferdinand of Spain know how to manipulate spectators as they brilliantly dissimulate, the ambassador does not just perform; he performs self-consciously. If, on the one hand, the ambassador is part of the audience, observing closely the workings of the foreign power, remaining deeply interested in the theatricality of much of court culture, on the other hand the ambassador is still always part of the spectacle, observed by a distant audience back at home, one of the actors being scrutinized for "the quality of the performance." The wise ambassador who maintains this double perspective will gather the requisite information yet maintain the proper distance. He will see himself as his prince sees him, as part of the spectacle rather than as part of the audience, as someone who cannot not act.

Yet even as the ambassador acts and acts self-consciously, he can never be entirely sure of the role he is playing within the larger scheme of things. In a maxim placed prominently at the beginning of the A version of the *Ricordi* and then substantially revised and placed second in the final text, Guicciardini indicates that, to be persuasive and to act one's role with absolute conviction as an ambassador, one does not always have to be good or even secretive; sometimes one can be downright ignorant of the true motive of having been sent away in the first place:

> Some princes confide to their ambassadors all their secret intentions, and tell them the goals they intend to achieve in their negotiations with the other princes. Others deem it better to tell their ambassador only as much as they want the other prince to believe. For if they wish to deceive, it seems almost necessary to deceive first their own ambassador, the agent and instrument who must deal with and convince the other prince. Each of these opinions has its reason. On the one hand, an ambassador who knows his prince means to deceive will hardly be able to speak and treat as warmly, effectively, and firmly as he would if he believed the negotiations were sincere and not fake. Furthermore, either levity or ill will might cause him to reveal the intentions of his prince—and that an ambassador ignorant of the truth could not do. On the other hand, it often happens that an ambassador who believes his false instructions to be genuine will be more insistent than the matter requires. For if he believes his prince really wishes to achieve a specific end, he will not be as moderate and circumspect in his negotiations as he would have been had he known the truth. It is impossible to give ambassadors instructions so detailed as to cover every circumstance; rather discretion must teach them to accommodate themselves to the end generally being pursued. But if the ambassador does not fully know that end, he cannot pursue it, and therefore he may err in a thousand ways.
>
> In my opinion, a prince who has prudent and honest ambassadors, well-disposed toward him, and well-provided for, so that they have no reason to depend on others, would do better to reveal his intentions. But if he cannot be sure that his ambassadors completely fit this description, it is safer to leave them ignorant and to let the ground for convincing others be the same grounds that convince the ambassadors themselves.[36] (C 2)

Regarding the ambassador's relationship to his principals, Guicciardini with this observation has come strikingly close in conception to Gorgias's description of the tragedian's relationship to his actors. Like the actor, the

36. The earlier version of this maxim, B 24, addresses only the need to deceive.

ambassador must sometimes be deceived in order to function properly and persuade effectively; by extension, the prince, in creating a deception that keeps the ambassador in the dark, behaves like the dramatist, thereby rendering the deceiver, in Gorgias's scheme of things, "more honest than the non-deceiver, and the deceived . . . wiser than the non-deceived." "Discretion" may therefore be required of a good ambassador, for discretion not only provides ambassadors with a "good and perspicacious eye" (C 117) that will allow them to sort out tiny differences and make fine distinctions; it teaches ambassadors how "to accommodate themselves to the end generally being pursued" and therefore (hopefully) how to attain their goal. Yet sometimes discretion simply is not enough to ensure that the quality of the ambassador's performance will be effective and persuasive. Sometimes an ambassador needs to be kept completely in the dark, precisely as Guicciardini had been on occasion during his stay in Spain. Being an ambassador, it would seem, consequently means accepting a condition of work in which you are at times philosophically knowledgeable about your own ignorance yet, practically speaking, still constrained to act on the grand scale, as if you were completely in control of the part you are expected to play.

From the early Q^1 maxims to the final version of his *Ricordi,* Guicciardini thus reflected both directly and indirectly on what it is like to be an ambassador in a particularly critical and difficult moment of Italian history, repeatedly drawing on his own experience as he composed and revised his book of flexible rules.[37] He also drew on his own experience as an ambassador when he wrote his *History of Italy* and included in it extended observations that seem to blossom out of the maxims of the *Ricordi.*[38] One particular observation that pertains directly to Guicciardini's ambassadorial experience addresses the risks of neutrality the Florentine government faced in the time of the Florentine Republic of 1494–1512. Guicciardini discussed this topic of neutrality as early as the Q^2 version of the *Ricordi* and then returned to it in the A, B, and C versions. In the *History of Italy,* however, he develops his thought in extended prose,

37. "Read these *Ricordi* often, and ponder them well. For it is easier to know and understand them than to put them into practice. But this too becomes easier if you grow so accustomed to them that they are always fresh in your memory" (C 9).

38. See, for example, Phillips, "F. Guicciardini: The Historian as Aphorist"; Rubinstein, "Introduction," in Guicciardini, *Maxims and Reflections,* 20; and the interspersed comments in Alexander's translation of Guicciardini's *History of Italy.* Asor Rosa ("*Ricordi* di Francesco Guicciardini," 18–22) observes how the *ricordi* also inversely seem to be drawn from Guicciardini's works of continuous prose.

rather than leaving it in the isolated, lapidary state of a collected fragment. Midway through this great work of humanist history, Guicciardini describes the debates held within his divided city. These debates took place in 1511, just before Guicciardini left for Spain, which is to say, during the period when the city of Florence was trying to remain neutral and enjoy the "benefit of time."

> Amid these contentions, one faction interrupting the advice of the other, they did not decide to declare themselves or to remain entirely neutral; which gave rise to counsels often uncertain and deliberations repugnant in themselves, without bringing reputation or merit to anyone. Instead, growing out of these uncertainties, they sent as ambassador to the King of Aragon (to the great displeasure of the King of France) Francesco Guicciardini, Doctor of Law, he who wrote this history, who at that time was still so young that in respect of his age, according to the laws of his country, he was unable to exercise any office whatever; and yet they did not give him commissions such as might lessen in any way the ill will of the allies.[39] (*HI,* 242–43; *SdI,* 1087)

Introducing himself for the first time into his *History of Italy,* Guicciardini here inserts himself into a narrative rhetorically structured, according to so many scholars, as a tragedy.[40] In doing so, Guicciardini gazes with mournful eyes at a brighter moment, at a time when he was not one of the successful deceivers writing a tragedy but, as Gorgias would have it, one of those who are ever so wisely deceived. For it was then, as a young ambassador writing his *Discorso di Logrogno,* that Guicciardini first optimistically articulated an ideal vision of his city reconstructed along the lines of a Venetian republic composed of "wise men." Now, some twenty-five years later, the older, far more skeptical Guicciardini views his own ineffectual role in averting the tragic course of history of which, while no longer a wise ambassador for the fallen Florentine Republic, he is still ineluctably a part.

Reflections on Ambassadorial Work in the History of Italy

The first appearance of ambassadors in the *History of Italy,* which covers the political events that occurred in Europe from 1490 to 1534, is a

39. See also Guicciardini, *HI,* 255; *SdI,* 1168–69.

40. Gilbert, *Machiavelli and Guicciardini,* 285 and 287. See also Ramat, *Il Guicciardini e la tragedia d'Italia,* 107–8; Bondanella, *Francesco Guicciardini,* 108–110; and Sapegno, "*Storia d'Italia* di Francesco Guicciardini," esp. 128, 140–42, 150, 152–55.

revealing one. Guicciardini has just described (in book 1, chapter 1) a happy mythic past for Italy. The country, viewed as a geographical rather than a political unity, was tranquil and integrated thanks to the brilliant diplomatic work of Lorenzo de' Medici. Though Lorenzo de' Medici (1449–1492) was not a powerful man, he nevertheless managed to maintain a perfect balance among unequals in Italy through a combination of skillful negotiation and good luck, through *virtù* and *fortuna*. Lorenzo's death, however, prefigured the end to this golden age of diplomacy, and it coincided with a series of "calamities." One such calamity, which would lead to the far greater calamities that set in motion the tragic history of Italy, was Ludovico Sforza's decision to manipulate the customary practice of sending ambassadors to Rome so that they might pay tribute to the newly elected pope, in this case to Alexander VI. Sforza's apparent aim in altering this accepted diplomatic custom is to make all of Italy seem politically unified. His underlying aim, however, is to expose an alliance—an "understanding" viewed as "the seed and source of all the misfortunes to come"—between King Ferdinand of Naples and Piero de' Medici of Florence (*HI,* 14). "According to long-established practice," Guicciardini observes,

> princes all over Christendom had to send ambassadors to pay homage to the new Pontiff and declare their obeisance to him as Vicar of Christ on earth. Ludovico Sforza (who was always seeking ways to appear, by means of hitherto unthought-of devices, wiser than anybody else) had proposed that all the ambassadors of the league should enter Rome on the same day and that one of them should speak in the name of all. In this way they would demonstrate to all of Italy that not only was there an alliance and friendship among them, but even more, they were so united that they seemed almost a single body under one head, and this would increase the reputation of the entire league. Reason, as well as a recent example, demonstrated the usefulness of such a procedure; for it was believed that the Pope who had recently died had been more disposed to attack the kingdom of Naples, finding a pretext in the disunion among the allies who had sent separate legations at various times to lend him obedience.
>
> Ferdinand [of Naples] readily approved Ludovico's scheme, as did the Florentines; nor did Piero de' Medici oppose the plan in a public meeting, although privately he was much annoyed by it. Having been chosen as one of the ambassadors elected in the name of the republic, and having decided to make his legation illustrious with a very proud and almost royal ostentation, Piero was aware that in entering Rome and presenting himself to the Pope together with the other ambassadors of the league, all his splendor and pomp would not make much display in such a multitude. This juvenile vanity of

> Piero's was supported by the ambitious counsel of Gentile, Bishop of Arezzo, who was also one of the elected ambassadors. The Bishop of Arezzo had been chosen to speak in the name of the Florentines in view of his Episcopal dignity and the reputation which he had in those studies called humanistic; the Bishop was vexed at losing the opportunity of displaying his eloquence in so honored and solemn a setting, as a result of Sforza's unusual and unexpected scheme. (*HI,* 14; *SdI,* 12–13)

With one fell stroke, Ludovico ingeniously aims to rob Piero de' Medici of his ability to engage in the pomp and circumstance of diplomatic mummery. This rankles not just Piero de' Medici, but also his fellow humanist ambassador, who has been training for the occasion. An ambassador without an oration has no performance, and Piero de' Medici and his fellow ambassador want to appear center stage, to foreground the power and glory not only of their republic but of themselves as well. Piero therefore objects to Sforza's scheme, "goaded partly by his own frivolity and partly by the Bishop's ambition" (*HI,* 14; *SdI,* 13), and he enlists King Ferdinand's aid in seeing to it that these altered ceremonies never comes to pass. Seeing this, Ludovico Sforza then swiftly comes to realize that "Piero de' Medici had a secret understanding with Ferdinand" (*HI,* 15; *SdI,* 14), and this suspicion marks the first visible breach in the already fragile league. How ambassadors appear, how they are maneuvered and manipulated, thus clearly matters in fifteenth-century Italy, and Guicciardini has chosen to reveal this at the very beginning of his *History of Italy.*

Ludovico Sforza, who manages to manipulate the king of France's ambassadors, is the first of many villains of the *History of Italy,* "the author and promoter of all these evils" (*HI,* 27; *SdI,* 45). He initially upsets the hard-won balance of counterpoised elements in Italy by inviting the king of France to enter and conquer Naples. But in point of fact it is the eloquence of Sforza's ambassador, Carlo da Barbiano, whose oration is the first in Guicciardini's text and magnificent in its length, that helps convince the king of France to invade Italy and take over Naples (see *SdI,* 30–34). Moreover, the Milanese ambassador, who delivers his oration before the royal council in 1493, has meanwhile greased the palms of King Charles's sycophant counselors, so many of whom are mere "yes" men, and so many of whom are easily "corrupted by money and promises put forward by Ludovico's ambassador, who left no stone unturned to win over those sympathetic to [the duke's] proposition" (*HI,* 24; *SdI,* 37). Ludovico Sforza's ambassador is not only strikingly eloquent and persuasive, but also crafty, manipulative, and secretive, tough and cunning, the way so many of the ambassadors are in Guicciardini's *History of Italy.* Consider, for example, in book 9 the Spanish resident ambassador, Jerónimo Cabanillas di Valenza, who in 1511 speaks to the king of France with "the sweetest words," extending brotherly friendship, but all while delivering a "tacit threat," a threat King Ferdinand himself delivers to the French resident ambassador, that Spain would "take up arms in favor of the Pope" (*HI,* 219; *SdI,* 995). Consider as well the tough-minded Florentine ambassadors of book 3, who refuse to be bullied by the duke of Milan, who wanted to know what the emperor Maximilian had said to them: the Florentines refused, claiming that the law of their republic did not permit them to divulge such information, though they were of course certainly free to hear anything the duke might wish to tell them. "They were not prohibited from listening," these sly ambassadors tell the angered duke, "any more than they could prohibit others from speaking." The duke of Milan, Guicciardini then observes, "dismissed the ambassadors and all those whom he had called together, since he had ended up being in part the butt of the disdain that he would have wanted the others to feel" (*SdI,* 328). Rather than being shamed by the duke's dismissal, these clever ambassadors end up shaming him. Consider yet again in book 3 the Venetian ambassador who in 1497 "artfully" [artificiosamente] proposes one thing, aware that by doing so he will gain precisely the desired opposite effect:

> The Duke wrought that the Pope and the ambassadors of the King of Spain, both of whom were threatened by such Venetian power, should propose that, in order to leave the French no possible foundation in Italy and to reduce all of Italy into harmony, it would be necessary to force the Florentines to enter into the common league by returning Pisa to them, since otherwise they could not be so induced. For, he argued, so long as the Florentines were separated from the others they would not cease to goad the king of France to come to Italy, and in case he should come, they would be able, by means of their money and men, especially since they are for the most part situated in the middle of Italy, to bring about consequences of no little importance. But this proposition was rejected by the Venetian ambassador as very harmful to the common welfare, alleging the inclination of the Florentines toward the King of France to be such that, even with this reward, they were not to be trusted if they did not give sufficient security to observe what they might promise, and in matters of such moment no other guarantee would suffice except to place Livorno into the hands of the allies. The Venetian ambassador cunningly proposed this because he knew the Florentines would never consent to place a city of such importance into their hands, and thus he would have all the more reasons to argue against the scheme. The matter then succeeding as he had anticipated, he opposed the proposal so vehemently that

> the Pope and the Duke of Milan's ambassador did not dare raise objections for fear of alienating the Venetians from their alliance, and so they did not pursue this line of argument further. (*HI,* 121; *SdI,* 349–50)

For Guicciardini, the dignity of the ambassador, which reflects the value of the government he represents, must be maintained at all costs. This is not always a simple task, however, especially when a power has been defeated or senses that it is in decline. In book 8, for example, Venice is desperate, confined largely to its canals and lagoons soon after having lost the crucial battle of Agnadello on May 14, 1509. Never before had Venice suffered such a devastating and ignominious defeat. In the face of this "calamity," with absolutely no hope that their captains can save Venice, the city chooses to send an ambassador to the emperor as a last resort. The ambassador, Antonio Giustiniano, must plead for clemency before Maximilian and ask him to intervene to assure peace. Venice has lost her pride of place, her *dignitas* as an empire, and it is Giustiniano's job to see that she does not sink any lower. Giustiniano therefore begins his oration by recalling the models of classical antiquity. In typical humanist fashion, he hopes that the emperor will emulate the models he sets before him: those of Scipio and Caesar Augustus. According to Giustiniano, it is one thing to conquer others and quite another to conquer oneself, as these emperors in antiquity did (*SdI,* 824–27). The emperor Maximilian need only adhere to these models of mercy and self-restraint, and he will be praised by Venetians as the "progenitor" and "founder" of their city (*SdI,* 826). The dignity of Venice will be maintained by making it a city worthy of an emperor, and Maximilian's "great merits" will be placed in the "annals" of the city, handed down from father to son (*SdI,* 826). The eloquence of the ambassador further serves as proof that the Venetians can write the humanist history that will adequately glorify the emperor's name for future generations. Yet despite his conspicuous eloquence, Giustiniano speaks in the dark. He pronounces many of the well-worn themes of humanist literature but all his words, as Guicciardini notes, are spoken "in vain" (*SdI,* 824). The emperor will have nothing to do with these matters, and so he leaves Venice isolated, defenseless, with "calamity on top of calamity accumulating" (*SdI,* 829).

In the tragedy of the *History of Italy,* which unfolds in twenty books and selectively covers the period when Italy increasingly became the contested site of domination by invading foreign powers, Guicciardini provides a veritable array of ambassadors at work. Some of them are singled out and praised for special characteristics. There is the Venetian ambassador, Girolamo Donato (1454–1511), a friend of Ermolao Barbaro and an important Italian humanist, who is commended for his "prudence and dexterity" (*SdI,* 1056), and the French humanist Guillaume Budé (1468–1540), who is described as "a man of the highest and perhaps unique erudition of humane letters, both Greek and Latin, among all the men of our time" (*SdI,* 1338). More often than not, however, the ambassadors in Guicciardini's *History of Italy* are the faceless drones who carry out others' policies as they go back and forth between potentates, sometimes at great risk to their own lives. In the first book alone they are sent to pay tribute (1.4); seal pacts (1.4); arrange marriages (1.5); feel out alliances, interests, commitments (1.5); maintain friendships (1.5); explain a military mission and seek assurance of safe conduct (1.6); request aid (1.7); draw others into a conflict for protection (1.8); hear and report complaints while assuring solidarity (1.8); appease and threaten (1.14); mark a separation within a sovereign power (1.15); establish how and when to enter a city (1.16); represent a power within a recently won territory (1.16); report threats (1.16); oversee events (1.16); request safe entrance into a domain and assure the peaceful intent of those who live there (1.17); and shift alliance (1.19). So present are ambassadors in Guicciardini's *History* that Alberico Gentili (1552–1608), an Italian in exile writing and teaching at Oxford at the end of the sixteenth century, would rely on it more than any other contemporary work when he turned to compose his treatise on the office of the ambassador, *De legationibus libri tres* (1585).

However, while ambassadors fill the pages of Guicciardini's history, they should not be taken as timeless examples illustrating how ambassadors should behave at all times and places. In keeping with Guicciardini's vision of exemplarity as an unreliable mode for understanding how to behave from one moment to the next,[41] the success or failure of ambassadors at any given moment in the *History of Italy*—the success of Carlo da Barbiano in fomenting war and the failure of Antonio Giustiniano in ensuring peace—has less to do with the *virtù* of a particular ambassador than with the completely unpredictable whim of *fortuna.* The successful ambassador's work can therefore never be construed as exemplary in Guicciardini's *History of Italy* because the conditions that prevailed when the ambassador succeeded will never be perfectly duplicated. Ultimately, ambassadors, along with everyone else in the *History of Italy,* are caught

41. "To judge by example is very misleading. Unless they are similar in every respect, examples are useless, since every tiny difference in the case may be a cause of great variations in the effects. And to discern these tiny differences takes a good and perspicacious eye" (C 117; see also C 110). See also *SdI,* 107 (bk. 1, chap. 14).

up in the grand sweep of historical events over which they have no real control. In this regard, the dense presence of ambassadors in Guicciardini's history signals not the efficacy of Renaissance diplomacy but the increased need for it in a world in which one event occurring in one place powerfully effects another event occurring elsewhere.[42] In the *History of Italy,* "the quality of the performance" of individual ambassadors matters far less than the network they collectively construct in an intricately connected world of newly emergent competing sovereign powers—a world, as Guicciardini pessimistically envisioned it, that was steadily and tragically falling apart, from the death of Lorenzo de' Medici in 1492 to the death of his nephew, the second Medici pope, Clement VII, in 1534.

42. See Gilbert, *Machiavelli and Guicciardini,* 294–96.

Secretaries

Six

OPEN SECRETS

The Place of the Renaissance Secretary

> The secret subject is always an open secret. . . . Yet, curiously enough, the fact that the secret is always known—and, in some obscure sense, known to be known—never interferes with the incessant activity of keeping it. . . . In this light, it becomes clear that the social function of secrecy . . . is not to conceal knowledge, so much as to conceal the knowledge of the knowledge. No doubt an analysis of the kinds of knowledge that it is felt needful to cover in secrecy would tell us much about a given culture or historical period. . . . But when the game of secrecy is played beyond those contexts that obviously call for suppression, it is evident that the need to "keep secret" takes precedence over whatever social exigencies exist for keeping one or another secret in particular. Instead of the question "What does secrecy cover?" we had better ask "What covers secrecy?" What, that is, takes secrecy for its field of operations?
>
> —DAVID MILLER

Portraits of a Secretary

In Sebastiano del Piombo's *Ferry Carondelet and His Secretaries,* completed in Rome sometime in 1511 or 1512, there seems to be little glamour or authority associated with the secretary's profession. All the glamour and authority instead belong to the dominant figure of Carondelet, who is wearing a plush robe that envelopes him in a sort of bow of spotted fur.[1] Nor is this a scene of intimacy between Carondelet and his trusted

1. The epigraph is from Miller, *The Novel and the Police,* 205–7. On Sebastiano del Piombo, see in general Hirst, *Sebastiano del Piombo.* On this painting, and its relationship to Titian's, which is discussed below, I am indebted to Jaffé, "The Picture of the Secretary of Titian." In my discussion of the Italian secretary and Torquato Accetto, I am indebted to and rely heavily

confidant. Though secretaries were commonly considered by definition "keepers of secrets" in the sixteenth century,[2] there can be little doubt that Sebastiano del Piombo has represented a public rather than a private moment. The figure of the second secretary, entering from the rear with a message, assures us that the two men in front are not engaged in deeply private affairs. The gaze of the second secretary, moreover, reaches out to reinforce the gaze of Carondelet and establish an implied observer: the spectator(s) of the painting, along with—presumably at the imagined moment of its execution—Sebastiano del Piombo himself. Carondelet is thus surrounded by people who are either gazing at, or attending upon, him. He is the center of attention; all eyes are drawn to him, even by the very lines of the carpeted table, each of which recedes toward a vanishing point just to the left of Carondelet's shoulder.

Carondelet was probably working in Rome as ambassador for the Emperor Maximilian and Margaret of Austria when Sebastiano del Piombo painted this portrait.[3] Carondelet's dominance in the picture plane, with his elbow pushed forward, establishes his superior stature and social status as an orator. He governs all the work, making and sending dispatches. He is a busy and important man, engaged in a flurry of activity of which he is in full control and from which he has taken a moment's pause to look up at his spectators. But Carondelet is not just a busy and important man. He is also a lofty one. We are expected to look up to the orator. By contrast, in his obvious submissive posture, the secretary to the right typifies the subordinate status of the secretary in early cinquecento Italy. His place, with respect to the orator who directs his activity, is low. He looks up to the orator as the kneeling New Testament scribe was traditionally represented taking down the word of God. Poised to write, the secretary waits to be instructed by the orator, who, fully illumined, will enlighten the

---

on the excellent studies by Nigro: *"Scriptor necans,"* "Lezione sull'ombra," "Le livre masqué d'un secrétaire du xviie siècle," and *Il segretario di lettere.* I am also indebted to Quondam, "Varianti di Proteo" and "Dal 'formulario' al 'formulario'"; Bulzoni, "Il segretario neoplatonico"; Basso, *Le genre épistolaire en langue italienne;* Iucci, "La trattatistica sul segretario"; Bonora, "Tra oratori, cortigiani e uomini di lettere: Il trattato sul segretario," chap. 4 in *Ricerche su Francesco Sansovino,* 139–62; and the excellent study by Fiorato, "Grandeur et servitude du secrétaire." For an account of an earlier period, see Dibben, "Secretaries in the Thirteenth and Fourteenth Centuries." I have also benefited from Rambuss, *Spenser's Secret Career.*

2. See, for example, Tasso, *Del secretario,* in *Le prose diverse,* 260. Tasso's *secretario* went through numerous printings and first appeared in 1587. The definition is longstanding, consistent with that of, say, the *Secretum secretorum;* see Bacon, *Opera hactenus inedita,* 5.146–47. The definition persists well into the eighteenth century, in one of the later Italian secretarial treatises; see Nardi, *Il segretario principiante,* 236.

3. Russell, *Diplomats at Work,* 19.

Sebastiano del Piombo, *Ferry Carondelet and His Secretaries,* 1511–1512.
© Museo Thyssen-Bornemisza, Madrid.

secretary with his thoughts. The orator speaks to the humbled secretary, who is there by the grace of his master. The secretary's gaze therefore rests reverently on the cardinal as he waits for the cardinal to turn and recognize him, at which point his work of taking dictation will resume.

The secretary is not thinking, much less inventing. Like the scribe upon whom he is modeled, the foregrounded secretary is recording rather than counseling. He is an instrument of the will of the cardinal, an extension of the pen he wields. He is there to serve: a marginal figure, he is pushed so far to the right edge of the canvas that only part of his head is visible.[4] It is unmistakably the orator, the man who speaks, who matters here, not the man who writes.

We may compare this vision of the secretary as humbled functionary with Titian's painting of *Georges d'Armagnac and His Secretary,* completed in about 1540. Though clearly modeled on Sebastiano del Piombo's painting, much has been changed in Titian's version. Rather than placing three men out in the open, on a sort of second-story loggia, Titian has created a studied portrait of two men in a closed interior setting. The secretary still kneels,[5] and his gaze is directed upward toward his master, but he is not so dramatically downstaged, and his head, completely framed by the window, is now fully in view. Titian's secretary has a place and dignity of his own within the picture plane. Moreover, the less stern commanding gaze of d'Armagnac, who is momentarily lost in thought, is turned away from the viewer of the painting. And rather than clutching his letters and folding his arms in upon himself as Carondelet does, d'Armagnac extends the letter toward his secretary, as if he were engaging his secretary in his own thought process. No one intrudes on the scene. The two sitters have been caught, to use Michael Fried's term, in a moment of "absorption,"[6] the conceptual trick here being that no one is present, including even the implied painter, to view the scene. For unlike the implied painter of Sebastiano del Piombo's canvas, who is recognized by the incoming secretary to the left and by Carondelet himself, the hidden representer in Titian's painting is acknowledged by no one in the double portrait. The two men, whom Titian has placed side by side in a more conversational pose, are absolutely alone. Shrouded in partial darkness, the light now falls on both men equally, illuminating each one's collar in much the same way. Even the expressions on their bearded faces seem identical: the same curved eyebrows, heavy eyelids, highlighted noses. The secretary,

4. Thomas Willette and Alexandra Wettlaufer suggested to me that the canvas could have been cut since the cropping of the secretary is so unusual. However, Hirst, in *Sebastiano del Piombo,* makes no mention of this, and Jaffé, in "The Picture," 114, treats the painting as unaltered.

5. In stating that the secretary kneels in Titian's painting, I follow Gould, *Titian as Portraitist,* 19.

6. Fried, *Absorption and Theatricality.*

in this respect, visually emerges as the writerly complement to the master who speaks. He is, to borrow the terms of one seventeenth-century secretarial treatise, the "good man who writes well" [huomo buono perito dello scrivere] as the structural counterpart to the orator, whom Quintilian describes as "the good man who speaks well" [vir bonus dicendi peritus].[7]

The secretary in Titian's painting was for many years thought to be Machiavelli posed with either Duke Sforza of Milan or Cosimo de' Medici. Machiavelli never worked for either of these men.[8] But it is both

Titian, *Georges d'Armagnac and His Secretary,* ca. 1540. Collection of the Duke of Northumberland.

7. Persico, *Del segretario, libri quattro,* 18; I cite from this edition throughout. First printed in 1620. On the secretary as the double of his master, with a focus on the English secretaries, see Rambuss, *Spenser's Secret Career.*

8. Jaffé, "The Picture," 117–18.

significant and appropriate that Machiavelli, who worked for fourteen years as secretary to the Florentine Republic, should be identified with Titian's secretary. In comparison with Sebastiano del Piombo's painting, the importance Titian has ascribed to the role of the secretary is precisely what Machiavelli actively sought to create for himself in discourse. In *The Prince,* Machiavelli not only "transfers" himself into his past as he draws on things learned from experience as a secretary "over so many years and with so much affliction and peril" (proem, 21).[9] He also reconceptualizes his past, expanding the scope of his prior administrative duties as secretary to the Florentine Republic and self-consciously elevating his subordinate status to the point where he conceives of himself as the secret counselor of a prince. Though this shift may at first seem minimal, it was in fact enormously significant, in terms of both personal prestige and social power, for men such as Francesco Sansovino (1521–1586), the Venetian polymath who wrote some fifty years after Machiavelli's drafting of *The Prince* that "of the great secretaries some serve principalities, others republics. Those that serve princes have greater weight and more responsibilities than the others, whence as a result they are more esteemed and honored in the world. And in the isle of England in our own times they are made knights of the order of the same king. And today the best governed courts make great capital of their secretaries, whence it has happened that sometimes the secretary has been elevated to become the prince of the signoria."[10] Secretaries may have greater liberty in republics, but they have less prestige and power. The important secretaries, the great ones, are those who work for princes.

This chapter focuses on Machiavelli's *The Prince,* but I also discuss at length, and examine *The Prince* in light of, the many treatises written on the secretary in the late sixteenth and early seventeenth centuries, when Italy was essentially dominated by court culture. In these late Renaissance treatises, the secretary, who was expected to have been fully trained in the *studia humanitatis,* was often viewed as the keeper of secrets, though his silence, which makes the secretary seem a cipher, actually functions to suggest a secret interior existing within him and thus ironically confers on him an identity, a private self, he would otherwise seem to lack. Before turning to these late Renaissance treatises on the secretary, however, I

9. The notion that Machiavelli may be "transferring" himself into precisely his previous role as secretary when writing *The Prince* is suggested, but not developed, by de Grazia in *Machiavelli in Hell,* 372.

10. Sansovino, *L'avvocato e il segretario,* 152–53, hereafter cited by page number in my text; first published in 1564.

seek to reconstruct the writer of *The Prince* as the humanist secretary of the failed Florentine Republic of 1498–1512, the keeper of secrets who not only wrote about secretaries in *The Prince* but identified himself soon after his fall from fortune as "quondam segretario" (*Let.* 9 April 1513; 1132),[11] still unsure whether he should speak his mind or take a vow of silence on questions of governance only months before he began drafting his most famous work. As Machiavelli creates a place for secretaries in his discourse on princes, however, he figures himself in *The Prince* as a completely atypical secretary of the Renaissance and thus undermines trust in his own position within *The Prince* as a reliable secretarial advisor. Machiavelli, who practiced the profession of secretary, undercuts the definition of that profession he offers in *The Prince* by presenting himself in that work not as the keeper of secrets but—unlike the secretaries in either Sebastiano del Piombo's or Titian's portraits—as their deliberate revealer.

Disclosing Secrets: Machiavelli as the Atypical Secretarial Advisor of The Prince

Federico Chabod asserted some years ago in *Il segretario fiorentino* that Machiavelli was always just a functionary, a person who could be counted on to carry out faithfully delicate and important missions but never an important player who held a high public office. As secretary to the Second Chancery, in a government within which his administrative function was not to offer counsel (even though he sometimes tried to do so), Machiavelli's duties varied greatly: "egli fa un po' di tutto" [he does a bit of just about everything]. He was a sort of mid-level civil servant who, by virtue of the Florentine law of 1483 promulgated during the reforms of Bartolomeo Scala, was expected to keep faithfully and prudently the secrets of state with which he had been entrusted.[12] Among the many

11. All citations of the Italian, hereafter indicated in my text by date and page number (with regard to letters) or chapter and page numbers (with regard to all other writings), are from Machiavelli, *Tutte le opere.* Translations, modified on occasion, are from George Bull's translation, *The Prince;* I have provided the page number from Bull's translation when the English is cited, followed generally by the page number from the Italian.

12. Chabod's comments, loosely paraphrased here, appear in "Il segretario fiorentino," in *Scritti su Machiavelli,* 274. On the Florentine law, see Marzi, *La cancelleria,* 599, which is cited as well in Rubinstein's informative "Beginnings of Niccolò Machiavelli's Career in the Florentine Chancery," and again in Brown, *Bartolomeo Scala,* 180.

things that Machiavelli did in his position as secretary, a position that had been open to humanists eager for political advancement since the beginning of the fifteenth century, was compose letters of state during the brief Florentine Republic. Among the letters Machiavelli composed were those sent to the Ten of War when he traveled both inside and outside Florentine boundaries, or when he accompanied ambassadors on various diplomatic and fact-finding missions. Fredi Chiappelli studied a large body of these letters in an article titled "Machiavelli as Secretary." Chiappelli concluded that "there is no essential distinction between the secretary and the writer," which is to say, the humanist writer of *The Prince*. The texts of the chancery letters, Chiappelli argues, "show that if Machiavelli's terminology is not yet fully ripened, as it will be in the years after 1512, the typical prose structure—the sentence, the grammatical polynomy, in which his thinking becomes organized—is already completely formed."[13] The humanist secretary of the chancery is already, in style and substantially in wit for Chiappelli, essentially the humanist writer of *The Prince*.

There are various reasons for envisioning the writer of *The Prince* as still a secretary, though by no means the same secretary who for more than ten years concluded many of his legations with the title "servitor, Nicolaus Machiavellus, Secretarius," a title Machiavelli was attached to and even continued to use right up to the publication of his *Arte della guerra* in 1521, nine years after he had been dismissed from the chancery.[14] In the first place, even as a secretary to the commune of Florence—and to the chagrin of many in the Florentine government—Machiavelli attempted to extend his bureaucratic duties to the policy-making office of the advisor,[15] which is putatively the office that Machiavelli takes up

13. Chiappelli, "Machiavelli as Secretary," 42 and 33 respectively. See also Najemy, *Between Friends*, 63–94.

14. In *From Poliziano to Machiavelli*, 235–36, Godman observes that Machiavelli "published a blatant lie" when he continued to refer to himself as "segretario Fiorentino" right on up to his *Arte della guerra* in 1521, long after he had been dismissed. See in general the chapter "The Shadow of the Chancery," in *From Poliziano to Machiavelli*, 235–91.

15. On the assertiveness of Machiavelli in his legations, on his taking on the role of advisor rather than that of secretary, which would have confined him to fact-finding and letter-writing, see Najemy, *Between Friends*, 62; and Najemy, "The Controversy Surrounding Machiavelli's Service to the Republic." The administrative function of the chancery officials was *not* to offer advice about Florentine politics, though Rubinstein addresses ways in which they could exercise influence in "Machiavelli and the World of Florentine Politics." On Machiavelli as secretary to Florence, see Chabod, "Il segretario fiorentino"; Rubinstein, "The Beginnings of Niccolò Machiavelli's Career"; Ridolfi, *The Life of Niccolò Machiavelli*, esp. 15–21 but see also 22–119; and Black, "Machiavelli, Servant of the Florentine Republic." See also Black, "Florentine

in *The Prince* by offering "the gift of counsel."[16] Moreover, from time to time Italians, in the course of writing treatises that defined the duties of the secretary in the late cinquecento, conceptualized the Machiavelli of *The Prince* as a secretary. Machiavelli, in other words, was sometimes thought of and referred to as a secretary when Italians wrote about the office of the secretary in the sixteenth and early seventeenth centuries, and the Machiavelli they were thinking of is unmistakably the author of *The Prince.* According to the Sienese humanist, statesman, and Valdesian Bartolomeo Carli Piccolomini (1503–ca.1537),[17] for example, Machiavelli was a particularly insightful thinker precisely because he had occupied the office of secretary in the Florentine chancery. "In such an office," Carli wrote in his *Del perfetto cancelliere,* "men will become experienced and expert in the infinity of things that they will be managing, as Niccolò Machiavelli did as secretary in the Florentine chancery, there having acquired various and great news, and a profound and rare discourse of the things of the world, whence came the inspiration for his esteemed works about the princedom, the war, the discourses on Livy, and his histories." Machiavelli's humanist writings, which draw so much on Roman models, are for Carli the product of a "great mind" that brings everything into "a perfect harmony," but they are also indebted to his "great experience"—an experience grounded in his work as secretary to the republic of Florence—"of various things that have to do with human life." Machiavelli's profession as a secretary has thus, according to Carli, profoundly shaped his genius as a humanist.[18] Machiavelli, it is important to point out, seems to say as much in the proem to *The Prince* when he

Political Traditions and Machiavelli's Election to the Chancery"; the concise statements in Skinner, *Machiavelli,* 3–20; and Hale, *Machiavelli and Renaissance Italy,* 1–134. Though not the central topic of his essay, the gradual bureaucratization of the chancery is an underlying issue traced in Garin, "I cancellieri umanisti della repubblica fiorentina," though for a positive reappraisal of reforms of the chancery under Accolti, see Black, *Benedetto Accolti and the Florentine Renaissance;* and for Florence during the Medici rule in the quattrocento, see Brown, *Bartolomeo Scala.*

16. Ascoli, "Machiavelli's Gift of Counsel."

17. On Piccolomini, see Belladonna, "Cenni biografici su Bartolomeo Carli Piccolomini," who describes him as having "reached the apex of humanist culture" (508; my translation) by the 1530s. Piccolomini studied both classical Latin and Greek, having received, as Belladonna puts it, a "traditional type of humanistic education" (509; my translation). He began to feel the influence of Erasmus and Valdensians toward 1531, but he was also strongly influenced by Machiavelli.

18. B. Carli Piccolomini, *Del perfetto cancelliere,* 61r–61v, as cited in Belladonna, "Pontanus, Machiavelli, and a Case of Religious Dissimulation," 381; my translation. Belladonna indicates that the manuscript version is dated 7 November 1529.

insists that he has achieved an "understanding of the deeds of great men" not just through the "continuous study of the ancient world," as one might naturally expect a humanist would, but from the "long acquaintance [*lunga esperienza*] with contemporary affairs" (proem, 29; 257) he acquired during his fourteen years as an interested and inquisitive secretary within the Florentine government. For Machiavelli, his secretarial past still had a powerful claim on his present theoretical work.

Along with this, Machiavelli wrote in *The Prince* not only as a former secretary but about secretaries, creating a place for secretaries, and thus a place for himself as a "quondam segretario" writing with an eye to return to power one day. In chapter 22 Machiavelli turns to talk about "the secretaries that a prince must choose" [De his quos a secretis principes habent]. The origins of the term *a secretis,* here used in the title heading, are unclear. In his *Trattato del segretario,* published in 1588, Andrea Nati observes that all the things he has mentioned in his treatise regarding the work of secretaries "in no small way agree with the descriptions of the Latins, from which the secretary was called . . . 'a secretis', the master of letters."[19] The Vicentian historian Giacomo Marzari, author of *La prattica e theorica del cancelliere* (1602), seems to be of much the same mind when he distinguishes the secretary of princes from those of republics and reinforces the longstanding assumption in the late Renaissance that a secretarial career was a ladder to success. Going all the way back to antiquity, secretaries—or *a secretis* as they are now sometimes called—succeeded to the highest possible office at a given time:

> But the Greeks and Persians used to call them secretaries, and they were held in such high esteem that secretaries were often seen to succeed to the position of the prince. . . . Nor are secretaries held in less esteem nowadays; we have heard about and seen many secretaries at the Roman court carried forward because of their virtues and their great valor. . . . Nowadays secretaries are held in such high esteem in some courts of Christian princes that they not only have a voice in parliament but also a vote in the deliberations; for which reason those working for a prince have a better reputation than the secretaries who serve republics, since, even if they assist in the consultations that are made with regard to the advice about things of the state, they do not have any part in the deliberations of the rulers. And as in the Roman Empire they were called "Silentiarii" . . . so Secretaries are now called "a secretis," presumably because they must have a constant and solid secrecy in them, that they will never speak freely, for any reason whatsoever, about the affairs of their prince,

19. Nati, *Trattato del segretario,* a7v. Hereafter cited by page number in text when the author is mentioned.

but the secretary must keep these affairs to himself, not otherwise as if he were mute.[20]

Marzari turns to classical culture to understand through analogy the origins of *a secretis* as a term designating in his own time the secretarial profession, whereas Pierre de Miraulmont, writing his *Traité de la Chancellerie* in 1610, imagines the term to have roots in antiquity. It is probable, however, that *a secretis* is of medieval origin.[21] The citations in the *Lexicon latinitatis medii aevi,* for example, record an early usage in the reign of Charlemagne; and *a secretis* as a term had wide currency in ecclesiastical circles.[22] In any event, *a secretis* was certainly used to designate secretaries during the Italian Renaissance and in Machiavelli's time. In the records of the Florentine chancery, for instance, in a document dated May 27, 1502, Machiavelli is described as "the principal secretary in the Second Chancery" [N. Malclavello, a secretis in secunda Cancellaria primario].[23] The man who often signed his letters as "secretarius" thus held a position within the Second Chancery as "a secretis"; his official position then becomes (at least to judge by the title) identical with the position of the character who advises the prince in the treatise Machiavelli wrote after his fall from power.[24] Machiavelli—the "quondam segretario"—has surreptitiously inscribed his prior office into his discourse on new princes, though the nature of that office has now substantially changed as he turns to discuss the role of "a secretis" in a political body far different from the Florentine Republic. Indeed, the secretary (*a secretis*) described

20. Marzari, *La prattica e theorica del cancelliere,* 1r.

21. Millar, in *The Emperor in the Roman World,* mentions only the familiar terms *ab epistulis, a libellis,* indicating that the term *a secretis* is of very late Roman origin, if it is even Roman at all. On Pierre de Miraulmont, Bizer writes in *Les lettres romaines,* 215 n. 140: "Dans son *Traité de la Chancellerie* (1610), Pierre de Miraulmont relève aussi le cas des scribes romains, 'qui servoient les rois & Empereurs, *ideo domestici vocati, quod imperatori essent à secretis, eiusque arcana scriberent.*' "

22. Bacci, *Lexicon vocabulorum,* 696.

23. Marzi, *La cancelleria,* 297: "The register of letters, which are written under a master, by votes of the highest authorities, with N. Machiavelli, the principal secretary in the Second Chancery, dictating afterwards or giving the order."

24. Machiavelli mentions the term only once, in the title of his twenty-second chapter, but he treats it as though it has a global significance. He then switches to the term *ministri* [ministers]: "Non è di poca importanzia a uno principe la elezione de' ministri" (chap. 22, 293), which he uses from that point on. Being a secretary, as Machiavelli had been, turns out not to be just one administrative position among others; rather, it comprises and encapsulates in titular form all the other positions within chap. 22 and, by extension, chap. 23, which discusses "flatterers." Modern English editions often substitute the term "ministers" for "secretaries" in the title of chap. 22, but the term Machiavelli uses is secretaries, which fact was acknowledged in even the earliest editions that provided vernacular translations of the Latin.

in Machiavelli's treatise is now fundamentally an advisor to princes—what we might best term a "secretarial advisor."

As secretary to the Florentine Republic, Machiavelli came into contact with the secretarial advisors to various princes. On one memorable occasion he observed with awe how Cesare Borgia refused to inform even his secretaries of his plans, much less seek their advice:

> As I have many times written to Your Lordships, this Lord is very secretive [*è segretissimo*], and I do not believe that what he is going to do is known to anybody but himself. And his chief secretaries [*secretarii*] have many times asserted to me that he does not tell anything except when he orders it, and he orders it when necessity compels and when it is to be done, and not otherwise. Hence I beg that Your Lordships will excuse me and not impute it to my negligence if I do not satisfy Your Lordships with information, because most of the time I do not satisfy myself. (*Let.* 26 December 1502; 479)

Machiavelli's description of Cesare Borgia's forceful and successful action, for which he never sought counsel from his "secretarii," precedes the description of how everyone in Cesena witnessed Remirro de Orco's body set out in the town square, chopped in half the morning after Christmas, precisely because "it so pleased the Prince [Cesare Borgia], who shows that he can make and unmake men as he likes, according to their deserts" (*Let.* 26 December 1502; 479). From the prince's ability to be secretive we move to his ability to demonstrate his authoritative power over subjects. We move from mystified intention to exteriorized theatrical representation in a moment so memorable that it would be recorded once again in *The Prince* as a sign of Borgia's absolute control of his subjects through spectacle:[25]

> Knowing also that the severities of the past had earned [Remirro de Orco] a certain amount of hatred, to purge the minds of the people and to win them over completely, he determined to show that if cruelties had been inflicted they were not his doing but prompted by the harsh nature of his minister. This gave Cesare a pretext; then, one morning, Remirro's body was found cut in two pieces on the piazza at Cesena, with a block of wood [*pezzo di legno*] and a bloody knife beside it. The brutality of this spectacle [*spettaculo*] kept the people of the Romagna for a time appeased and stupefied. (chap. 7, 57–58; 267)

In the version of the spectacle described in *The Prince,* there is an object associated with the execution—a dagger—but no agent. There are traces

25. On Machiavelli's elaborate strategy in this example, see Rebhorn, *Foxes and Lions,* 117–24; and Kahn, "Virtù and the Example of Agathocles," 72–74.

of the prince's judgment—a body chopped in half—but no prince himself. The prince has disappeared to let the drama, the *spettaculo,* speak for itself and have full mimetic effect. Moreover, if we understand the "pezzo di legno" in this spectacle to form "part of the iconography before the judges' bench in deciding capital offenses,"[26] then the implied judicial setting, grounded in the traditional imagery of the Last Judgment,[27] forever cuts Remirro de Orco off from salvation, despite his being executed, we know from Machiavelli's secretarial letter, the very day after the anniversary of Christ's birth. The carefully staged spectacle described in *The Prince* models the justice of the absent prince upon the justice of an absent God, whose traces of power may everywhere be witnessed in specific instances in history but whose separation of the good from the bad will occur only at the end of time. The *virtù* of the prince, who here appears to be motivated by righteous wrath, thereby "saves" virtuous people by forestalling their own passions of revenge, their committing an act of *ferocità* that they desired to perform, through this dramatic spectacle of justice. The prince's authority has thus been mystified and sanctified, transforming the absent prince into an almost inscrutable god of justice.

As a strategy for ruling, secretiveness itself may therefore be admired in *The Prince* as one more aspect of Machiavellian *virtù,* the ability of an individual like Borgia who "knew so well how to dissimulate his own mind" [seppe tanto dissimulare l'animo suo, chap. 7, my translation; 267]. But secretiveness on the part of the prince with regard to his secretarial advisors, which Machiavelli admired in his letter to the Florentine chancery, is never explicitly praised in *The Prince.* The one prince who is secretive with his secretarial advisors in *The Prince* is the emperor Maximilian, and Machiavelli's description of him is entirely negative. The emperor repeatedly fails as a ruler not only because he refuses to act swiftly and decisively but also because he does not communicate his plans to his secretarial advisors or, for that matter, receive advice from them. "The emperor," Machiavelli writes,

> is a secretive man, he does not tell anyone of his plans, and he accepts no advice. But as soon as he puts his plans into effect, and they come to be known, they meet with opposition from those around him; and then he is only too easily diverted from his purpose. The result is that whatever he does one day is undone the next, what he wants or plans to do is never clear,

26. De Grazia, *Machiavelli in Hell,* 327.

27. Edgerton discusses the iconography of the Last Judgment in *Pictures and Punishment,* esp. 22–58.

> and no reliance can be placed on his deliberations. A prince must, therefore, always seek advice. But he must do so when he wants to, not when others want him to; indeed, he must discourage everyone from tendering advice about anything unless it is asked for.[28] (chap. 23, 126–27; 294)

The risks of being a secretive prince, Machiavelli suggests through "the modern example" [esemplo moderno, chap. 23, my translation; 294] of the emperor Maximilian, is that you will not seek counsel from your own secretarial advisors. Being secretive as a prince and not accepting advice may be logically separate activities, but they seem to go hand in hand, to be stylistically joined as one more way of explaining Maximilian's failures: "non comunica li sua disegni con persona, non ne piglia parere" (chap. 23, 294). If a prince is going to be secretive, he presumably needs to behave like Cesare Borgia, who acted swiftly, deliberately, and single-mindedly, never asking for advice and never wavering from his purpose once he had put it into effect. The example of Borgia in Machiavelli's correspondence would further seem to indicate that for a prince to hold onto a secret with his own *secretari* invariably provides him with potential control over his subjects. Where there is secrecy there is, in short, power, an implicit relation of master and slave. As Stefano Guazzo (1530–1593), a writer with experience as both an ambassador and a secretary, warns in the context of talking about secretaries in his *La civil conversazione* (1574), "according to the proverb, one transforms oneself into the servant of another when you tell a secret to one who doesn't know it."[29]

In *The Prince* itself Machiavelli does not admire secrecy between the prince and his secretarial advisors, however, because secretive princes are arguably ill-inclined to receive advice, and at the very moment in which he is writing, Machiavelli is engaged as a "quondam segretario" in precisely the work of giving advice. Yet if this is the case, it is by no means clear whether a former secretary like Machiavelli can ever even be trusted in the first place to keep the secrets of the prince. The infallible rule for

28. Machiavelli rehearses the judgment he made of Maximilian when he was a secretary and presented in his discourses on Germany, *Rapporto delle cose della Magna* (1508) and *Discorso sopre le cose della Magna e sopra l'Imperatore* (1509). See Machiavelli, *Opere,* 65 and 68.

29. Guazzo, *La civil conversazione,* 1.50. I would like to thank Marc Bizer for first pointing out to me the relevance of Guazzo's text. Francesco Guicciardini claimed in his *Ricordi,* which was written but never printed in either Machiavelli's or Guicciardini's lifetime: "For you become a slave to those who know your secrets—aside from all of the other evils that knowledge of them can bring about" (B 49). Translation from Guicciardini, *Maxims and Reflections.* As Quondam points out in his extensive commentary to *La civil conversazione,* 122 n. 434, the proverbial expression derives from the latin *vis esse tacitum, nulli dixeris;* on which, see Tosi, *Dizionario delle sentenze latine e greche,* 9.

detecting trustworthiness, according to Machiavelli, is to decide whether a person has his own interests in mind rather than the prince's: "But as for how a prince can assess his minister, here is an infallible guide [*non falla mai*]: when you see a minister thinking more of himself than of you, and seeking his own profit in everything he does, such a one will never be a good minister, you will never be able to trust him. This is because a man entrusted with the task of government must never think of himself but of the prince, and must never concern himself with anything except the prince's affairs [*non debbe pensare mai a sé, ma al principe, e non li ricordare mai cosa che non appartenga a lui*]" (chap. 22, 125; 293).[30] But how can any person ever think more of the prince than himself given that human nature demands, in a manner entirely consistent with Machiavelli's overall view of humankind, that "de' consiglieri, ciascuno penserà alla proprietà sua" [each counselor will consult his own interests, chap. 23, 127, my translation; 294].[31] In *The Prince* we are made so keenly aware that men of *virtù* know exactly how and when to mask their own self-interests for the purposes of self-advancement and self-preservation that it is difficult to believe that this advice-giving "quondam segretario" is doing anything other than inviting trust though mechanisms of deception, appearing to have the prince's interests in mind while secretly concealing his own all along. Nor is it a solution to assume that a person bent on giving free advice may engage the trust of a prince by foregrounding the ways in which both he and the prince are not to be trusted, as if mutual mistrust could ever be the proper foundation for creating a stable bond that will never fail: "non falla mai." Princes and secretarial advisors may recognize each other as confidence men, but that is no reason for them to have confidence in one another.[32] Their knowledge only provides them with one more reason to recognize their mutual aim to acquire, and at best share, power.

Throughout *The Prince,* we are in the presence of a "quondam segretario" who reveals not his status as a typical subordinate but his ability to stand on an equal footing with the prince in a fruitful, horizontal dialogue of exchange. Rather than waiting to be asked for advice, Machiavelli actively volunteers it, thus setting him apart from the secretarial advisors within *The Prince,* who are expected to remain silent until addressed by their master. Far from being a mid-level functionary who responds to

30. Machiavelli is here repeating advice as old as the *Secretum secretorum*. See Gilbert, *Machiavelli's "Prince" and Its Forerunners,* 179–80.

31. Ascoli ("Machiavelli's Gift of Counsel," 246–48) argues this point in depth.

32. See on this Rebhorn, *Foxes and Lions,* 188–227.

the prince only when questioned, and then in a predetermined chancery style, this "quondam segretario," to borrow Nancy Struever's phrase, is a "discursive ruffian," revealing at every turn a rigorous, personal independence of mind.[33] Everything about *The Prince* discloses a resolutely antibureaucratic writer shunning familiar stylistic and argumentative formulas. He is given not to executing prescribed programs but to creating a strand of richly descriptive and often conflicting possibilities.[34] Machiavelli stands above the very group of typical, subordinate, secretarial advisors he claims the prince must choose. He establishes the rules, he enlightens the prince. *The Prince,* after all, presents itself not as one piece of advice literature among many but as a political program that the prudent prince (who has not even requested the treatise) should follow: disregard it and you reign at your own peril. In this respect, as Machiavelli draws on his secretarial past as *a secretis* within the chancery, evoking it in both the prologue and the title to chapter 22, he simultaneously creates an image of himself as a secretarial advisor within *The Prince* that is so atypical as to be barely recognizable in conventional terms. Rhetorically speaking, the term "secretary" may be applied to the author of *The Prince* only as catachresis—an abuse of language. There is a family resemblance between the author of *The Prince* as a "quondam segretario" and the secretarial advisory duties described in his text. Yet when viewed within the category of *a secretis,* the category he once occupied as secretary to the Florentine Republic and now recreates for the advisors to the prince, Machiavelli remains tenaciously atypical.

Machiavelli was among the first in the Italian Renaissance to address, however obliquely, the work of the secretary in treatise form, but he obviously devotes his treatise instead to a full and novel discussion of the role of the prince, and in particular, the new prince. To identify the role of the new humanist secretary of the Renaissance, however, and to discover infallible mechanisms for how a prince should detect faithfulness in *secretari,* as well as how the typical secretary may prove his trustworthiness to a prince, we must turn instead to such authors as Francesco Sansovino (1521–1586). An enormously prolific writer, Sansovino spent most of his life in Venice, where he early on received a humanist education typical of the socially elevated in Venice; he composed, edited, and translated some eighty works; he made a living from his books (he briefly pursued

33. Struever, *Theory as Practice,* 175.

34. Struever, "Machiavelli: Narrative as Argument," in *Theory as Practice,* 147–81; see also Hampton, *Writing from History,* 62–80, for a discussion of the crisis of exemplarity in Machiavelli.

the possibility of careers in both law and the papal court, but they did not appeal to him); and he played an important role in the popularizing of history in late Renaissance Italy.[35] In 1564, he published the first of what would eventually become a flourishing genre of Italian treatises codifying the profession of the secretary. In his *Il segretario,* which went through numerous editions and revisions, Sansovino addresses the growing professional class of *secretari* who formed one of the largest bodies of humanists in Renaissance Italy. In writing on this topic, Sansovino is also highly conscious of the spectacular success and political importance of such remarkable secretarial figures as Pietro Bembo, not to mention those who have risen through the ranks to become popes.[36] The office of the secretary is a ladder to success for humanists, and Sansovino means to offer concrete, realizable techniques for guaranteeing achievement, both within and through the secretarial profession. His treatise is therefore bent on giving prescriptive rules rather than a broad, conflicting range of examples. He aims to write a practical manual, from which a professional secretary can learn everything from what kinds of punctuation exist to how to use them; how to address in various ways everyone from a pope to a soldier; how to seal a letter; what books to consult; what "hand" to imitate. And amid this technical information, Sansovino provides the customary preliminary advice—already found, though arguably never practiced, in *The Prince*—that the secretary should think always more of his "signore che il suo proprio e particolar bene" [his master rather than his own particular welfare, 172].

But unlike Machiavelli, Sansovino—along with so many others writing treatises about the secretary in the late sixteenth and early seventeenth centuries—identifies the secretary not merely by his ability to be secretive but—and this is all-important for Salvatore Nigro—by his ability to be silent outside of counsel. "The secretary is named from the secrecy that one presupposes must be in him," Sansovino declares, "because acting as a principal member of the body of the prince's counsel, he must have eyes and mind, but not a tongue outside of counsel" (152). The secretary, rewarded for that faith one can also call "faithful silence," knows how to "hold his tongue," "whence his taciturnity will be equal to the greatness of his task" (162–63). Similarly, Guazzo will insist that "if we are expected

35. On Sansovino, see the synthetic study by Grendler, "Francesco Sansovino and Italian Popular History 1560–1600." For a more extended treatment, see Bonora, *Ricerche su Francesco Sansovino,* 17–19, for a discussion of his early education.

36. Sansovino, *L'avvocato e il segretario,* 153–54. This is a commonplace assumption in Italian secretarial treatises, voiced, for example, in Zucchi, *L'idea del segretario,* 38.

to keep silent about the secret of a friend, all the more so are we expected as secretaries to be silent about the secret of our master, who pays us so that we keep silent."[37] The secretary's tongue, according to Nati, must therefore not only be imprisoned behind bars of teeth but bound,

> to keep it under control and moderate and not used very often. He should not use it, letting it free and completely unleashed, in which case it would offend others' ears and upset the stomachs of many. . . . And like that vase that, being full of cracks, leaks and therefore should not be held in any consideration and has no value whatsoever, so, in my opinion, are those who do not retain anything but at the first opportunity spill the beans. The secretary should further bear in mind that he must always be silent, and never reveal a thing, because in doing so he would become himself a problem and of little value. . . . He must always be silent. (a8r–b1r)

The author and tragedian Gabriele Zinano (ca. 1557–ca. 1637), who worked as a secretary for noble families in Naples, asserts in his *Segretario* (1625) that "to be silent itself is greater than to speak, whence the Greeks said that humans speak, whereas the gods were masters of being silent" [onde i Greci dissero, che del parlare gli huomini, e del tacere eran maestri gli Dei].[38]

Panfilo Persico (d. 1625), who had a long and successful career as a secretary principally in Rome, observes in his *Del segretario* (1620) that Machiavelli, of all people, was an example of a "buon segretario" [good secretary] if not, Persico hastens to explain, a "huomo buono" [good man].[39] Moreover, as Persico remarks, the author of *The Prince* is a modern master of Tacitean diplomacy. What enables Machiavelli to penetrate hidden Tacitean mysteries of state is, above all, "acume,"

> the acumen one calls the eye of prudence, because it sees from afar the principles and beginnings of things, it penetrates right down to the marrow, the reasons, motives, counsels, but in understanding these things the mind tends often toward evil, either because such is the tendency of all people by nature, or because of the imperfection in all things human. In this manner all kinds of bad policies occur, in such a way that all things are brought to the utility of the prince, to the interest of ruling, without regard to the public

37. Guazzo, *La civil conversazione,* 1.50. Relevant to these injunctions that the secretary be silent are the commonplaces of proverbial expressions of "il silenzio e la loquacità" listed in Tosi, *Dizionario delle sentenze latine e greche,* 9–17. See also below, chapter 7, note 10.

38. Zinano, *Il segretario,* 7.

39. Persico, *Del segretario,* 19.

> good, to justice, to religion. And of all the ancient writers the most aware of this was Cornelius Tacitus; of the moderns it is Machiavelli.[40]

Machiavelli faithfully served his superiors, however, and in this respect, both in his obedience and in his ability to execute assigned tasks, Persico considers Machiavelli exemplary as a secretary: "Let us take as an example Niccolò Machiavelli, who at different times was secretary."[41] Yet as much as Persico seeks to define Machiavelli as an obedient servant in relation to his superiors, and thus to salvage him as a good secretary if not a good man, it is difficult to see how the Machiavelli of *The Prince* could ever be considered a "buon segretario." A good secretary, after all, is the obedient vessel—a "most holy and safe vessel" (Sansovino, 162)—for the prince's thoughts. He is a minister theologically in relation to the prince as the highest angels are to God (151), much as the secretary will be for writers such as such as Nati (a7r) and the Neapolitan Giulio Cesare Capaccio (1552–1634).[42] This being the case, Machiavelli appears in retrospect to be the worst of all possible secretaries, as he aspires to establish himself on an equal footing with his master in a reciprocal dialogue of exchange.

Far more importantly, Machiavelli cannot be trusted as a secretary not because he over-aspires, dissimulates, or belongs to the opposing political party, but because at bottom he talks too much about things better kept—to borrow from David Miller's epigraph above—as "open secrets." It is scandalous of Machiavelli ever to think that as a trained "keeper of secrets" he might now effectively uncover what covers secrecy. A "buon segretario" does not expose, as Machiavelli claims he does, what "è suta insegnata a' principi *copertamente* dagli antichi scrittori" [has been taught to princes *covertly* by ancient writers, chap. 18, my emphasis and translation; 283], even if the advice delivered by Machiavelli in *The Prince* may be known information, *arcana imperii,*[43] information available to anyone who goes about observing with acumen the daily workings of such princes as Cesare Borgia. What is scandalous, Reginald Pole's assumptions to the contrary, is not so much *what* Machiavelli tells us as *that* he is telling us this information at all, that he is trying to let the cat out of the bag. Machiavelli is disclosing not so much secret knowledge

40. Ibid., 130.

41. Ibid., 19.

42. Capaccio, *Il secretario,* 1r–2r. First printed in 1589.

43. On *The Prince* treated as containing sacred mysteries of the state, *arcana imperii,* which were as important to advisors as to princes, see Donaldson, *Machiavelli and Mystery of State.*

as the knowledge of the knowledge of secrecy, the "field of operations" that makes secrecy possible and necessary at a given time. Needless to say, this is not what secretaries, as keepers of secrets, are supposed to do. Secretaries are supposed to keep their mouths shut and thereby conceal "high mysteries" of state.[44] By so doing, secretaries dutifully proved their worth to their masters and, with their tongues safely and tightly bound, found a secure place in a vulnerable world.

Constructing a Profession: The Silent Resistance of the Renaissance Secretary

"In a world," David Miller writes,

> where the explicit exposure of the subject would manifest how thoroughly he has been inscribed within a socially given totality, secrecy would be the spiritual exercise by which the subject is allowed to conceive of himself as a resistance: a friction in the smooth functioning of the social order, a margin to which its far-reaching discourse does not reach. Secrecy would thus be the subjective practice in which the oppositions of private/public, inside/outside, subject/object are established, and the sanctity of their first term kept inviolate. And the phenomenon of the "open secret" does not, as one might think, bring about the collapse of these binarisms and their ideological effects, but rather attests to their fantasmatic recovery. In a mechanism reminiscent of Freudian disavowal, we know perfectly well that the secret is known, but nonetheless we must persist, however ineptly, in guarding it. The paradox of the open secret registers the subject's accommodation to a totalizing system that has obliterated the difference he would make—the difference he does make, in the imaginary denial of this system "even so."[45]

Likewise, secrecy had a double role to play in the many treatises defining the secretarial profession in late sixteenth- and early seventeenth-century Italy. Sometimes represented with the prince in a horizontal dialogue of exchange, the secretary was more often envisioned in these treatises as the instrument of the prince's mind, his absolute subject. Italian treatises of the sixteenth and seventeenth centuries often articulate this double vision of the secretary by favorably comparing his profession, whose principal duties were traditionally those of keeping secrets and writing letters, with that of other administrators, above all counselors. In the process, some

44. Nati, *Trattato del segretario,* a7r.
45. Miller, *The Novel and the Police,* 207.

authors claimed that the duties of the secretary overlapped with those of the counselor. The humanist author, poet, and playwright Angelo Ingegneri (ca. 1550–1613), a friend of Tasso and a secretary for many years to Cardinal Cinzio Aldobrandini in Rome, remarks "that he is a man of counsel . . . even if the office of the counselor is distinct from that of the secretary; nevertheless sometimes it occurs that whoever does one does the other also."[46] Bonifatio Vannozzi (d. 1621), secretary for a total of more than twenty years to, among others, the Medici in Florence and Cardinal Cinzio Aldobrandini in Rome, went so far as to claim that "a secretary who does not arrive at becoming a counselor to a prince does not arrive at the highest level, and the true preeminence, of the secretary."[47] Similarly, Vincenzo Gramigna (ca. 1580–1627), author of various treatises, orations, dialogues, and poetry, and secretary in Rome to cardinals Scipione Borghese, Scipione Cobelluzzi, and Tiberio Muti, writes "that the secretary is foremost called upon by the prince of good sense into counsel [and that] he holds, even more than ten counselors combined, the keys to the heart, so to speak, of the prince himself."[48] As Salvatore Nigro has argued, however, by the end of the cinquecento, and certainly toward the beginning of the seicento, the secretary had become emblematic of the perfect subordinate and submissive functionary, not an advisor but a copyist, not a thinker and inventor but a mere executor of fine form, a "pigmy," as Capaccio would have it, working and running amid "giants."[49] For Zinano, who neatly separates the office of the counselor from that of the secretary in two distinct books, the last thing the secretary was expected to do was to speak his mind to offer his master advice:

> Keep the will of the master as a fixed rule, according to which you should measure all his sayings and deeds. Nor must you concern yourself whether it is right or wrong, but only labor to know and observe his will, and to bring into effect the things demanded of you, not according to what seems to the secretary appropriately done, but according to what the master has ordered him to do. So that if he should want to propose his own advice above and

46. Ingegneri, *Del buon segretario libri tre,* 20–21. Tasso dedicates a poem to Ingegneri at the outset of *Del buon segretario.*

47. Vannozzi, *Della suppellettile,* 3.119. For information about Vannozzi, I rely on Basso, *Le genre épistolaire,* 399.

48. Gramigna, *Il segretario dialogo,* 64. On Gramigna, see Salvatore, *Antichi e moderni in Italia nel Seicento,* i–xii; Basso, *Le genre épistolaire,* 493; Iucci, "La trattatistica sul segretario," 93 n. 42.

49. Capaccio, *Il secretario,* not paginated in address to reader: "apresso ai Giganti corrano i Pigmei."

> beyond the orders given him, the obedience that he owes his master—and that is the proper virtue of the servant—will be destroyed. . . . Therefore let the secretary be obedient, because this is his role just as the master's is to command.[50]

Even while they may admire the protean capacity of the secretary trained in the *studia humanitatis* to do many things, the authors of these treatises by and large seek to restrict the secretary's field of operations. They seek to narrow down, to borrow Andrew Abbott's terminology, the secretary's "jurisdictional claim" over certain types of professional work.[51] "He can do what he knows and what he wants," Gramigna warns, "because even if he is Proteus, I will bind him so tightly, that after he has changed into all the shapes that he can, he will in the end be forced to take on his original shape and form, and still, not wishing to, be forced to satisfy our common desire."[52] On the one hand, Gramigna argues that the secretary should possess prudence and insight into the affairs of man. As Sigismondo Sigismondi succinctly put it in his *Prattica cortigiana morale, et economica* (1604), a work that is not specifically about secretaries but nevertheless contributes to the general discourse about them, a secretary must be a "perfect humanist" [perfetto humanista], a man "learned in the sciences of philosophy, and trained in other doctrines."[53] On the other hand, Gramigna typically depicts not so much the "Gran segretario" he admires as the "Segretario idiota" he deplores, a learned secretary ("segretario dotto") who, for all his training in the *studia humanitatis,* paradoxically needs only a superficial knowledge of philosophy.[54] This is because what mattered most for Gramigna was not the fullness of the secretary's urbane wit and his deep prolonged meditations on history and humanity (precisely what Machiavelli prided himself on as a humanist secretary and in his prologue to *The Prince*!), but the ability of the humanist secretary to cancel his own identity in order to effect the prince's wishes at any time and at any place. For this reason Gramigna describes the perfect secretary as an "octopus" [polpo] who spontaneously changes

50. Zinano, *Il segretario,* 9.

51. Abbott, *The System of Professions.*

52. As in Gramigna, *Il segretario dialogo,* 12. See as well in general the discussion of Quondam, "Varianti di Proteo."

53. Sigismondi, *Prattica cortigiana morale, et economica,* 43, as cited in Fragnito, "Buone maniere e professionalità," 93, but see also 91–97. On secretaries in these treatises as the heirs of "la culture humaniste" of the early cinquecento, even as the value of that humanist culture experiences a crisis, see Fiorato, "Grandeur et servitude," 143, 149, 151–53.

54. Gramigna, *Il segretario dialogo,* 27 and 29, and on his knowledge of philosophy 56.

color in order to mask his true identity and blend into, as well as mirror, his patron's will:

> *Cont. Alf.* And what must the secretary therefore do?
>
> *Quer.* He must conform to the will of the master, and to satisfy his every whim, he must not think at all about going against his aim.
>
> *Con. Alf.* In such a way that the person, who with praise wants to exercise this art, should act as the octopus, which is, namely, to take on the color of the thing to which one is near. So the secretary should liken himself in all things to the master whom he serves.[55]

The humanist secretary, maneuvering like a *polpo* in a dangerous environment within which "the favor of the powerful is a fragile thing,"[56] was rewarded not for his speech and thoughts, his rhetorical expertise and insight into human affairs, but for his silence as a mark of absolute personal effacement. To this effect, the secretary, however broad his training in the *studia humanitatis* and however "perfetto" a humanist he might be, could be imaged as just a puppet, a mere "man of wood" [huomo di legno],[57] whose material function was to contain the prince's innermost thoughts and to act mechanically according to his master's will. For that matter, the secretary might even be characterized as a stomach, where all the villainous or virtuous secrets of the prince could be safely stored from public view yet putrefied as in a garbage bin, thereby compromising the secretary's own breath: "A secretary," Vannozzi writes, "said that his breath stank because the many secrets held in his stomach had putrefied" [Disse un Segretario, a cui puzzava il fiato, ciò essergli avvenuto, perche *multa secreta computruerant in pectore suo*].[58] Stefano Guazzo was no warmer in his estimation.[59]

By way of compensation, the secretary, as the keeper of secrets, had access to the inner recesses of the prince's cabinet: "the Lord's ministers all govern the bark, but the secretary penetrates into the marrow."[60] According to the humanist courtier and writer Giambattista Guarini (1538–

55. Ibid., 142.

56. Guarini, *Il segretario dialogo,* 59.

57. Gramigna, *Il segretario dialogo,* 29.

58. Vannozzi, *Della suppellettile,* 400.

59. Guazzo, *La civil conversazione,* 1.50. As Amedeo Quondam points out in his commentary to Guazzo, *La civil conversazione,* 2.122, the source for this may have been Euripides, as transmitted through Erasmus and then adapted to the secretary's peculiar function as the person who has to stomach, as it were, his master's secrets. Erasmus, *Apophthegmatum,* 688: "Solent autem res in occulto congestae computrescere."

60. Guarini, *Il segretario dialogo,* from preface letter to Cardinal Ascanio Colonna.

1612), who served for a time as secretary to Alfonso II d'Este and wrote his *Il segretario dialogo* at the end of the sixteenth century, the secretary often passes his time in the prince's locked archives, which he can "enter at his own ease, and [where he can] leisurely turn over papers and writings, making himself master of it all. . . . That is his office, that his workshop, that, in short, to speak in an old-fashioned way, his 'secretary' " [Quella è la sua bottega, quell'è il suo fontaco, quell'è in somma per parlar all'antica il suo Segretario].[61] The secretary, for Ingegneri, should even be provided with a room of his own in the palace, "separated but luminous and airy, where he would never have to eat or sleep, and where he could avoid having to let certain inappropriate people enter."[62] The Neapolitan poet, historian, literary scholar, and editor Tomaso Costo (ca. 1560–ca. 1613), who worked for many years as secretary to various noble families and participated marginally in the literary polemic over the *Liberata,* counseled his nephew on how to become a perfect secretary in his *Discorso* (1602), insisting in one instance that his nephew must make every effort to have "a room all by yourself" [camera da te solo],[63] where he might compose his letters and exercise his profession in private. The secretary, the quintessential "insider," consequently had a secure place within the prince's cabinet because he knew how to be silent and, like the "sileni" that conceal their jewels within,[64] he knew how to hold the prince's valuable secrets far from the public gaze.

Secrecy thus became one of the privileged mechanisms by which the humanist secretary in the late Renaissance proved his worth to his master. Secrecy secured the secretary's profession in a vulnerable world and effectively allowed him to accommodate himself to a totalizing system that had thoroughly obliterated any potential he might ever have to make a difference. Nevertheless, secrecy also became the mechanism by which a secretary sought self-expression "even so." Secrecy could also constitute a personal mark of resistance to the very system that absorbed and contained him. Torquato Accetto (b. ca. 1600), a poet and professional secretary, is a case in point. Best known for his slim treatise titled *Della dissimulazione onesta* (1641), Accetto is concerned about not only the need to dissimulate, but also, in Salvatore Nigro's brilliant argument, the need

61. Ibid., 60.

62. Ingegneri, *Del buon segretario libri tre,* 106.

63. Costo, *Discorso pratico fatto,* 381. On Costo, see V. Lettere, "Costo, Tomaso."

64. See Nigro, "Lezione sull'ombra," v, for the image of the perfect functionary as a silenus figure.

to dissimulate dissimulation, much as a secretary needs to know how to hide the knowledge of the knowledge of secrecy in order to keep the very "game of secrecy" operating smoothly. For this reason, Accetto calls attention to his own silence in his text as a calculated strategy of resistance. He writes:

> A year ago this treatise was three times longer than what you see now, and that is known by many; and if I had wanted to delay even more in bringing it out to be published, the book itself would have been reduced to nothing on account of all the continual wounds [*ferite*] that destroy more than emend it. These scars [*cicatrici*] will still be recognized by all readers of good judgment; and so you must excuse me in bringing this book out in this condition, almost bloodless [*esangue*], since writing about dissimulation has demanded that I dissimulate; for this reason it is a far shorter book than the one I had initially written.[65]

The treatise we read has been mutilated by its own author and, as Nigro observes, it discreetly bares its wounds. But about what lies behind those wounds, what has been not playfully but savagely cut from the text, Accetto, trained "keeper of secrets," is cunningly silent. Unlike Machiavelli, Accetto adamantly refuses to talk. He is not, to adapt Nancy Struever's phrase, a discursive ruffian but a resiliently elliptical one, having now become—in Guazzo's view of things—a "secretary to himself."[66] The secretary may therefore have been for Sansovino and other writers the obedient angel in relation to the divine prince as a god. But when it came to Accetto's own form of self-expression as a secretary, his text responds through ellipsis, denial, silence, taunting disobedience, and self-sacrifice.

Accetto's statement, rendered with characteristic brazen-faced guile toward the end of the treatise, is thus particularly helpful in pinpointing his innovative strategy of concealment as a form of personal resistance:

> One readily admires in the greatness of men of high state, the way they reside in palaces—there in their secret rooms [*camere segrete*], fenced in by iron and by men guarding their own persons and interests. Yet it is clear that, without much expense at all, every man, though exposed to the gaze of all [*ancorch'esposto alla vista di tutti*], can still hide his own affairs in the vast and simultaneously secret house of his own heart [*nella vasta e insieme segreta casa del suo cuore*]. (79–80)

65. Accetto, *Della dissimulazione onesta,* 31–32, hereafter cited by page number. My argument closely follows the excellent discussion of Nigro, *"Scriptor necans,"* 22–26, to which I am indebted.

66. Guazzo, *La civil conversazione,* 1.50.

Fearlessly pitting his own "segreta casa" against the "camere segrete" of the court, Accetto goads his readers into believing that his "affari," securely hidden away in the deep, vast space of his heart, contain thoughts that we, along with the prince, may never glimpse. But then again, these secrets, like perhaps all such secrets according to David Miller, are still somehow always already known. What matters most in *Della dissimulazione onesta* is not so much *what* Torquato Accetto says as, in a radical reversal of the discursive strategy of *The Prince, that* he tells us he will not speak his mind at all. The scandal in *Della dissimulazione onesta,* in short, is not that the author speaks too much, as Machiavelli did as a humanist and former secretary aggressively offering advice, but that he openly and steadfastly refuses to talk. Transforming his text into a kind of personal secretary, Accetto takes all the strategies of the vulnerable secretarial office—self-effacement, secrecy, and silence—and literally "underwrites" himself. He cancels his own text in order to bring himself publicly into existence as an inaccessible, private being. Rather than letting his text function as a "treasury"[67] for another, whose valuable secrets he conserves, Accetto inversely makes *Della dissimulazione onesta* function as a secretarial treasury for him alone. And by doing so Accetto acquires—not by concealing but by openly revealing that he has secrets—a voice and authority all his own.

67. Nati, *Trattato del segretario,* a7v.

Seven

THE SECRETARIAL PROFESSION AMONG OTHERS

Tasso's Enabling Analogies

> In drawing on Marcus Tullius, and of the usefulness that the modern secretary can draw from him, Tasso grossly exaggerates and openly discloses lies; but that shouldn't come much as a surprise, since—without offending Torquato—we can say that he was never a secretary. And so in speaking of the office, as he had been asked to do by others, he preferred to touch on matters of speculative rather than practical concern, and so he embraced generalities, which is a less cumbersome task, and left aside the particulars, which is indeed the art and profession [*professione*] of persons who have had long experience.
>
> —BONIFACIO VANNOZZI

In his *Gerusalemme liberata,* Tasso describes various arts, often providing contrasting, representative figures from each one. This is certainly the case with regard to the art of diplomacy exercised by ambassadors, who have, Tasso informs us in his *Il messaggiero* (1580–83), a "most noble profession."[1] In book 2, for example, Alete, who has come to the Christian camp to persuade Goffredo not to wage war, embodies everything negative about the ambassador. Alete, whose name means "not hiding," "not simulating," ironically disguises the fact that he is an arch-dissembler, a manipulator who uses his conspicuous eloquence not to reveal the truth and motivate people to positive action but to lie and keep the Christians

1. The epigraph is drawn from a letter from Bonifacio Vannozzi to Bartolomeo Sozzifanti, as transcribed in Solerti, *Vita di Torquato Tasso,* 2.426, my translation. Tasso, *Il messaggiero,* in *Prose,* 60, my translation; hereafter cited by page number in my text.

KING ALFRED'S COLLEGE

from achieving their goal (2.57–58).[2] Alete "adorns" [adorne, 2.58] his bitter message of inevitable failure on the part of the crusaders in order to keep them from ever moving forward. The poet, by contrast, adorns the bitter message of war and suffering contained in his poem ("adorno . . . le carte," 1.2) in order to push his epic tale forward so that everyone—Goffredo, Alfonso, and the multitude of readers in a fragmented society of rival nations and beliefs within Christendom—will ultimately be persuaded to move toward a common goal: the liberation of Jerusalem, unity, and acquiescence to the church as the supreme authority. In this respect, Alete emerges as a potential rival to the author of the poem. If Goffredo listened seriously to Alete, took into consideration the ambassador's words of prudence, and accepted his offer of peace, there would be no poem: the crusaders would be left wandering in errant, purposeless behavior, and the readers, who are meant to imitate the example of the crusaders in their own time, would be stalled in the errancy of balanced political and religious rivalries rather than propelled into resolved, meaningful political and social action. But Goffredo, who is equally capable of adorning words (1.19), resists: "Whether or not he offends the law of nations and ancient custom, he gives it neither a thought nor care" [la ragion de le genti e l'uso antico / s'offenda o no, né 'l pensa egli, né 'l cura, 2.95]. To be effective, diplomacy requires not only the capacity to speak but the ability to hear and be moved. Goffredo hears Alete but refuses to be swayed by his false, adorning words. Goffredo will have no truck with Alete's diplomacy, for he operates outside of conventional diplomatic procedures and practices, having substituted inspired zeal (1.8, as elsewhere) for the practical prudence Alete appeals to. Indeed, Goffredo is not prudent at all, and he need not be, since his actions are guaranteed by a celestial messenger ("messaggier celeste," 1.14), Gabriel, the otherworldly "nunzio" (1.12) who is to be contrasted with Alete, the worldly pagan one.

Just as Tasso offers positive and negative examples of ambassadors engaged in the art of diplomacy, so too he provides examples of people engaged in other arts, such as, at the very outset, the art of ruling. Goffredo, for instance, represents the divinely appointed ruler, whose election takes place in a manner that both anticipates and validates the centralized authority of the late Renaissance, post-Tridentine absolutist state (1.12, 1.16). By contrast, Aladino, the pagan prince, operates as the evil Machiavellian new prince, whose singular aim at the beginning of the epic is to preserve the recently acquired city of Jerusalem through

2. Tasso, *Gerusalemme liberata,* with translations, slightly modified, from *Jerusalem Delivered.*

terror—though Aladino does recognize, as the innovative Machiavellian new prince should, that terror can backfire and eventually lead the suppressed populace to rise up and revolt. Tasso also provides extended examples of good and bad advisors exercising the art of giving counsel. Ismeno, the nefarious pagan advisor to Aladino, meddles in affairs, delays the inevitable, and remains blind to the underlying significance of such events as the disappearance of the effigy of the Virgin Mary. Pietro, the righteous Christian hermit who advises Goffredo, has access to divine dispensation and foresees not just the liberation of Jerusalem but the return of Rinaldo. Along with this, Tasso describes the art of the secretary, an art of extraordinary importance to humanists in the Italian Renaissance, though this time he does not provide a balance of positive and negative examples and, oddly enough, describes it only briefly. Toward the beginning of the seventeenth canto of the *Gerusalemme liberata,* Tasso through circumlocution identifies the secretary as one of the most important pagan leaders. The secretary, he writes, stands right beside the king of Egypt, who is overlooking his pagan troops now amassed in preparation for the war with the Christians and now parading before him:

> Stannogli, a destra l'un, l'altro a sinistra,
> due satrapi, i maggiori: alza il più degno
> la nuda spada, del rigor ministra,
> l'altro il sigillo ha del suo officio in segno.
> Custode un de' secreti, al re ministra
> opra civil ne' grandi affar del regno,
> ma prence de gli esserciti e con piena
> possanza è l'altro ordinator di pena.
>
> (17.12)

[Two satraps stand beside him, his greatest men, the one on his right the other on his left; the noblest holds aloft the naked sword, instrument of his rigor; the other in token of his office keeps the seal. Custodian of secrets is the one, who wields for the king the civil power in grand affairs of state; but prince of the armies is the other, and with full power the dispenser of punishments.]

Late in the seventeenth century, Michele Benvenga took notice of Tasso's verses as he considered in his *Proteo segretario* (1689) the manifold roles the secretary assumes in society: "The first crowns of Europe call each of [the secretaries] in their own states either great chancellor of the kingdom or first minister. Such are they in effect; nor should it be construed otherwise, even if Tasso placed the secretary after the leader of the pagan troops, there where he sings."[3] Tasso's verses on the secretary go unnoticed for the most part in modern critical editions, and there is a similar silence in earlier commentaries. Those early commentators focus instead on the rival profession of the ambassador, which has a far more prominent role in Tasso's poem, beginning with Alete in canto 2 and extending to the pagan and Christian messengers traveling about the land, along with the angelic messengers flying through the air. In his commentary on Tasso's *Gerusalemme conquistata,* for example, Francesco Birago on two different occasions departs significantly from the text at hand to discuss the behavior of the many *messaggieri* in the poem in the context of ambassadorial immunity and accepted diplomatic practices.[4] Alessandro Manzoni, of course, ridiculed such commentaries in his highly ironic, historicized rereading of the late sixteenth- and early seventeenth-century obsession with defining rules and formal appearances.[5] Yet Tasso made these readings possible, both by incorporating different professions into his poem and by writing about and codifying some of them in treatise form. One profession Tasso never officially practiced yet felt obliged to write about in treatise form was in fact that of secretary, and it is his treatise on the secretary that I will principally discuss in this final chapter. For Tasso's treatise not only addresses in a historically determined manner the systemic nature of professional identity as it was conceived by humanists in Renaissance Italy; it illuminates in a particularly concise way the tension between past and present inherent in virtually every serious humanist engagement with professions discussed in this book. In the final pages of this chapter I then briefly address how Tasso identifies with yet coopts the authority of the humanist secretary as he occupies the profession of the poet within the court.

In his little treatise titled *Del secretario,* written in Mantua and dated January 7, 1587, Tasso says he knows what the obligations of friendship compel

3. Benvenga, *Proteo segretario,* in Nigro, *Il segretario di lettere,* 106–7, my translation.

4. Birago, *Dichiarationi et avertimenti,* 82, 154–56. As Rhu (*Genesis of Tasso's Narrative Theory,* 21 and 165 n. 16) points out, the classical models for Alete can be located in Homer, Livy, and Silius Italicus, though Virgil's Drances from book 11 of the *Aeneid* probably influenced Tasso as well. Modern scholars also focus on the angelic *messaggieri,* on which see, for example, Greene, *Descent from Heaven,* 183–202.

5. See, for example, Manzoni, *I promessi sposi,* 90 and Russo's note.

him to do.[6] He must please his friend by writing a treatise on the subject of secretarial work. But Tasso is initially confused as to how he must go about fulfilling the request. He is plagued by doubt. Is he to write a book about the "rules for writing letters," or is he to write a book that fashions the "perfect secretary"? To do both, he insists, would be "very difficult" (257). The verb "congiongere," which Tasso employs as he describes how difficult his task would be, is an important one. For Tasso's lifelong project was to bring together disparate elements, whether it be romance and epic, chivalric behavior and Christian piety, or early humanist praise for multiplicity and individualism and the late sixteenth-century emphasis on unity and centralized authority.[7] Yet Tasso chooses neither of the options he initially sets up for himself (he neither details how to write letters nor paints the portrait of the perfect secretary), and he certainly refuses to do both at the same time.

When Tasso claims that the task before him is difficult, he has in mind the work of Cicero, who, as he points out, "wrote in separate books about the idea of the perfect orator," which is to say his *Orator,* "and the rhetorical teachings" required to be one, which is to say his *De oratore* (257). At the very beginning of Tasso's *Del secretario,* we are thus explicitly drawn into making a comparison between what the author has been asked to do (provide rules of letter-writing or form a perfect secretary) and what Cicero accomplished in two distinctly different books.[8] In the *Orator,* Cicero raises our minds beyond the things written about on the page, elevating us into an almost ineffable place of thought. According to Tasso, Cicero creates an "I don't know what" [non so che, 257] that is far more exalted and exquisite [più alto; più esquisito, 257] than anything we can ever imagine. Cicero's style seems to lift itself up, so that the words no longer appear even adequate to express the concept toward which they point. Cicero's words remain pure signifiers in the *Orator,* forever striving to grasp the transcendent Idea that escapes them and their own materiality. By contrast, in *De oratore,* Cicero's style lowers itself ("s'abbassa," 257). It immerses itself in gritty details, "minute things and particulars" (257), a stylistic shift that for Tasso recalls a realist painter's

6. Tasso, *Del secretario,* in *Le prose diverse,* 260, cited by page number in my text hereafter. All translations are my own.

7. See in particular Zatti, *L'uniforme cristiano e il multiforme pagano.*

8. Tasso's turn to Cicero as a model for letter-writing and secretarial work is by no means unusual. It was the tendency to conflate oratory and letter-writing in both the Renaissance and the Middle Ages. Witt ("Medieval *Ars Dictaminis,*" 33) points out that Petrarch innovatively sought to separate oratorical and letter-writing traditions.

attention—overbearing in some contexts—to such mundane, superficial matter as "nails" and "hair" (257). The differences here traced between the *Orator* and *De oratore* thus correspond in Tasso's mind to the differences between the assumed incompatible styles of an idealizing painter, who seeks to express only the essence of the object represented, and a realist painter, who seeks to re-present reality. Normally, attempting to bring together two such seemingly irreconcilable stylistic projects—to join them [*congiungere*]—might excite Tasso. But Tasso here views his task with skepticism, and not just because he would be constrained to bring together into a single slim treatise what Cicero analogously worked out and developed expansively. Tasso views the task before him with skepticism because he has no classical model, no authorizing text, that illustrates how he might fruitfully "conjoin" the two, and for Tasso to conjoin means simultaneously to separate and to integrate, as well as to order hierarchically, in a secure and unthreatening way. The problem at bottom is, as it so often is for Tasso, how to order discourse and reality by locating a single authority that—like Goffredo with his errant knights and the poet with his fragmented European states in the *Gerusalemme liberata*—can securely subordinate the many to the one. Confusion for Tasso is always threatening where it cannot evolve dialectically into order.

While his two treatises cannot serve Tasso as a model for constructing his own small one, Cicero nevertheless remains important as the guiding model for secretarial work within Tasso's treatise itself. Cicero, Tasso observes early on, left behind, along with other works, "two books of letters, the Familiar letters and those addressed to Atticus" (258). These books "must never leave the secretary," Tasso admonishes, "because from them one learns not only about eloquence but prudence" (258). From Cicero the secretary also learns about copiousness, variety, and richness; about sincerity, the gravity of customs, the constancy of the will, and the inconstancy of fortune (259); about the art of accusing, defending, praising, and blaming (259); and about how to divide letters into three types and to use "gravity and ornament of words" (265). Cicero illustrates how it is possible to write long letters (266), which is a formidable task, as well as stylistically complex letters that mix the "magnifico" and the "veemente" (273). "There is not a gentile," Tasso thus observes, "more worthy of being imitated than Cicero" (259). Cicero's "authority" is the greatest and most "worthy of consideration" among the Romans (268). Cicero's is the supreme authority of classical Latin, and any humanist secretary worth his salt would do well to imitate him. "As Cicero desired" or "as Cicero said" or "as it pleased Cicero" are consequently phrases that riddle Tasso's treatise. The omnipresence of Cicero as the greatest authority for letter-writing would seem to indicate that when it comes to the professional identity of the secretary there is, for Tasso, nothing new here under the sun: *Nihil sub sole novum.*

Yet Tasso is also keenly aware that the Ciceronian model he has set up is fraught with difficulties. Tasso's and Cicero's projects *and* knowledge appear at radically different historical moments. "The world has changed form, and almost changed in face and appearance," Tasso observes, just after he has insisted that the secretary always keep Cicero's letters close at hand, "wherefore from the fall [*corruzione*] of the ancient kingdoms and ancient republics others have been born, and the new empire acquired and maintained with authority and arms, and the new and most holy religion and the most holy pontificate have introduced other customs and other ceremonial traditions, and almost another way of life" (258–59). Tasso writes in a brave new world, passionately aware that the republics and princedoms of Christian Italy in no way resemble the pagan republic of ancient Rome. Cicero, he notes, wrote "as the father of his fatherland, and as a lover of liberty," whereas "our secretary," he observes, "writes as a son of obedience, and as a friend of servitude" (259). Significantly, the difference rapidly sketched by Tasso is not only historical and genealogical, but personal. As we pass from ancient Rome to late sixteenth-century Italy, we pass not only from men in authority to men who are authorized but from Cicero as the greatest classical authority to eventually, it turns out, Tasso's own father as the greatest modern secretarial model.

Shortly after he marks out for the first time a clear historical distinction between the virtuous past of republican, Ciceronian Rome and the fallen present of his own times, Tasso holds up his father as the one modern who merits "much praise" for having carried over into our own language from ancient Greek and Latin "the concepts and the sayings [*i concetti e le sentenze*] and the other ornaments of speech." "Nor," Tasso observes, "was he left behind by any other" (259). Bernardo Tasso (1493–1569), who is second to none among the moderns as a humanist, is a letter-writer worthy both of imitation and of a place among the great ones of the classical past. Bernardo Tasso indeed appears for the first time just after his son praises both Cicero, for his ability subtly to incorporate into his epistles all the genres of the oration, and Pliny, for his ability to praise not only people but things: "Not only does one praise men, but the cities or towns [*i paesi*]; as Pliny did describing Laurentino, and my father in his description of Naples and of Sorrento" (259). Bernardo Tasso, who was in fact a secretary for many years of his life, emerges as the great

Christian model in the treatise, the privileged extension of the classical past. Yet the comparison made by Tasso is also potentially botched from the start. Bonifacio Vannozzi, who worked for years as a secretary in Rome and Florence, and whose words are cited in the epigraph of this chapter, considers it a gross and misleading exaggeration. Cicero may have written letters, but a letter-writer—as Vannozzi implicitly warns—is not the same thing as a secretary. Although all secretaries are necessarily letter-writers, not all letter-writers are necessarily secretaries. And Cicero, to be sure, was never a secretary. Tasso's father may have been successful as a secretary, but the realities of the present and the past, the realities of late sixteenth-century Italy and ancient republican Rome, make for dangerous comparisons when it comes to outlining the "particulars" of a profession, the very particulars that, according to Vannozzi, are acquired only through "long experience."

Though throughout his treatise Tasso constructs an analogy between the ancient classical orator and the modern secretarial *scriptor,* he also continually breaks that analogy down. On the one hand he draws out similarities: "And pleasing and consoling and recommending are also the office of the orator, from which the secretary learns" (259); "Our secretary is, therefore, an orator, and the art of writing letters is very similar to that of writing orations" (260).[9] On the other hand, Tasso marks out differences, first subtly and then more insistently, filling his treatise in the process with adversatives, all of which stylistically convey to us how much he is quibbling, qualifying, correcting: "the orator is not at all the same as the secretary; *but* the orator speaks to those present, the secretary to those far away" (271, my emphasis); "the orator reigns among judges, as one sees in our own times in Venice; *but* the action of the secretary is very far away from the noises of the palace and of the battling among litigants" (272, my emphasis). However similar, the orator works on the outside, the secretary on the inside; the one works far away, the other nearby. Moreover, secretarial and ambassadorial labors with language produce markedly different results: "*for* as we have said, the letter is not an oration" (273, my emphasis). "Whence," Tasso writes, separating the work of the one from the other, "I cannot in any way praise those who make of the letter and the oration the same genre" [non posso in modo alcuno lodar coloro i quali fanno i generi medesimi quelli dell'epistole e dell'orazione, 271]. "What is acceptable in the

9. "The art of the secretary," Tasso confirms in the second part of his treatise, "is very similar to that of the orator" (271).

oration," Tasso affirms, "would be overbearing in the letter" (273). In no way, then, are the ancient classical orator and the modern secretarial scriptor as neatly analogous as Tasso might otherwise wish them to be. "Wherefore imitation in such dissimilarity and diversity of things," Tasso in fact cautions, "is not at all secure, except where judgment is without any defect and chooses only the appropriate things" (259).

Tasso's comparison of the classical orator and the sixteenth-century secretary eventually yields to a more refined and historically appropriate comparison between the ambassador and the secretary in his own time as he seeks to define, in Abbott's terms, their respective jurisdictional claims over work in the court and in relation to the prince. The position of the ambassador is a secure one in that it has a recognizably direct classical precedent. To be an ambassador was, for so many in the Renaissance, to be an "orator." As Tasso acknowledges in his *Messaggiero,* begun seven years before the composition of *Del secretario,* the two terms were largely interchangeable; "perhaps," Tasso even suggests, "in antiquity it was the same work" [e forse ne gli antichi secoli fu il medesimo essercizio, 58]. Yet the secretarial profession, which indirectly emerges from the work of the classical orator, turns out in *Del secretario* to be superior to the ambassadorial profession. "Nevertheless, most excellent," Tasso declares, "is [the office] of the secretary, and in second place is that of the ambassador" (267). For Tasso the secretary is superior because he is "closer to the prince" [più vicino al principe, 267]; because the secretary has received his information straight from the "will of the prince" (267); and because the ambassador receives his instructions from the secretary and therefore not directly from the prince. The instructions handed over to the ambassador from the secretary must be treated as "laws," and hence, Tasso insists, "the secretary is so much worthier than the ambassador as much as the legislator is to that person who observes the laws, and the judge to that person who interprets them" (267). In the end, for the greater glory of the prince, "the secretary and the ambassador must be friends, and almost conspire at the service of the prince; and if a sort of emulation should arise between them, it must function at the service of the prince; otherwise the virtue of one would be brighter because of the defect of the other" (267).

The secretary, then, is different not only from the ambassador but, above all, from the classical orator and in particular, as we have seen, the Ciceronian orator, who was a lover of liberty rather than of servitude. Given these differences, we should hardly be surprised that much of the information culled from rhetorical treatises such as Cicero's, Tasso claims, "non è molto utile al nostro secretario nello scriver egli" [is not very useful for our secretary in the art of writing, 272]. Indeed, it is in the very nature of the secretary, we are informed early on, to escape the authority of prescriptive rhetorical rules altogether: "si lascia libera l'elezione a la prudenza ed a l'accorgimento del secretario" [one leaves free choice to the prudence and understanding of the secretary, 257]. The excellence of the secretary, for whom "niuna cosa è data per legge inviolabile" [nothing is given as an inviolable law, 257], displays itself by devaluing (*disprezzo*) precepts "taught by rhetors" (257–58). Here Tasso's use of the term *disprezzo* indirectly recalls Castiglione's strategy of *sprezzatura* in *Il cortegiano,* the suave devaluing of all rules as the cardinal rule that art must conceal its own artifice. To have *grazia,* which is requisite in a *bon cortegiano,* one must also have *sprezzatura,* which requires devaluing, understatement. Yet *sprezzatura* also evolves in *Il cortegiano* as an eminently discursive practice as courtiers seek to demonstrate how they can both define and regulate their own highly selective boundaries as an elite group. Rhetorically, to persuade the prince that the courtier is a necessary component in the court requires language. Hence, all the talk of *Il cortegiano* serves many purposes, but it always remains talk, elegant talk, prolific talk, four long books of talk.

By contrast, Tasso's late sixteenth-century secretary, with all his devaluing of rules, persuades not like Castiglione's model courtier fashioned earlier in the century, but through silence, or what Tasso innovatively calls "tacita persuasione" [tacit persuasion, 258], which is "the whole life of the secretary" (258), for the secretary, he declares, "takes his name from silence" (260). Tacit persuasion enlists silence rather than words as a means of moving others to action. It cannot be learned through precepts any more than it can be learned in the schools or academies. It is learned, Tasso claims, above all in the courts. "He does not live among the schools of rhetors or of the sophists," Tasso writes, "but in the palaces and in the courts of princes; nor does he live in contemplation, but in action" (272). But what, then, is tacit persuasion and how can it be practically taught? How do you persuade silently in a court setting such as Castiglione imagines in Urbino, a setting like that Tasso returns to time and again in his treatises? How do you teach the art of silent persuasion through language? And how do you remain active, which Tasso insists the secretary must be, *and* silent?

One model for tacit persuasion might be the Augustinian "rhetoric of silence" identified by Joseph Mazzeo, and later developed by Jerrold Seigel, as central to Petrarch's humanist program and, in turn, to the

Renaissance.[10] But silence, according to Augustine, constituted not so much a means of persuasion as the end of persuasion, the final momentous act of giving up words (*verba*) for things (*res*). In transcending the physical vibration of speech, "true rhetoric," for Augustine, "culminates in silence, in which the mind is in immediate contact with reality," and "the movement of thought was through the words to the realities themselves, from the temporal realities to the eternal realities, from talk to silence, and from discourse to vision."[11] By contrast, the model of tacit persuasion germane to the role of the secretary in the late sixteenth century would be the one that seems to inform Tasso's own calculatingly brief treatise. Tasso will not provide precepts; instead he will communicate much as one might hint or wink among friends, disclosing only that much and not revealing the express commands of masters or teachers ("e quelli ch' io darò, saran più tosto simili a' cenni degli amici ch' a gli espressi commandamenti de' maestri," 257). We detect and learn tacit persuasion through the reception and practice of ellipsis. Tacit persuasion implies discursivity as a capacity, a competence suppressed so far that it cannot be detected as a performance. Tacit persuasion persuades because, as a self-authenticating device, it convinces us that something valuable is being withheld. Tacit persuasion does not work by saying one thing and meaning another, as *sprezzatura* does. Tacit persuasion works by not saying anything at all and by consequently implying that there exists a vast reservoir of untouched speech and meaning.[12] Unlike Castiglione's model courtier fashioned at the beginning of the century, then, Tasso's late sixteenth-century secretary is strikingly silent, and he remains silent because he would have us believe, through the conspicuous repression of speech, that he indeed has something valuable to say even as he persistently refuses to say it.

Now the secretary's knowledge, which includes all "things that must be kept secret and revealed" (260), comprises the hidden thoughts of the prince along with the secretary's own concealed concerns, but his knowledge is also general and vast. Tasso's secretary must know every-

10. Seigel, *Rhetoric and Philosophy in Renaissance Humanism,* 45–46; and Mazzeo, "St. Augustine's Rhetoric of Silence." On silence in the Renaissance, see Patrizi, "Pedagogie del silenzio." On silence in rhetoric, see the synthetic study by Franchi, "Le figure del silenzio."

11. Mazzeo, "St. Augustine's Rhetoric of Silence," 187 and 189.

12. As Tasso observes in his *Malpiglio, overo de la corte,* "the little part of oneself that is revealed can create a desire to know what is covered up; it can cause men generally and even the prince to believe that something rare, singular, and perfect is being hidden." See Tasso, *Tasso's Dialogues*, 175; hereafter cited by page number in my text.

thing that has to do with letter-writing (258) as well as all the forms of address and titles used, including those titles employed in ancient histories as well as new and reformed ones (262). Tasso's secretary knows all about the nature of things and the power, uses, and derivations of words (262). He must know about the forms and customs—both past and present—of honoring people (263). He must know about oratory to be a fine speaker but also the nature and names of things to be a philosopher (263). "He must know," Tasso remarks, "about wars, seditions, discords, victories, acquisitions and losses of provinces and kingdoms and troops, peace-making, truces, family lineages, births, deaths of great ones, and the rise and fall of famous men, and, in short, *all things that have ever happened in the world*" (276, my emphasis). The secretary's authority, Tasso further observes, derives from his knowledge of civil law and his ability to rise above it, along with the judges who dispense justice. The secretary dispenses power not through harsh laws but suavely and mercifully, through the fully disseminated authority of the state, which is manifested in the customs of the people, their deeply entrenched traditions and habits (262–63). The secretary consequently has a broad knowledge of his *own* culture, and this knowledge gives him power, for even kings, who are not subject to civil laws, are subject to customs. The secretary's knowledge, then, is unmistakably concrete, specific, contemporary, but it is also, as we have seen, general and vast. In short, the secretary knows about *his* prince, *his* society, *his* culture in the very moment that he knows about "all things that have ever happened in the world" (276).

Tasso's treatise, like so many humanist treatises, is thus tellingly torn between the culturally distinct models of the present and the highly valued yet flawed models of the past. As Tasso looks to Cicero for a unifying authority, he confronts the familiar humanist problem of applying timeless models of antiquity to the historically determined moment of the present. The recognition that the past radically differed from the present did not, however, keep Tasso from constructing professions in and for his own time, any more than it kept Tasso—or, for that matter, other Italian Renaissance humanists—from locating specific strategies for ensuring professional success and development. For Tasso, the secretary was the functionary appropriate to the period in which he lived, a period that needed—as classical Rome never did—just this kind of obsequious filial servant in a centralized and increasingly bureaucratic state. Hence, the secretary had a specific jurisdictional claim over work, and it was a claim that marked off his profession from that of the ambassador in a friendly rivalry that characterized the secretary as ultimately the superior of the two (267). Moreover, the secretary had a specific strategy for communication rooted in a time, as Tasso puts it in his *Malpiglio, overo de la corte* (ca. 1585), when "concealment becomes the courtier more than showing off" (175), when "tacit persuasion" was best suited to the needs of an administrator exercising his *professione* at court, when silence and dissimulation and slavish self-effacement were more appropriate than prolific talk. Yet the past, as the competing authoritative model for thinking about behavior and constructing identities, always had a formidable claim upon the present, not only for Tasso but for so many Italian humanists writing about professions during the Renaissance. The distinctions therefore made between the orator and the secretary, which are so carefully mapped out in Tasso's treatise, are only important for the "small orator" and the "small secretary" ("questa distinzione e quasi divisione de' confini è tra 'l picciolo oratore e 'l picciolo secretario," 260). For the great ones, there is—Tasso fudges—an "amichevole confusione" [a friendly confusion] of abilities, as "one passes from the power of one to the other" (260). The great ones of the present are no different from the great ones of the past. So it was for a host of Italian humanists writing in Tasso's own time, just as it had been for Petrarch two and a half centuries earlier, when he sought to imitate the imagined laureate poets of antiquity, to fashion the "profession of the poet," and to have himself crowned before the senate on the Capitoline after a lapse of more than a thousand years.

I end with Tasso, for though he never officially occupied the profession of secretary, he did in a very real way occupy the profession of poet, the profession with which we began and the profession Petrarch created for himself and other humanists in his coronation oration. Tasso was one of a number of Italian humanists who managed to survive, to the degree that he was willing to stay put in Ferrara and behave himself, as a hired poet. "He had," Tasso's biographer Angelo Solerti writes, "the title and place of a gentleman, a room, a place at the table in court, and no particular duty other than to write rhymes, whenever the occasion warranted it."[13] Tasso occupied in a sufficiently remunerated way the office of the poet at court, though he did not always feel that he was being treated in a genuinely dignified manner. He makes this clear enough in one of the letters included in the epistolary collection that followed his treatise on

13. Solerti, *Vita di Torquato Tasso,* 1.162–63.

the secretary as it was printed in 1588. "Now I am not seeking work but quiet," Tasso writes,

> not obligations but entertainment, not masters but friends. And I would willingly quit the service of this most serene prince, since it seems to me that I have been almost completely severed from his friendship. I know what is due to his greatness and what is due to the modesty of a gentleman who has always had the profession of letters [*professione di lettere*]. . . . But after seven years of imprisonment, after nine of illness, thirty-two of exile (if I may call it that), after thousands of anxious moments and thousands of pains, and the continuous horror of seeing my own works lacerated [*lacerate l'opere mie*], I would put aside, if I could, all the other troubles, which impede me from correcting my works, expanding them, beautifying them.[14]

The letters accompanying Tasso's treatise were taken (or rather, mistaken, Vannozzi would insist) as models for the kinds of letters a secretary would or should write.[15] Yet within this collection of letters, which are the product of an often anguished, self-conscious poet who is hardly self-effacing, as secretaries were supposed to be, Tasso announces that he practices the profession of letters, which we may understand here as both the profession of the poet and the humanist, of *humanae litterae* in general. And foremost among the lacerated writings that Tasso in his "professione di lettere" hopes to amend is surely his epic poem, which had been printed in an unfinished state.

The humanist poet and the secretary are distinct. Yet much of what Tasso writes about the secretary, I would like to suggest in conclusion, conforms at one level to his presentation of what an epic poet should be, especially if we take into consideration Tasso's discourses on the art of poetry and his presentation of himself in the *Gerusalemme liberata*. The secretary, like the epic poet, must not only deal with the realm of probability but be capable of operating with all registers of style (265), which Tasso does in an epic that stylistically appropriates the genres of lyric, romance, tragedy, and pastoral. The secretary's province of expertise is not, like the philosopher's, dialectic or sophistic argumentation, but, like the epic poet's, moral persuasion (266). Unlike the orator, who speaks, the secretary, like the epic poet, writes, and in his writings the epic poet

14. Tasso, *Il secretario et il primo volume, delle lettere,* letter 48. The first printing of the treatise on the secretary appeared in 1587. The portion of the letter cited can be sampled in Tasso, *Lettere,* 3.112–13.

15. Nor should this be surprising given the placement of these familial letters as a collection often directly after the secretarial treatise and the printer's recommendation in Tasso, *Il secretario et il primo volume,* a4r, that they be treated as models.

ideally demonstrates, like the secretary, a sort of field knowledge of his culture in his own time as well as a broad-based understanding of the past. Along with this, the secretary must be "a child of obedience, and a friend of servitude" (259), which mirrors exactly how Tasso presents himself in the proem in relation to his father-figure, Alfonso d'Este, to whom he dutifully brings an "offering" [voto, 1.4]. Finally, like the secretary, the epic poet of the *Liberata* is a keeper of secrets who communicates through tacit persuasion. The *Gerusalemme liberata* is not just a nocturnal poem in which characters hide and feign and dissimulate, but a poem that dissimulates as part of its own narrative strategy, a deeply secretive poem, as Sergio Zatti brilliantly argues,[16] composed by an author who, unlike the discursive and deliberately open Ariostan narrator, is self-effacing, elliptical, tight-lipped.

The epic poet and the secretary are thus somewhat alike in their shared strategies of writing, their breadth of knowledge as humanists, and their recognition that they must submit—or at least feign to submit completely—to absolute authority. The humanist professional poet, who distanced himself from his father by refusing to follow in his footsteps and officially become a secretary, not only defines his father's profession for future generations in treatise form but, in a far more subtle way, strategically absorbs aspects of it into his own poetic practice as an author embellishing his "carte" [pages, 2.1]. Yet for all that they may resemble one another, the epic poet and the secretary are fundamentally different. Most noticeably, the epic poet writes predominantly in the high style, the secretary in the middle style; one writes about heroic matters, the other about daily affairs; one chooses his *materia,* the other has it assigned; one writes verse, the other prose letters. In the end, the *Gerusalemme liberata* is no more a poem written by a secretary than it is a poem written by a doctor or an ambassador, however much Tasso likens himself to a physician as he borrows from Lucretius's *De rerum natura* or sets himself

16. Zatti, "Il linguaggio della dissimulazione," 423–47. On Tasso as a secretive poet who hides, and for a view of the *Liberata* as a nocturnal poem, see Quint, *Origin and Originality in Renaissance Literature,* esp. 108–10. See also Cermolacce, "La nuit dans la 'Gerusalemme liberata.'" That Tasso is a secretive poet who moves us by deliberately suppressing information underpins much of the psychoanalytic reading provided in Ferguson, *Trials of Desire,* 54–136. This notion also underpins as well the rereading of Tasso's allegory in Stephens, "Metaphor, Sacrament, and the Problem of Allegory," 235: "he evidently came to fear that, if the structuring of the poem were discerned, he would seem to be meddling in sacramental theology. So he attempted to cover his tracks in letters and treatises." Tasso, it would seem, is secretive about even the secretive nature of allegory. On the figure of the poet in Tasso, still indispensable is the seminal study by Durling, *The Figure of the Poet in Renaissance Epic,* 182–210.

up as a rival messenger adorning his words as Alete did. The *Gerusalemme liberata* is ultimately a poem composed by a professional poet who—as if in defense of poetry against Socrates' accusation in Plato's *Republic*—writes with presumed authority about all the arts contained and coopted in his poem. "Let us not, then, demand a reckoning from Homer," Socrates observes in book 10 of the *Republic,* "or any other of the poets on other matters by asking them, if any one of them was a physician and not merely an imitator of a physician's talk, what men any poet, old or new, is reported to have restored to health as Asclepius did, or what disciples of the medical art he left after him as Asclepius did his descendants, and let us dismiss the other arts and not question them about them" (*Republic,* 599 b–d).[17] For Socrates, the Homeric poet—and thus all epic poets—only feigns knowing what he speaks about when he describes various arts in his poems. By contrast, the poet—as Tasso expressed it in the greatest of his enabling analogies[18]—is nothing other than a sort of God, who oversees the workings of humankind and its myriad activities in the world in the very moment that he melancholically exercises his profession with humility in the service of his master at court.

17. Plato, *Collected Dialogues*.

18. See Rhu, *Genesis of Tasso's Narrative Theory,* 130–31, for Tasso's description of the poet as a god ruling his poem. On Tasso's analogy, see Durling, *The Figure of the Poet,* esp. 201–2.

Bibliography

Abbott, Andrew. *The System of Professions: An Essay on the Division of Expert Labor.* Chicago: University of Chicago Press, 1988.

Accetto, Torquato. *Della dissimulazione onesta.* Ed. S. Nigro. Genoa: Costa & Nolan, 1983.

Alford, John A. "Medicine in the Middle Ages: The Theory of a Profession." *Centennial Review* 23 (1979): 377–96.

Amundsen, Darrel W. *Medicine, Society, and Faith in the Ancient and Medieval Worlds.* Baltimore: Johns Hopkins University Press, 1996.

Aquinas, St. Thomas. *Summa Theologiae.* 61 vols. New York: McGraw-Hill, 1964–81.

Aristotle. *Aristotle's "Poetics."* Trans. James Hutton. New York: Norton, 1982.

Arrizabalaga, Jon. "Facing the Black Death: Perceptions and Reactions of University Medical Practitioners." In *Practical Medicine from Salerno to the Black Death,* ed. Luis García-Ballester et al., 237–88. Cambridge: Cambridge University Press, 1994.

Arrizabalaga, Jon, John Henderson, and Roger French. *The Great Pox: The French Disease in Renaissance Europe.* New Haven, Conn.: Yale University Press, 1997.

Ascoli, Albert R. "Machiavelli's Gift of Counsel." In *Machiavelli and the Discourse of Literature,* ed. A. Ascoli and V. Kahn, 219–57. Ithaca, N.Y.: Cornell University Press, 1993.

Asor Rosa, Alberto. "*Ricordi* di Francesco Guicciardini." In *Letteratura italiana: Le opere,* vol. 2, ed. Alberto Asor Rosa, 3–94. Turin: Einaudi, 1993.

Bacci, Antonio. *Lexicon vocabulorum quae difficilius latine redduntur.* 4th ed. Rome: Societas Libraria Studium, 1963.

Bacon, Roger. *Opera hactenus inedita.* Ed. Robert Steele. Oxford: Oxford University Press, 1920.

Barbaro, Ermolao. *De coelibatu—De officio legati.* Ed. Vittore Branca. Florence: Olschki, 1969.

———. *Epistolae, orationes et carmina.* Ed. Vittore Branca. Florence: Bibliopolis, 1943.

Baron, Hans. *The Crisis of the Early Italian Renaissance: Civic Humanism and Republican Liberty in an Age of Classicism and Tyranny.* Princeton, N.J.: Princeton University Press, 1966.

Basso, Jeannine. *Le genre épistolaire en langue italienne, 1538–1662: Répertoire chronologique et analytique.* Rome: Bulzoni, 1990.

Battaglia, Salvatore. *Grande dizionario della lingua italiana.* Turin: Unione Tipografico-Editrice Torinese, 1961–.

Bec, Christian. "Lo statuto socio-professionale degli scrittori (Trecento e Cinquecento)." In *Letteratura italiana: Produzione e consumo,* vol. 2, ed. Alberto Asor Rosa, 229–67. Turin: Einaudi, 1983.

Behrens, B. "Treatises on the Ambassador Written in the Fifteenth and Early Sixteenth Centuries." *English Historical Review* 51 (1936): 616–27.

Belladonna, Rita. "Cenni biografici su Bartolomeo Carli Piccolomini." *Critica storica* 11 (1974): 507–16.

———. "Pontanus, Machiavelli and a Case of Religious Dissimulation in Early Sixteenth-Century Siena (Carli's *Trattati nove della prudenza*)." *Bibliothèque d'Humanisme et Renaissance* 37 (1975): 377–85.

Benedek, Thomas G. "The Medical Autobiography of Petrarch." *Bulletin of the History of Medicine* 41 (1967): 332–41.

Benivieni, Antonio. *De abditis nonnullis ac mirandis morborum et sanationum causis.* Florence: Philippi Giuntae, 1507.

Benjamin, Walter. *Illuminations.* Trans. Harry Zohn, with an introduction by Hannah Arendt. New York: Schocken Books, 1969.

Bernardo, Aldo S. "The Plague as Key to Meaning in Boccaccio's *Decameron.*" In *The Black Death: The Impact of the Fourteenth-Century Plague,* ed. D. Williman, 39–64. Binghamton, N.Y.: Center for Medieval and Early Renaissance Studies, 1982.

Bigi, E. "Barbaro, Ermolao." In *DBI* 6 (1964): 96–99.

Biow, Douglas. *Mirabile Dictu: Representations of the Marvelous in Medieval and Renaissance Epic.* Ann Arbor: University of Michigan Press, 1996.

Birago, Francesco. *Dichiarationi et avertimenti poetici, istorici, politici, cavallereschi e morali nella Gerusalemme Conquistata.* Milan: Benedetto Somasco, 1616.

Bizer, Marc. "Letters from Home: The Epistolary Aspects of Joachim Du Bellay's *Regrets.*" *Renaissance Quarterly* 52 (1999): 140–79.

———. *Les lettres romaines de Du Bellay: "Les Regrets" et la tradition épistolaire.* Montreal: Les Presses de l'Université de Montréal, 2001.

Black, Robert. *Benedetto Accolti and the Florentine Renaissance.* Cambridge: Cambridge University Press, 1985.

———. "Florentine Political Traditions and Machiavelli's Election to the Chancery." *Italian Studies* 40 (1985): 1–16.

———. "Machiavelli, Servant of the Florentine Republic." In *Machiavelli and Republicanism,* ed. Gisela Bock, Quentin Skinner, and Maurizio Viroli, 71–99. Cambridge: Cambridge University Press, 1990.

Boccaccio, Giovanni. *The Decameron.* Trans. G. H. McWilliam. Middlesex: Penguin, 1972.

———. *Il Decameron.* Ed. Vittore Branca. Vol. 4 of *Tutte le opere,* ed. Vittore Branca. Milan: Mondadori, 1976.

Bondanella, Peter E. *Francesco Guicciardini.* Boston: Twayne, 1976.

Bonora, Elena. *Ricerche su Francesco Sansovino imprenditore librario e letterato.* Venice: Istituto Veneto di Scienze, Lettere ed Arti, 1994.

Bonora, Fausto, and George Kern. "Does Anyone Really Know the Life of Gentile da Foligno?" *Medicina nei secoli* 9 (1972): 29–53.

Branca, Vittore. *Boccaccio medievale e nuovi studi sul "Decameron."* Florence: Sansoni, 1981.

———. "Ermolao Barbaro and Late Quattrocento Venetian Humanism." In *Renaissance Venice,* ed. John Hale, 218–43. London: Faber and Faber, 1973.

———. "L'umanesimo veneziano alla fine del Quattrocento: Ermolao Barbaro e il suo circolo." In *Storia della cultura veneta,* ed. G. Arnaldi and M. Pastore Stocchi, vol. 3, pt. 1, 123–75. Vicenza: Neri Pozza, 1981.

Brown, Alison. *Bartolomeo Scala, 1430–97, Chancellor of Florence: The Humanist as Bureaucrat.* Princeton, N.J.: Princeton University Press, 1979.

Bullough, Vern L. *The Development of Medicine as a Profession: The Contribution of the Medieval University to Modern Medicine.* New York and Basel: Karger, 1966.

Bulzoni, Lina. "Il segretario neoplatonico (F. Patrizi, A. Querenghi, V. Gramigna)." In *La Corte e il "Cortegiano,"* vol. 2, ed. Adriano Prosperi, 133–69. Rome: Bulzoni, 1981.

Burke, Peter. *The Fortunes of the "Courtier": The European Reception of Castiglione's "Cortegiano."* Cambridge: Polity Press, 1995.

———. "The Renaissance, Individualism, and the Portrait." *History of European Ideas* 21 (1995): 393–400.

Bushnell, Rebecca W. *A Culture of Teaching: Early Modern Humanism in Theory and Practice.* Ithaca, N.Y.: Cornell University Press, 1996.

Bylebyl, Jerome L. "Medicine, Philosophy, and Humanism in Renaissance Italy." In *Science and the Arts in the Renaissance,* ed. John W. Shirley and F. David Hoeniger, 27–49. Washington, D.C.: Folger Shakespeare Library, 1985.

Calcaterra, Carlo. *Nella selva di Petrarca.* Bologna: Cappelli, 1942.

Calvi, Giulia. *Histories of a Plague Year: The Social and the Imaginary in Baroque Florence.* Trans. D. Biocca and B. Ragan Jr. Berkeley: University of California Press, 1989.

Campana, Augusto. "The Origin of the Word 'Humanist.'" *Journal of the Warburg and Courtauld Institute* 9 (1946): 60–73.

Campbell, Anna M. *The Black Death and Men of Learning.* New York: Columbia University Press, 1931.

Capaccio, Giulio Cesare. *Il secretario.* Venice: Vicenzo Somascho, 1599.

Carmichael, Ann G. *Plague and the Poor in Renaissance Florence.* Cambridge: Cambridge University Press, 1986.

———. "Plague Legislation in the Italian Renaissance." *Bulletin of the History of Medicine* 57 (1983): 508–25.

Carrara, Daniela Mugnai. "Fra causalità astrologica e causalità naturale: Gli interventi di Nicolò Leoniceno e della sua scuola sul morbo gallico." *Physis* 21 (1979): 37–54.

Cassian, John. *Opera omnia.* Vol. 49 of *Patrologiae Latinae Cursus Completus,* ed. J. P. Migne. Paris: Thibaud, 1874.

———. *A Select Library of Nicene and Post-Nicene Fathers,* 2d ser., vol. 11. Trans. Edgar C. S. Gibson. Reprint. Grand Rapids, Mich.: William B. Eerdmans, 1964.

Castiglione, Baldesar. *The Book of the Courtier.* Trans. Charles S. Singleton. New York: Anchor Books, 1959.

———. *Il cortegiano.* 3d ed. Ed. Vittorio Cian. Florence: Sansoni, 1929.

———. *Lettere del Conte Baldessar Castiglione.* Ed. P. Serassi. Padua: Comino, 1769.

Castiglioni, Arturo. "I libri italiani della pestilenza." In *Il volto di Ippocrate: Istorie di medici e medicine d'altri tempi,* 147–69. Milan: Società Editrice Unitas, 1925.

Ceccarelli, L. "Gentile da Foligno." In *DBI* 53 (1999): 162–67.

Cermolacce, Jean. "La nuit dans la 'Gerusalemme liberata.'" *Revue des études italiennes* 19 (1973): 244–59.

Chabod, Federico. *Scritti su Machiavelli.* Turin: Einaudi, 1964.

Cheney, Patrick Gerard. *Spenser's Famous Flight: A Renaissance Idea of a Literary Career.* Toronto: University of Toronto Press, 1993.

Chiappelli, Fredi. "Machiavelli as Secretary." *Italian Quarterly* 13 (1970): 27–44.

Cipolla, Carlo. *Miasmas and Disease: Public Health and the Environment in the Pre-Industrial Age.* Trans. E. Potter. New Haven, Conn.: Yale University Press, 1992.

———. "The Professions—The Long View." *Journal of European Economic History* 2 (1973): 37–51.

———. *Public Health and the Medical Profession in the Renaissance.* Cambridge: Cambridge University Press, 1976.

Clay, Diskin. *Lucretius and Epicurus.* Ithaca, N.Y.: Cornell University Press, 1983.

———. "The Tragic and Comic Poet of the *Symposium.*" *Arion,* n.s., 2 (1975): 238–61.

Corner, George W. *Anatomical Texts of the Earlier Middle Ages: A Study in the Transmission of Culture.* Washington, D.C.: Carnegie Institution of Washington, 1927.

Corradi, Alfonso. *Annali delle epidemie occorse in Italia dalle prime memorie fino al 1850.* Vol. 4. Reprint. Bologna: Litografia, 1973.

Corsini, Andrea. "Il 'De Vita' di Marsilio Ficino." *Rivista di storia critica delle scienze mediche e naturali* 10 (1919): 5–13.

Costo, Tomaso. *Discorso pratico fatto ad un suo nipote ad alcune qualità che debba haver un buon segretario.* Venice: Barezzo Barezzi, 1602.

Cottino-Jones, Marga. "Boccaccio e la scienze." In *Letteratura e scienza nella storia della cultura italiana: Atti del IX Congresso dell'AISLLI,* 356–70. Palermo: Manfredi, 1978.

D'Agramont, Jacme. "Regiment de Preservacio a Epidimia o Pestilencia e Mortaldats." Trans. M. L. Duran-Reynals and C.-E. A. Winslow. *Bulletin of the History of Medicine* 23 (1949): 57–89.

D'Anghiera, Pietro Martire. *De rebus oceanicis et orbe novo.* Basel: Ioannem Bebelium, 1533.

Daston, Lorraine, and Katharine Park. *Wonders and the Order of Nature, 1150–1750.* New York: Zone Books, 1998.

de Caprio, Vincenzo. "Aristocrazia e clero dalla crisi dell'Umanesimo alla Controriforma." In *Letteratura italiana: Produzione e consumo,* vol. 2, ed. Alberto Asor Rosa, 299–361. Turin: Einaudi, 1983.

Defaux, Gérard. *Le curieux, le glorieux et la sagesse du monde dans la première moitié du XVIe siècle: L'exemple de Panurge (Ulysse, Démosthène, Empédocle).* Lexington: French Forum, 1982.

de Grazia, Sebastian. *Machiavelli in Hell.* Princeton, N.J.: Princeton University Press, 1989.

Dehio, Ludwig. *The Precarious Balance: Four Centuries of the European Power Struggle.* Trans. Charles Fullman. New York: Vintage, 1962.

Del Panta, Lorenzo. *Le epidemie nella storia demografica italiana (secoli XIV–XIX).* Turin: Loescher Editore, 1980.

Dibben, L. B. "Secretaries in the Thirteenth and Fourteenth Centuries." *English Historical Review* 25 (1910): 430–44.

Dionisotti, Carlo. *Geografia e storia della letteratura italiana.* Turin: Einaudi, 1967.

Dizionario biografico degli italiani [*DBI*]. Rome: Istituto della Enciclopedia Italiana, 1960–.

Doglio, Maria Luisa. "Ambasciatore e principe: L'*Institutio legati* di Ermolao Barbaro."

In *Umanesimo e rinascimento a Firenze e Venezia,* vol. 1, 297–310. Florence: Olschki, 1983.

Dolet, Étienne. "Étienne Dolet on the Functions of the Ambassador, 1541." Trans. James E. Dunlap, with an introduction by Jesse S. Reeves. *American Journal of International Law* 27 (1933): 80–95.

———. *Stephani Doleti Galli aurelii liber unus de officio legati, quem vulgo ambasciatorum vocant.* Lugdani: Apud Steph. Doletum, 1541.

Donaldson, Peter S. *Machiavelli and Mystery of State.* Cambridge: Cambridge University Press, 1988.

Dotti, Ugo. *Vita di Petrarca.* Bari: Laterza, 1987.

Douglas, Richard M. "Talent and Vocation in Humanist and Protestant Thought." In *Action and Conviction in Early Modern Europe: Essays in Memory of E. H. Harbison,* ed. T. K. Rabb and J. E. Seigel, 261–98. Princeton, N.J.: Princeton University Press, 1969.

Du Cange, Charles Du Fresne. *Glossarium mediae et infimae Latinitatis.* Graz: Akademische Druck, 1954.

Durling, Robert M. *The Figure of the Poet in Renaissance Epic.* Cambridge: Harvard University Press, 1965.

Eden, Richard. *The First Three English Books on America.* Ed. Edward Arber. New York: Kraus Reprint, 1971.

Edgerton, Samuel Y. Jr. *Pictures and Punishment: Art and Criminal Prosecution during the Florentine Renaissance.* Ithaca, N.Y.: Cornell University Press, 1985.

Erasmus, Desiderius. *Apophthegmatum ex optimis utriusque linguae scriptoribus.* Basel: Nicolaum et Eusebium Episcopios, 1565.

Ferguson, Margaret. *Trials of Desire: Renaissance Defenses of Poetry.* New Haven, Conn.: Yale University Press, 1983.

Ferriguto, Arnaldo. *Almorò Barbaro, l'alta cultura nel settentrione d'Italia nel '400, i "sacri canones" di Roma e le "santissime leze" di Venezia.* Venice: Miscellanea di Storia Veneta, 1922.

Ficino, Marsilio. *Commentary on Plato's Symposium on Love.* Trans. Sears Jayne. Dallas, Tex.: Spring Publications, 1985.

———. *Consilio contro la pestilenzia.* Ed. E. Musacchio, with an introduction by G. Moraglia. Bologna: Cappelli, 1983.

———. *Three Books on Life.* Ed. and trans. Carol V. Kaske and John R. Clark. Binghamton, N.Y.: Medieval and Renaissance Texts and Studies, 1989.

Figliuolo, Bruno. *Il diplomatico e il trattatista: Ermolao Barbaro ambasciatore della Serenissima e il "De officio legati."* Naples: Guida, 1999.

Fiorato, Adelin Charles. "Grandeur et servitude du secrétaire: du savoir rhétorique à la collaboration politique." In *Culture et professions en Italie (fin XVe–début XVIIe siècles),* ed. A. C. Fiorato, 133–84. Paris: Publications de la Sorbonne, 1989.

Fish, Stanley. *Doing What Comes Naturally: Change, Rhetoric, and the Practice of Theory in Literary and Legal Studies.* Durham, N.C.: Duke University Press, 1989.

Foa, Anna. "The New and the Old: The Spread of Syphilis (1494–1530)." Trans. Carole C. Gallucci. In *Sex and Gender in Historical Perspective,* ed. Edward Muir and Guido Ruggiero, 26–45. Baltimore: Johns Hopkins University Press, 1990.

Foucault, Michel. *The Birth of the Clinic: An Archeology of Medical Perception.* Trans. A. M. Sheridan Smith. New York: Vintage, 1973.

———. *The Order of Things.* Trans. A. M. Sheridan Smith. New York: Vintage, 1970.

Fracastoro, Girolamo. *De contagione et contagiosis morbis et eorum curatione, libri III.* Ed. and trans. Wilmer Cave Wright. New York: Putnam's Sons, 1930.

———. *Fracastoro's "Syphilis": Introduction, Text, Translation and Notes with a Computer-Generated Word Index.* Ed. and trans. Geoffrey Eatough. Liverpool: Francis Cairns, 1984.

———. *Naugerius, sive de poetica dialogus.* Trans. Ruth Kelso, with an introduction by Murray W. Bundy. *University of Illinois Studies in Language and Literature,* vol. 9. Urbana: University of Illinois Press, 1924.

———. *Opera omnia.* Venice: Iuntas, 1555.

———. *Scritti inediti di Girolamo Fracastoro.* Ed. Francesco Pellegrini. Verona: Edizioni Valdonega, 1954.

———. *Trattato inedito in prosa di Gerolamo Fracastoro sulla sifilide.* Ed. Francesco Pellegrini. Verona: La Tipografica Veronese, 1939.

Fragnito, Gigliola. "Buone maniere e professionalità nelle Corti Romane del Cinque e Seicento." In *Educare il corpo, educare la parola nella trattatisica del Rinascimento,* ed. Giorgio Patrizi and Amedeo Quondam, 77–109. Rome: Bulzoni, 1998.

Franchi, Piero Luxardo. "Le figure del silenzio: Statuto retorico dei fenomeni ellittici." In *Studi in onore di Vittorio Zaccaria,* ed. M. Pecoraro, 439–55. Milan: Unicopli, 1987.

Frazier, Alison. "Reforming Hagiography: Aurelio Brandolini (ca. 1454–97) and Raffaele Maffei (1445–1522)." Unpublished manuscript.

Freccero, John. *Dante: The Poetics of Conversion.* Ed. Rachel Jacoff. Cambridge: Harvard University Press, 1986.

Freeman, Kathleen. *Ancilla to the Pre-Socratic Philosophers.* Cambridge: Harvard University Press, 1956.

French, Roger. "Gentile da Foligno and the *Via Medicorum.*" In *The Light of Nature: Essays in the History and Philosophy of Science Presented to A. C. Crombie,* ed. J. D. North and J. J. Roche, 21–34. Dordrecht: Martinus Nijhoff, 1985.

Fried, Michael. *Absorption and Theatricality: Painting and Beholder in the Age of Diderot.* Berkeley: University of California Press, 1980.

Frye, Northrop. *Secular Scripture: A Study of the Structure of Romance.* Cambridge: Harvard University Press, 1976.

Fubini, Mario. "Le quattro redazioni dei *Ricordi* del Guicciardini." In *Studi sulla letteratura del Rinascimento,* 138–207. Florence: Centro Nazionale di Studi sul Rinascimento, 1948.

Fubini, Riccardo. "L'ambasciatore nel XV secolo: Due trattati e una biografia (Bernard de Rosier, Ermolao Barbaro, Vespasiano da Bisticci)." *Mélanges de l'école française de Rome* 108 (1996): 645–65.

Gage, Monica. *Myth and Poetry in Lucretius.* Cambridge: Cambridge University Press, 1994.

Gagneux, Marcel. "Reflets et jalons de la carrière d'un homme politique: Les trois rédactions des *Pensées* de François Ghuicardin." In *Réécritures II: Commentaires, parodies, variations dans la littérature italienne de la Renaissance,* 69–99. Paris: Université de la Sorbonne Nouvelle, 1984.

Garin, Eugenio. "I cancellieri umanisti della repubblica fiorentina da Coluccio Salutati a Bartolomeo Scala." *Rivista storica italiana* 71 (1959): 185–208.

———. *La disputa delle arti nel Quattrocento.* Florence: Vallecchi Editore, 1947.

———. *Italian Humanism: Philosophy and Civic Life in the Renaissance.* Trans. Peter Munz. New York: Harper & Row, 1965.

Garzoni, Tomaso. *Piazza universale di tutte le professioni del mondo.* Ed. Paolo Cherchi. Turin: Einaudi, 1996.

Gaskoin, George. *The Medical Works of Francisco López de Villalobos, the Celebrated Court Physician of Spain.* London: Churchill, 1870.

Gensini, Stefano. " 'Poeta et historicus': L'episodio della laurea nella carriera e nella prospettiva culturale di Francesco Petrarca." *La cultura* 18 (1980): 166–94.

Gentile da Foligno. *Consilia.* Pavia: Antonius Carcanus, ca. 1488.

———. *Consilium contra pestilentiam.* Colle di Valdelsa: Bonus Gallus, ca. 1479.

———. *Super prima fen quarti Canonis Avicennae.* Padua: Nicolaus Petri de Harlen, 1476.

Gentili, Alberico. *De legationibus libri tres.* With an introduction by Ernest Nys. New York: Oxford University Press, 1924.

Gerbi, Antonello. *La natura delle Indie nove: Da Cristoforo Colombo a Gonzalo Fernandez de Oviedo.* Milan: Ricciardi, 1975.

Gilbert, Allan H. *Machiavelli's "Prince" and Its Forerunners: The "Prince" as a Typical Book de regimine principum.* Durham, N.C.: Duke University Press, 1938.

Gilbert, Felix. *Machiavelli and Guicciardini: Politics and History in Sixteenth-Century Florence.* Reprint. New York: Norton, 1984.

Gilmore, Myron P. *Humanists and Jurists: Six Studies in the Renaissance.* Cambridge: Harvard University Press, 1963.

———. "*Studia Humanitatis* and the Professions in Fifteenth-Century Florence." In *Florence and Venice: Comparisons and Relations,* vol. 1, ed. S. Bertelli, N. Rubinstein, and C. H. Smyth, 27–40. Florence: La Nuova Italia Editrice, 1979.

Godi, Carlo. "La 'Collatio laureationis' del Petrarca." *Italia medioevale e umanistica* 13 (1970): 13–27.

Godman, Peter. *From Poliziano to Machiavelli: Florentine Humanism in the High Renaissance.* Princeton, N.J.: Princeton University Press, 1998.

Goldberg, Jonathan. "The Politics of Renaissance Literature: A Review Essay." *English Literary History* 49 (1982): 514–42.

Goodwin, Charles. "Professional Vision." *American Anthropologist* 96 (1994): 606–33.

Gould, Cecil. *Titian as Portraitist.* London: National Gallery, 1976.

Grafton, Anthony. "The New Science and the Traditions of Humanism." In *The Cambridge Companion to Renaissance Humanism,* ed. Jill Kraye, 203–23. Cambridge: Cambridge University Press, 1996.

———. "Renaissance Readers and Ancient Texts: Comments on Some Commentaries." *Renaissance Quarterly* 38 (1985): 615–49.

Grafton, Anthony, April Shelford, and Nancy G. Siraisi. *New Worlds, Ancient Texts: The Power of Tradition and the Shock of Discovery.* Cambridge: Harvard University Press, 1992.

Grafton, Anthony, and Lisa Jardine. *From Humanism to the Humanities: Education and the Liberal Arts in Fifteenth- and Sixteenth-Century Europe.* London: Duckworth, 1986.

Gramigna, Vincenzo. *Il segretario dialogo.* Florence: Pietro Cecconcelli, 1620.

Gray, Hanna H. "Renaissance Humanism: The Pursuit of Eloquence." *Journal of the History of Ideas* 24 (1963): 497–514.

Greenblatt, Stephen. *Marvelous Possessions: The Wonder of the New World.* Chicago: University of Chicago Press, 1991.

———. *Renaissance Self-Fashioning: From More to Shakespeare.* Chicago: University of Chicago Press, 1980.

Greene, Thomas. *The Descent from Heaven: A Study in Epic Continuity.* New Haven, Conn.: Yale University Press, 1963.

———. "The Flexibility of the Self in Renaissance Literature." In *The Disciplines of Criticism,* ed. Peter Demetz, Thomas Greene, and Lowry Nelson Jr., 241–64. New Haven, Conn.: Yale University Press, 1968.

———. *The Light in Troy: Imitation and Discovery in Renaissance Poetry.* New Haven, Conn.: Yale University Press, 1982.

Grendler, Paul F. "Francesco Sansovino and Italian Popular History 1560–1600." *Studies in the Renaissance* 16 (1969): 139–80.

———. *Schooling in Renaissance Italy: Literacy and Learning, 1300–1600.* Baltimore: Johns Hopkins University Press, 1989.

Grmek, Mirko D. "Les vicissitudes des notions d'infection, de contagion et de germe dans la médecine antique." In *Mémoires V: Textes Médicaux Latins Antiques,* ed. G. Sabbah, 53–70. Saint-Étienne: Publications de l'Université de Saint-Étienne, 1984.

Gruner, Christian Gottfried. *Aphrodisiacus sive de lue venera.* Jena: Apud C. H. Cunonis Heredes, 1789.

Guarini, Giambattista. *Il segretario dialogo.* Venice: Megietti, 1594.

Guazzo, Stefano. *La civil conversazione.* Ed. Amedeo Quondam. Vols. 1 and 2. Ferrara: Franco Cosimo Panini, 1993.

Guicciardini, Francesco. *The History of Italy.* Ed. and trans. Sidney Alexander. Princeton, N.J.: Princeton University Press, 1969.

———. *Le lettere.* Ed. Pierre Jodogne. Vols. 1 and 2. Rome: Istituto Storico Italiano per l'Età Moderna e Contemporanea, 1986.

———. *Maxims and Reflections of a Renaissance Statesman.* Trans. Mario Domandi, with an introduction by Nicolai Rubinstein. New York: Harper and Row, 1965.

———. *Opere.* Ed. Emanuella Lugnani Scarano. Vol. 1. Turin: Unione Tipografico-Editrice Torinese, 1970.

———. *Report from Spain.* Ed. and trans. Sheila Ffolliott. "Francesco Guicciardini's *Report from Spain.*" *Allegorica* 7 (1982): 60–115.

———. *Ricordi.* Ed. Ettore Barelli, with an introduction by Mario Fubini. 2d ed. Milan: Rizzoli, 1984.

———. *Ricordi.* Ed. Raffaele Spongano. Florence: Sansoni, 1951.

———. *Scritti autobiografici e rari.* Ed. Roberto Palmarocchi. Bari: Laterza, 1936.

———. *Storia d'Italia.* Ed. Ettore Mazzali, with an introduction by Emilio Pasquini. 3 vols. Milan: Garzanti, 1988.

Guidi, José. "Baldassar Castiglione et le pouvoir politique: du gentilhomme de cour au nonce pontifical." In *Les écrivains et le pouvoir en Italie à l'époque de la Renaissance,* ed. André Rochon, vol. 2, 243–78. Paris: Université de la Sorbonne Nouvelle, 1973.

Hale, John R. "Castiglione's Military Career." In *Castiglione: The Ideal and the Real* in *Renaissance Culture,* ed. Robert W. Hanning and David Rosand, 143–64. New Haven, Conn.: Yale University Press, 1983.

———. *Machiavelli and Renaissance Italy.* New York: Macmillan, 1960.

Hale, John R., ed. *Renaissance Venice.* London: Faber and Faber, 1973.

Hampton, Timothy. *Writing from History: The Rhetoric of Exemplarity in Renaissance Literature.* Ithaca, N.Y.: Cornell University Press, 1990.

Harrison, Fraser. *Strange Land, The Countryside: Myth and Reality.* London: Sidgwick & Jackson, 1982.

Helgerson, Richard. *Self-Crowned Laureates: Spenser, Jonson, Milton, and the Literary System.* Berkeley: University of California Press, 1983.

Henderson, John. "The Black Death in Florence: Medical and Communal Responses." In *Death in Towns: Urban Responses to the Dying and the Dead, 100–1600,* ed. Steven Bassett, 136–50. Leicester and New York: Leicester University Press, 1992.

———. "Epidemics in Renaissance Florence: Medical Theory and Government Response." In *Maladie et societé (xiie–xviiie siècles). Actes du colloque de Bielefeld,* 165–86. Paris: CNRS, 1989.

Hendrickson, G. L. "The 'Syphilis' of Girolamo Fracastoro." *Bulletin of the Institute of the History of Medicine* 2 (1934): 515–46.

Hippocrates. Trans. W. H. S. Jones, E. T. Withington, and Paul Potter. Reprint. 6 vols. Cambridge: Harvard University Press, 1972–88.

Hirst, Michael. *Sebastiano del Piombo.* Oxford: Oxford University Press, 1981.

Hoffmann, George. *Montaigne's Career.* Oxford: Clarendon Press, 1998.

Hrabar, Vladimir E., ed. *De legatis et legationibus tractatus varii.* Dorpat: Mattieseniano, 1905.

Ingegneri, Angelo. *Del buon segretario libri tre.* Rome: Guglielmo Faciotto, 1594.

Iucci, Stefano. "La trattatistica sul segretario tra la fine del cinquecento e il primo ventennio del seicento." *Roma moderna e contemporanea* 3 (1995): 81–96.

Isidore of Seville. *Etymologiarum sive originum libri XX.* Oxford: Oxford University Press, 1911.

Jacquart, Danielle. "Theory, Everyday Practice, and Three Fifteenth-Century Physicians." *Osiris* 6 (1990): 140–60.

Jaffé, Michael. "The Picture of the Secretary of Titian." *Burlington Magazine* 108 (1966): 114–26.

Javitch, Daniel. "Poetry and Court Conduct: Puttenham's *Arte of English Poesie* in the Light of Castiglione's *Cortegiano.*" *Modern Language Notes* 87 (1972): 865–82.

———. *Poetry and Courtliness in Renaissance England.* Princeton, N.J.: Princeton University Press, 1978.

Kahn, Victoria. *Rhetoric, Prudence, and Skepticism in the Renaissance.* Ithaca, N.Y.: Cornell University Press, 1985.

———. "Virtù and the Example of Agathocles in Machiavelli's *Prince.*" *Representations* 13 (1986): 63–83.

Kennedy, William J. *Authorizing Petrarch.* Ithaca, N.Y.: Cornell University Press, 1994.

King, Margaret L. "Caldiera and the Barbaros on Marriage and the Family: Humanist Reflections of Venetian Realities." *Journal of Medieval and Renaissance Studies* 6 (1976): 19–50.

———. *Venetian Humanism in an Age of Patrician Dominance.* Princeton, N.J.: Princeton University Press, 1986.

Kirkham, Victoria. "Painters at Play on the Judgment Day (*Decameron* VIII, 9)." *Studi sul Boccaccio* 14 (1983–84): 256–77.

Klibansky, Raymond, Erwin Panofsky, and Fritz Saxl. *Saturn and Melancholy: Studies in the History of Natural Philosophy, Religion and Art.* New York: Basic Books, 1964.

Kristeller, Paul Oskar. "Philosophy and Medicine in Medieval and Renaissance Italy." In *Organism, Medicine, and Metaphysics: Essays in Honor of Hans Jonas,* ed. Stuart F. Spicker, 29–40. Dordrecht and Boston: Reidel, 1978.

———. *Renaissance Thought: The Classic, Scholastic, and Humanist Strains.* New York: Harper Torchbooks, 1961.

La piccola Treccani. Rome: Istituto della Enciclopedia Italiana, 1995.

Larson, Magali Sarfatti. *The Rise of Professionalism: A Sociological Analysis.* Berkeley: University of California Press, 1977.

Lettere, V. "Costo, Tommaso." *DBI* 30 (1984): 411–15.

Liber, Elinor. "Galen on Contaminated Cereals as a Cause of Epidemics." *Bulletin of the History of Medicine* 44 (1970): 332–45.

Lipking, Lawrence. "The Dialectic of *Il cortegiano.*" *Publications of the Modern Language Association* 81 (1966): 355–62.

Logan, Oliver. *Culture and Society in Venice, 1470–1790: The Renaissance and Its Heritage.* New York: Charles Scribner's Sons, 1972.

Long, Esmond R. "Antonio Benivieni and His Contribution to Pathological Anatomy." In *De abditis nonnullis ac mirandis morborum et sanationum causis,* trans. Charles Singer, with an introduction by Esmond R. Long, xvii–xlvi. Springfield, Ill.: Charles C. Thomas, 1954.

Lopez de Villalobos, Francisco. *The Text and Concordance of the "Sumario de la medicina," 1–1169, Biblioteca Nacional, Madrid.* Ed. Mariá Nieves Sánchez. Madison, Wis.: Hispanic Seminary of Medieval Studies, 1987.

Luciani, Vincent. "Il Guicciardini e la Spagna." *Publications of the Modern Language Association* 56 (1941): 992–1006.

Lucretius. *De rerum natura.* Ed. W. H. D. Rouse. Cambridge: Harvard University Press, 1924.

Luigini, Luigi. *De morbo Gallico omnia quae extant apud omnes medicos cuiuscunque nationis.* 3 vols. Venice: J. Zilettus, 1566–67.

Machiavelli, Niccolò. *The Prince.* Trans. George Bull. London: Penguin, 1961.

———. *Tutte le opere.* Ed. Mario Martelli. Florence: Sansoni, 1971.

Maggi, Ottaviano. *De legato libri duo.* Venice: Ruscellius, 1566.

———. *L'Epistole di M. Tullio Cicerone Scritte a Marco Bruto.* Venice: Aldus, 1556.

Malatesta, Maria. "Introduction: The Italian Professions from a Comparative Perspective." In *Society and the Professions in Italy, 1860–1914,* ed. M. Malatesta, trans. Adrian Belton, 1–23. Cambridge: Cambridge University Press, 1995.

Malatesta, Maria, ed. *I professionisti.* Annali 10 of *Storia d'Italia.* Turin: Einaudi, 1996.

Mann, Thomas. *Death in Venice and Other Stories.* Trans. H. T. Lowe-Porter. New York: Vintage, 1989.

Manzoni, Alessandro. *I promessi sposi.* Ed. Luigi Russo. Florence: La Nuova Italia, 1976.

Marcus, Leah S. "Renaissance/Early Modern Studies." In *Redrawing the Boundaries,* ed.

Stephen Greenblatt and Giles Gunn, 41–63. New York: The Modern Language Association of America, 1992.

Markulin, Joseph. "Guicciardini's *Ricordi* and the Idea of a Book." *Italica* 59 (1982): 296–305.

Martin, John. "Inventing Sincerity, Refashioning Prudence: The Discovery of the Individual in Renaissance Europe." *American Historical Review* 102 (1997): 1309–42.

Martinelli, Bortolo. "Il Petrarca e la medicina." In Francesco Petrarca, *Invective contra medicum,* ed. Pier Giorgio Ricci, 205–49. Rome: Edizione di Storia e Letteratura, 1978.

Martines, Lauro. *Lawyers and Statecraft in Renaissance Florence.* Princeton, N.J.: Princeton University Press, 1968.

———. *Power and Imagination: City-States in Renaissance Italy.* New York: Knopf, 1979.

———. *The Social World of the Florentine Humanists, 1390–1460.* Princeton, N.J.: Princeton University Press, 1963.

Marzari, M. Giacomo. *La prattica e theorica del cancelliere.* Vicenza: Giorgio Greco, 1602.

Marzi, Demetrio. *La cancelleria della repubblica fiorentina.* Rocca S. Casciano: Licinio Cappelli, 1910.

Mattingly, Garrett. "The First Resident Embassies: Medieval Italian Origins of Modern Diplomacy." *Speculum* 12 (1937): 423–39.

———. *Renaissance Diplomacy.* Reprint. New York: Dover, 1988.

Mazzeo, Joseph Anthony. "St. Augustine's Rhetoric of Silence." *Journal of the History of Ideas* 22 (1962): 175–96.

Mazzotta, Giuseppe. *Dante's Vision and the Circle of Knowledge.* Princeton, N.J.: Princeton University Press, 1993.

———. *The World at Play in Boccaccio's "Decameron."* Princeton, N.J.: Princeton University Press, 1986.

McClure, George W. "The *Artes* and the *Ars moriendi* in Late Renaissance Venice: The Professions in Fabio Glissenti's *Discorsi morali contra il dispiacer del morire, detto Athanatophilia* (1596)." *Renaissance Quarterly* 51 (1998): 92–127.

———. "Healing Eloquence: Petrarch, Salutati, and the Physicians." *Journal of Medieval and Renaissance Studies* 15 (1985): 317–46.

———. *Sorrow and Consolation in Italian Humanism.* Princeton, N.J.: Princeton University Press, 1991.

McGovern, John. "The Rise of New Economic Attitudes—Economic Humanism, Economic Nationalism—during the Later Middle Ages and the Renaissance, A.D. 1200–1550." *Traditio* 26 (1970): 217–53.

Millar, Fergus. *The Emperor in the Roman World (31 B.C.–A.D. 337).* London: Duckworth, 1977.

Miller, David A. *The Novel and the Police.* Berkeley: University of California Press, 1988.

Monfasani, John. "Episodes of Anti-Quintilianism in the Italian Renaissance: Quarrels on the Orator as a *Vir Bonus* and Rhetoric as the *Scientia Bene Dicendi.*" *Rhetorica* 10 (1992): 119–38.

Muir, Edward. *Civic Ritual in Renaissance Venice.* Princeton, N.J.: Princeton University Press, 1981.

Muscetta, Carlo. "Crisi e sviluppi della cultura dal comune alle signorie." In Raffaele Amaturo, *Petrarca,* 1–35. Bari: Laterza, 1986.

Najemy, John M. *Between Friends: Discourses of Power and Desire in the Machiavelli-Vettori Letters of 1513–1515.* Princeton, N.J.: Princeton University Press, 1993.

———. "The Controversy Surrounding Machiavelli's Service to the Republic." In *Machiavelli and Republicanism,* ed. Gisela Bock, Quentin Skinner, and Maurizio Viroli, 101–17. Cambridge: Cambridge University Press, 1990.

Nardi, G. M. "Antonio Benivieni ed un suo scritto inedito sulla peste." *Atti e memorie dell'Accademia di storia d'arte sanitaria* 4 (1938): 124–33, 190–97.

Nardi, Isidoro. *Il segretario principiante, ed istruito.* Bologna: Longhi, 1711.

Nati, Andrea. *Trattato del segretario.* Florence: Giorgio Marescotti, 1588.

Navagero, Andrea. *Opera omnia.* Ed. J. A. Vulpius and C. Vulpius. Venice: Remondiniana, 1754.

Nigro, Salvatore. "Lezione sull'ombra." Introduction to Torquato Accetto, *Rime amorose,* v–xxi. Turin: Einaudi, 1987.

———. "Le livre masqué d'un secrétaire du xviie siècle." In *Le Temps de la réflexion* Fall (1984): 183–211.

———. "*Scriptor necans.*" Introduction to Torquato Accetto, *Della dissimulazione onesta,* ed. S. Nigro, 19–26. Genoa: Costa & Nolan, 1983.

———. *Il segretario di lettere.* Palermo: Sellerio, 1991.

Nutton, Vivian. "The Reception of Fracastoro's Theory of Contagion: The Seed that Fell among Thorns." *Osiris* 6 (1990): 196–234.

———. "The Seeds of Disease: An Explanation of Contagion and Infection from the Greeks to the Renaissance." *Medical History* 27 (1983): 1–34.

O'Day, Rosemary. *The Professions in Early Modern England, 1450–1800.* Harlow: Longman, 2000.

Olson, Glending. *Literature as Recreation in the Later Middle Ages.* Ithaca, N.Y.: Cornell University Press, 1982.

Otetea, André. *François Guichardin: Sa vie publique et sa pensée politique.* Paris: Librairie Picart, 1926.

Ottosson, Per-Gunnar. *Scholastic Medicine and Philosophy: A Study of Commentaries on Galen's "Tegni" (ca. 1300–1450).* Naples: Bibliopolis, 1984.

Palazzotto, D. "The Black Death and Medicine: A Report and Analysis of the Tractates Written between 1348–1350." Ph.D. dissertation, University of Kansas, 1973.

Palmarocchi, Roberto. "L'ambasceria del Guicciardini in Spagna." *Archivio storico italiano* 97 (1939): 145–69.

Palmer, Richard John. *The Control of Plague in Venice and Northern Italy, 1348–1600.* Ph.D. dissertation, University of Kent, 1978.

Palumbo, Matteo. *Francesco Guicciardini.* Naples: Liguori, 1988.

———. "Guicciardini, Gramsci e la forma-ricordo." *Modern Language Notes* 102 (1987): 76–95.

Panofsky, Erwin. *Problems in Titian, Mostly Iconographic.* New York: New York University Press, 1969.

Park, Katharine. *Doctors and Medicine in Early Renaissance Florence.* Princeton, N.J.: Princeton University Press, 1985.

———. "Medical Profession and Medical Practice in the Italian Renaissance." In *The*

Rational Arts of Living, ed. A. C. Crombie and N. Siraisi, 137–57. Smith College Studies in History 50. Northampton, Mass.: Department of History, Smith College, 1987.

———. "Medicine and Society in Medieval Europe, 500–1500." In *Medicine in Society: Historical Essays,* ed. Andrew Wear, 59–90. Cambridge: Cambridge University Press, 1992.

Parker, Patricia. *Inescapable Romance: Studies in the Poetics of a Mode.* Princeton, N.J.: Princeton University Press, 1979.

Paschini, Pio. *Tre illustri prelati del Rinascimento: Ermolao Barbaro, Adriano Castellesi, Giovanni Grimani.* Rome: Facultas Theologica Pontificii Athenaei Lateranensis, 1957.

Patrizi, Giorgio. "Il *Libro del Cortegiano* e la trattatistica del comportamento." In *Letteratura italiana,* ed. Alberto Asor Rosa, vol. 3, pt. 2, 855–90. Turin: Einaudi, 1984.

———. "Pedagogie del silenzio. Tacere e ascoltare come fondamenti dell'apprendere." In *Educare il corpo, educare la parola nella trattatisica del Rinascimento,* ed. Giorgio Patrizi and Amedeo Quondam, 415–24. Rome: Bulzoni, 1998.

Pearce, Spencer. "Intellect and Organism in Fracastoro's *Turrius.*" In *The Cultural Heritage of the Italian Renaissance: Essays in Honour of T. G. Griffith,* ed. Clive Griffiths and Robert Hastings, 235–70. Lewiston, N.Y.: Edwin Mellen Press, 1993.

———. "Nature and Supernature in the Dialogues of Girolamo Fracastoro." *Sixteenth Century Journal* 27 (1996): 111–31.

Pellegrini, Francesco. *La dottrina fracastoriana del "contagium vivum": Origini e primi sviluppi tratti da autografi inediti.* Verona: Valdonega, 1950.

Persico, Panfilo. *Del segretario, libri quattro.* Rome: Michele Cortellini, 1655.

Peruzzi, Enrico. "Antioccultismo e filosofia naturale nel *De sympathia et antipathia rerum* di Gerolamo Fracastoro." *Atti e memorie dell'Accademia Toscana di Scienze e Lettere La Colombaria* 45 (1980): 41–131.

Petrarch, Francesco. *Le familiari, I–XXIV.* Ed. V. Rossi and U. Bosco. 4 vols. In *Edizione Nazionale delle Opere di Francesco Petrarca,* vols. X–XIII. Florence: Sansoni, 1933–1942.

———. *Letters of Old Age.* Trans. Aldo S. Bernardo, Saul Levin, and Reta A. Bernardo. 2 vols. Baltimore: Johns Hopkins University Press, 1992.

———. *Letters on Familiar Matters.* Trans. Aldo S. Bernardo. Vol. 1. Albany: State University of New York Press, 1975. Vols. 2 and 3. Baltimore: Johns Hopkins University Press, 1982–1985.

———. *Librorum Francisci Petrarche impressorum annotatio.* Venice: Andree Torresani de Asula, 1501.

———. *Opere latine.* Ed. Antonietta Bufano. Vol. 2. Turin: Unione Tipografico-Editrice Torinese, 1975.

———. *Opera omnia.* Basel: Petri, 1554. Reprinted in 3 vols. Ridgewood, N.J.: Gregg Press, 1965.

———. *Il Petrarcha con l'espositione di M. Gio. Andrea Gesualdo.* Venice: Appresso Alessandro Griffe, 1581.

———. *Petrarch's Lyric Poems: The "Rime sparse" and Other Lyrics.* Ed. and trans. Robert M. Durling. Cambridge: Harvard University Press, 1976.

Phillips, Mark. "F. Guicciardini: The Historian as Aphorist." *Quaderni d'italianistica* 2 (1984): 110–22.

Pigman, G. W. III. "Living Examples: Exemplarity, the New Historicism, and Psychoanalysis." In *Creative Imitation: New Essays on Renaissance Literature in Honor of Thomas M. Greene,* ed. D. Quint et al., 281–95. Binghamton, N.Y.: Medieval and Renaissance Texts and Studies, 1992.

Plato. *The Collected Dialogues of Plato.* Ed. Edith Hamilton and Huntington Cairns. Princeton, N.J.: Princeton University Press, 1961.

Pocock, John G. A. *The Machiavellian Moment: Florentine Political Thought and the Atlantic Republican Tradition.* Princeton, N.J.: Princeton University Press, 1975.

Queller, Donald E. "The Civic Irresponsibility of the Venetian Nobility." In *Economy, Society, and Government in Medieval Italy: Essays in Memory of Robert L. Reynolds,* ed. David Herlihy et al., 223–35. Kent, Ohio: Kent State University Press, 1969.

———. "The Development of Ambassadorial Relazioni." In *Renaissance Venice,* ed. J. R. Hale, 174–96. London: Faber and Faber, 1973.

———. *Early Venetian Legislation on Ambassadors.* Geneva: Librarie Droz, 1966.

———. "How to Succeed as an Ambassador: A Sixteenth Century Venetian Document." *Studia Gratiana* 15 (1972): 653–71.

———. *The Office of Ambassador in the Middle Ages.* Princeton, N.J.: Princeton University Press, 1967.

———. *The Venetian Patriciate: Reality versus Myth.* Urbana: University of Illinois Press, 1986.

Quétel, Claude. *The History of Syphilis.* Trans. Judith Braddock and Brian Pike. Baltimore: Johns Hopkins University Press, 1990.

Quint, David. *Origin and Originality in Renaissance Literature: Versions of the Source.* New Haven, Conn.: Yale University Press, 1983.

Quintilian. *The Institutio Oratoria of Quintilian.* Trans. H. E. Butler. 4 vols. London: Putnam's Sons, 1922.

Quondam, Amedeo. "Dal 'formulario' al 'formulario': Cento anni di 'libri di lettere.'" In *Le "carte messaggiere": Retorica e modelli di comunicazione epistolare,* ed. A. Quondam, 13–156. Rome: Bulzoni, 1981.

———. "Varianti di Proteo: L'Accademico, il Segretario." In *Il segno barocco: Testo e metafora di una civiltà,* ed. Gigliola Nocera, 163–92. Rome: Bulzoni, 1983.

Rabil, Albert Jr., ed. *Renaissance Humanism: Foundations, Forms, and Legacy.* 3 vols. Philadelphia: University of Pennsylvania Press, 1988.

Ramat, Raffaello. *Il Guicciardini e la tragedia d'Italia.* Florence: Olschki, 1953.

Rambuss, Richard. *Spenser's Secret Career.* Cambridge: Cambridge University Press, 1993.

Ramusio, Gianbattista. *Delle navigationi e viaggi.* Vol. 3. Venice: Giunti, 1565.

Rebhorn, Wayne A. *Courtly Performances: Masking and Festivity in Castiglione's "Book of the Courtier."* Detroit, Mich.: Wayne State University Press, 1978.

———. *The Emperor of Men's Minds: Literature and the Renaissance Discourse of Rhetoric.* Ithaca, N.Y.: Cornell University Press, 1995.

———. *Foxes and Lions: Machiavelli's Confidence Men.* Ithaca, N.Y.: Cornell University Press, 1988.

Rhu, Lawrence F. *The Genesis of Tasso's Narrative Theory: English Translations of the Early Poetics and a Comparative Study of Their Significance.* Detroit, Mich.: Wayne State University Press, 1993.

Riddell, William Renwick. "Sebastian Brandt: *De Pestilentiali scorra sive impetigine anni XCVI.*" *Archives of Dermatology and Syphilography* 20 (1929): 63–74.

Ridolfi, Roberto. *The Life of Francesco Guicciardini.* Trans. Cecil Grayson. New York: Knopf, 1968.

———. *The Life of Niccolò Machiavelli.* Trans. Cecil Grayson. Chicago: University of Chicago Press, 1963.

Rosa, Mario. "La chiesa e gli stati regionali nell'età dell'assolutismo." In *Letteratura italiana: Il letterato e le istituzioni,* vol. 1, ed. Alberto Asor Rosa, 257–389. Turin: Einaudi, 1982.

Rubinstein, Nicolai. "The Beginnings of Niccolò Machiavelli's Career in the Florentine Chancery." *Italian Studies* 11 (1956): 72–91.

———. "Machiavelli and the World of Florentine Politics." In *Studies on Machiavelli,* ed. M. Gilmore, 5–28. Florence: Sansoni, 1972.

Russell, Joycelyne G. *Diplomats at Work: Three Renaissance Studies.* Wolfeboro Falls, N.H.: Alan Sutton, 1992.

Saccone, Eduardo. "Grazia, Sprezzatura, and Affettazione in the *Courtier.*" In *Castiglione: The Ideal and the Real in Renaissance Culture,* ed. Robert W. Hanning and David Rosand, 45–67. New Haven, Conn.: Yale University Press, 1983.

———. "Trattato e ritratto: L'introduzione del *Cortegiano.*" *Modern Language Notes* 93 (1978): 1–21.

Salvatore, Filippo. *Antichi e moderni in Italia nel Seicento.* Montreal: Guernica, 1987.

Sansovino, Francesco. *L'avvocato e il segretario.* Ed. Piero Calamandrei. Florence: Le Monnier, 1942.

Sapegno, Maria Serena. "*Storia d'Italia* di Francesco Guicciardini." In *Letteratura italiana: Le opere,* vol. 2, ed. Alberto Asor Rosa, 125–78. Turin: Einaudi, 1993.

Sasso, Gennaro. *Per Francesco Guicciardini: Quattro studi.* Rome: Istituto Storico Italiano per il Medio Evo, 1984.

Scarano, Emanuella Lugnani. "Le redazioni dei *Ricordi* e la storia del pensiero guicciardiniano dal 1512 al 1530." *Giornale storico della letteratura italiana* 147 (1970): 183–259.

Schleiner, Winfried, "Infection and Cure through Women: Renaissance Constructions of Syphilis." *Journal of Medieval and Renaissance Studies* 24 (1994): 499–517.

———. "Moral Attitudes toward Syphilis and Its Prevention in the Renaissance." *Bulletin of the History of Medicine* 68 (1994): 389–410.

Schoeck, Richard J. "Humanism and Jurisprudence." In *Renaissance Humanism: Foundations, Forms, and Legacy,* vol. 3, ed. Albert Rabil Jr., 310–26. Philadelphia: University of Pennsylvania Press, 1988.

Seigel, Jerrold E. *Rhetoric and Philosophy in Renaissance Humanism: The Union of Eloquence and Wisdom, Petrarch to Valla.* Princeton, N.J.: Princeton University Press, 1968.

Sigismondi, Sigismondo. *Prattica cortigiana morale, et economica. Nella quale si discorre minutamente de' Ministri, che servono in Corto d'un Cardinale.* Ferrara: Vittorio Baldini, 1604.

Sillar, Frederick Cameron, and Ruth Mary Meyler. *The Symbolic Pig: An Anthology of Pigs in Literature and Art.* Edinburgh and London: Oliver and Boyd, 1961.

Singer, Charles, and Dorothea Singer. "The Scientific Position of Girolamo Fracastoro." *Annals of Medical History* 1 (1917): 1–34.

Singer, Dorothea Waley. "Some Plague Tractates (Fourteenth and Fifteenth Centuries)." *Proceedings of the Royal Society of Medicine* 9 (1915–16): 159–215.

Siraisi, Nancy G. *Arts and Sciences at Padua: The "Studium" of Padua before 1350.* Toronto: Pontifical Institute of Mediaeval Studies, 1973.

———. *Avicenna in Renaissance Italy: The "Canon" and Medical Teaching in Italian Universities after 1500.* Princeton, N.J.: Princeton University Press, 1987.

———. *The Clock and the Mirror: Girolamo Cardano and Renaissance Medicine.* Princeton, N.J.: Princeton University Press, 1997.

———. *Medieval & Early Renaissance Medicine: An Introduction to Knowledge and Practice.* Chicago: University of Chicago Press, 1990.

———. "The Physician's Task: Medical Reputations in Humanist Collective Biographies." In *The Rational Arts of Living,* ed. A. C. Crombie and N. Siraisi, 105–33. Smith College Studies in History 50. Northampton, Mass.: Department of History, Smith College, 1987.

———. *Taddeo Alderotti and His Pupils: Two Generations of Italian Medical Learning.* Princeton, N.J.: Princeton University Press, 1981.

Siraisi, Nancy G., and Michael McVaugh. "Introduction." *Osiris* 6 (1990): 7–15.

Skinner, Quentin. *The Foundations of Modern Political Thought.* Vol. 1. Cambridge: Cambridge University Press, 1978.

———. *Machiavelli.* New York: Hill and Wang, 1981.

Solerti, Angelo. *Vita di Torquato Tasso.* 2 vols. Rome: Loescher, 1895.

Sontag, Susan. *Illness as Metaphors: AIDs and Its Metaphors.* London: Penguin, 1991.

Stallybrass, Peter, and Allon White. *The Politics and Poetics of Transgression.* Ithaca, N.Y.: Cornell University Press, 1986.

Stanford, William. *The Ulysses Theme: A Study in the Adaptability of a Traditional Hero.* Oxford: Blackwell, 1954.

Stefanutti, U. "Benivieni, Antonio." *DBI* 8 (1966): 543–45.

Stephens, Walter. "Metaphor, Sacrament, and the Problem of Allegory in Tasso's *Gerusalemme liberata.*" *I Tatti Studies* 4 (1991): 217–47.

Struever, Nancy S. *The Language of History in the Renaissance: Rhetoric and Historical Consciousness in Florentine Humanism.* Princeton, N.J.: Princeton University Press, 1970.

———. "Petrarch's *Invective contra medicum:* An Early Confrontation of Rhetoric and Medicine." *Modern Language Notes* 108 (1993): 659–79.

———. "Rhetoric and Medicine in Descartes' *Passions de l'âme:* The Issue of Intervention." In *Renaissance-Rhetorik/Renaissance Rhetoric,* ed. Heinrich F. Plett, 196–212. Berlin: Walter de Gruyter, 1993.

———. *Theory as Practice: Ethical Inquiry in the Renaissance.* Chicago: University of Chicago Press, 1992.

Sudhoff, Karl, ed. *The Earliest Printed Literature on Syphilis, Being Ten Tractates from the Years 1495–1498.* Florence: R. Lier & Co., 1925.

———. "Pestschriften aus den ersten 150 Jahren nach der Epidemie des 'schwarzen Todes' 1348." In *Archiv für Geschichte der Medizin.* Reprint. Wiesbaden: Verlag, 1964.

———. "Pestschriften aus den ersten 150 Jahren nach der Epidemie des 'schwarzen Todes' 1348." *Archiv für Geschichte der Medizin* 4 (1910–11): 191–222, 389–424; 5 (1911–12): 36–87, 332–96; 6 (1912–13): 313–79; 7 (1913–14): 57–114; 8 (1914–15): 175–215, 236–89; 9 (1915–15): 53–78, 117–67; 11 (1918–19): 44–92, 121–76; 14

(1922–23): 1–25, 79–105, 129–68; 16 (1924–25) 1–69, 77–188; 17 (1925) 12–139, 241–91.

Tasso, Torquato. *Gerusalemme liberata*. Ed. Lanfranco Caretti. 2 vols. Bari: Laterza, 1967.

———. *Jerusalem Delivered*. Ed. and trans. Ralph Nash. Detroit, Mich.: Wayne State University Press, 1987.

———. *Le lettere*. Ed. Cesare Guasti. Vol. 3. Florence: Le Monnier, 1853.

———. *Prose*. Ed. Ettore Mazzali. Milan: Ricciardi, 1959.

———. *Le prose diverse*. Ed. Cesare Guasti. Florence: Le Monnier, 1875.

———. *Il secretario et il primo volume, delle lettere familiari, del Sig. Torquato Tasso, nuovamente ristampate*. Venice: Giacomo Vincenzi, 1588.

———. *Tasso's Dialogues: A Selection, with the "Discourse on the Art of the Dialogue."* Ed. and trans. Carnes Lord and Dain A. Trafton. Berkeley: University of California Press, 1982.

Temkin, Owsei. *The Double Face of Janus and Other Essays in the History of Medicine*. Baltimore: Johns Hopkins University Press, 1977.

Thorndike, Lynn. "*Consilia* and More Works in Manuscript by Gentile da Foligno." *Medical History* 3 (1959): 8–19.

———. *A History of Magic and Experimental Science*. Vol. 3. New York: Columbia University Press, 1934.

———. "Medicine versus Law." In *Science and Thought in the Fifteenth Century: Studies in the History of Medicine and Surgery, Natural and Mathematical Science, Philosophy, and Politics*, 24–58. New York: Columbia University Press, 1929.

Tiraboschi, Girolamo. *Storia della letteratura italiana*. Vol. 7, pt. 3. Florence: Molini, Landi e c., 1812.

Tosi, Renzo. *Dizionario delle sentenze latine e greche*. Milan: Rizzoli, 1991.

Trapp, J. B. "*The Poet Laureate:* Rome, *Renovatio* and *Translatio Imperii*." In *Rome in the Renaissance: The City and the Myth*, ed. P. A. Ramsey, 93–130. Binghamton, N.Y.: Medieval and Renaissance Texts and Studies, 1982.

Trinkaus, Charles. *In Our Image and Likeness: Humanity and Divinity in Italian Humanist Thought*. Vol. 2. Chicago: University of Chicago Press, 1970.

Una famiglia veneziana nella storia: i Barbaro: Atti del Convegno di studi in occasione del quinto centenario della morte dell'umanista Ermolao, Venezia, 4–6 novembre, 1993. Venice: Istituto Veneto di Scienze, Lettere, ed Arti, 1996.

Vannozzi, Bonifatio. *Della suppellettile degli avvertimenti politici, morali, et christiani*. Vol. 3. Bologna: Heredi di Giovanni Rossi, 1613.

Vasoli, Cesare. "Le discipline e il sistema del sapere." In *Sapere e/è potere: Discipline, dispute e professioni nell'università medievale e moderna, il caso bolognese a confronto*, ed. Andrea Cristiani, vol. 2, 11–36. Bologna: Istituto per la Storia di Bologna, 1990.

Villani, Giovanni. *Historie universali dei suoi tempi*. Venice: Giunti, 1559.

Villani, Matteo. *Istorie*. Florence: Giunti, 1581.

Virgil. *Eclogues, Georgics, Aeneid*. Ed. and trans. H. Rushton Fairclough. 2 vols. Cambridge: Harvard University Press, 1986.

Vocabolario degli accademici della Crusca. Reprint of the 1612 edition. Florence: Le Lettere, 1987.

Whigham, Frank. *Ambition and Privilege: The Social Tropes of Elizabethan Courtesy Theory*. Berkeley: University of California Press, 1984.

White, Hayden. *Tropics of Discourse: Essays in Cultural Criticism*. Baltimore: Johns Hopkins University Press, 1978.

Wightman, W. P. D. *Science and the Renaissance: An Introduction to the Study of the Emergence of the Sciences in the Sixteenth Century*. Edinburgh: Oliver and Boyd, 1962.

Wilkins, Ernest Hatch. *The Life of Petrarch*. Chicago: University of Chicago Press, 1961.

———. *The Making of the "Canzoniere" and Other Petrarchan Studies*. Rome: Edizioni di Storia e Letteratura, 1951.

———. *Studies in the Life and Works of Petrarch*. Cambridge, Mass.: The Mediaeval Academy of America, 1955.

Witt, Ronald G. *"In the Footsteps of the Ancients": The Origins of Humanism from Lovato to Bruni*. Leiden: Brill, 2000.

———. "Medieval *Ars Dictaminis* and the Beginnings of Humanism: A New Construction of the Problem." *Renaissance Quarterly* 35 (1982): 1–35.

———. "Medieval Italian Culture and the Origins of Humanism as a Stylistic Ideal." In *Renaissance Humanism: Foundations, Forms, and Legacy*, ed. Albert Rabil Jr., vol. 1, 29–70. Philadelphia: University of Pennsylvania Press, 1988.

Woodhouse, John Robert. *Baldesar Castiglione: A Reassessment of "The Courtier."* Edinburgh: Edinburgh University Press, 1978.

Zatti, Sergio. "Il linguaggio della dissimulazione nella *Gerusalemme liberata*." In *Forma e parola: Studi in memoria di Fredi Chiappelli*, ed. Dennis J. Dutschke et al., 423–47. Rome: Bulzoni, 1992.

———. *L'uniforme cristiano e il multiforme pagano: Saggio sulla "Gerusalemme liberata."* Milan: Il Saggiatore, 1983.

Zimmerman, Ernest L. "Joseph Grünpeck's *Libellus de mentulagra alias morbo Gallico* of 1503." *American Journal of Syphilis, Gonorrhea, and Venereal Disease* 24 (1940): 364–85.

Zinano, Gabriele. *Il segretario*. Venice: Giovanni Guerigli, 1625.

Ziolkowski, John. "Epic Conventions in Fracastoro's Poem *Syphilis*." *Altro Polo* (1984): 57–73.

Zucchi, Bartolomeo. *L'idea del segretario*. Venice: Compagnia Minima, 1600.

Index

Page numbers in italics refer to illustrations.

Abbott, Andrew, 12–13, 14, 27, 176, 189
Accetto, Torquato, 178–80
Aeneid (Virgil): Fracastoro's *Syphilis sive morbus Gallicus* influenced by, 20, 24, 90–91, 92, 93–94, 96; Tasso's *Gerusalemme liberata* influenced by, 184n. 4
Alderotti, Taddeo, 53, 56
allegorical readings, 31
ambassadors, 99–152; Dolet's *De officio legati* on, 107–8, 120–21; evolution of resident, 108–9; function of, 102; humanists as, 15, 16, 109; humanist writings on, 122; Petrarch as, 40–42, 40n. 22, 44; Rosier on, 109, 138; and social mobility, 17; Tasso's *Del secretario* on, 189; Tasso's *Gerusalemme liberata* on, 181–82, 184; Venice in creation of resident, 102, 103; and wonder, 102. *See also* Barbaro, Ermolao; Guicciardini, Francesco
Ambaxiatorum brevilogus (Rosier), 138
Amundsen, Darrel, 15, 52
Apollo, 94–95
Apology (Plato), 68
Aristotle: Barbaro studying, 104–5; doctors quoting, 39; Fracastoro reading, 72; Gentile da Foligno influenced by, 54; on play, 33; *Poetics,* 88
Armagnac, Georges d', 158–61, *159*
arms, profession of, 8–9
Arrizabalaga, Jon, 49n. 3, 55
Asor Rosa, Alberto, 145n. 38
Augustine, St., 190
Avicenna, 54, 54n. 25

Bacon, Roger, 33
Bakhtin, Mikhail, 64
Barbaro, Ermolao: accompanying his father on diplomatic missions, 105; as ambassador, 105, 113, 114, 115–16, 117, 119, 120; Aristotle studied by, 104–5; biographical sketch of, 104–5; *Castigationes Plinianae et in Pomponium Melam,* 105; as at center of humanist culture, xiv; *De coelibatu liber,* 105, 105n; on exemplarity, 25; on humanism and ambassadorial work, 20; humanist associations of, 105; Maggi contrasted with, 126–27; as Patriarch of Aquileia, 105, 120; and Pico della Mirandola, 104; self-fashioning of, 23; Tasso on, 101. See also *De officio legati*
Barbaro, Francesco, 105
Barbaro, Marcantonio, 106–7, 123
Barbaro, Zaccaria: in Ermolao Barbaro's *De officio legati,* 113, 113n. 29, 114, 115, 116, 117; son Ermolao accompanying on diplomatic missions, 105
Barbiano, Carlo da, 148, 151
Bembo, Pietro, 17, 72, 73, 75, 98, 171
Benivieni, Antonio, 53
Benjamin, Walter, 65
Benvenga, Michele, 183–84
Birago, Francesco, 184
Bizer, Marc, 165n. 21
Black, Robert, xivn. 11
Boccaccio, Giovanni: and the literary, 25–26; and Petrarch on medicine, 65–66; as protohumanist, xiv, 19. See also *Decameron*
Bologna, 56, 64
Borgia, Cesare, 166–67, 168, 173
Branca, Vittore, 104n. 11, 105n, 109, 115n
Brasavola, Antonio Musa, 87n. 34
Bruni, Francesco, 35
Budé, Guillaume, 151

Burke, Peter, 115n
Bylebyl, Jerome, 66

Cabanillas di Valenza, Jerónimo, 149
Campbell, Anna, 54
Canon (Avicenna), 54, 54n. 25
Canzoniere, 168 (Petrarch), 42–43
Capaccio, Giulio Cesare, 173, 175
Carli Piccolomini, Bartolomeo, 163, 163n. 17
Carondelet, Ferry, 155–58, *157*
Cassian, John, 32–33
Castigationes Plinianae et in Pomponium Melam (Barbaro), 105
Castiglione, Baldesar: *Il libro del cortegiano,* 6–11, 190, 191; seeing himself as doing something new, 15
Cattaneo, Jacopo, 86
Catullus, 72
Chabod, Federico, 161
Chiappelli, Fredi, 162
Cicero: *De oratore,* 22, 185–86; doctors spouting phrases from, 39; letters of, 23, 106, 186–87; Maggi translating letters of, 106; Maggi writing in imitation of, 122, 126; and *meraviglia* elicited by the courtier, 10; *Orator,* 22, 185, 186; and Petrarch's coronation oration, 38; Tasso taking as model for secretaries, 22, 23, 25, 185–87, 189, 192
classical literature: humanism as devoted to study of, 1–2, 24; translation of, 106. *See also authors and works by name*
collatio, 27–28, 32, 35, 44
Collationes (Cassian), 32–33
Colonna, Giovanni, 41
Columbus, 94, 96
Commedia (Dante), 28–29
Commentary on Plato's Symposium on Love (Ficino), 68
Consilio contro la pestilenzia (Ficino), 67–70; and classical culture, 24; as conservative text, 67; Gentile referred to in, 50, 67; linking Ficino and his father, 50, 50n; on living happily to combat the plague, 67–68; scholastic medicine and classical literature in, 19, 67
Consilium contra pestilentiam (Gentile da Foligno), 51
Consolatoria (Guicciardini), 134
contagion: cyclic nature of, 97; demonic character attributed to, 92–93; Fracastoro's *De contagione et contagiosis morbis* on, 20, 74–83
conversation, 32, 55, 63
coronation oration of Petrarch, 27–36; on ascent to Parnassus, 28–30; at beginning of the Renaissance, 1; classical culture in, 24; as collatio, 27–28, 32, 35, 44; Easter Sunday as occasion of, 28–29; on the laurel branch, 34–35; as manifesto of humanism, 18; on poet's profession, 30–36; and romance, 26, 30, 31–32, 34; self-fashioning in, 23; Virgil's *Georgics* cited in, 28, 30–31
Corsini, Andrea, 70
cortegiano, Il (Castiglione), 6–11, 190, 191
Costo, Tomaso, 178
courtiers, 8–11, 190

Da Monte, Giovanni Battista, 77, 77n. 8
Dante, 28–29, 60, 64, 92, 137
De anatomia porci, 60
Decades (Peter Martyr), 84
Decameron (Boccaccio), 57–65; on doctors, 19, 50, 57–59, 63–65; on dying properly, 63; Maestro Alberto, 63–64; Maestro Simone, 50, 58–59, 63–64; pigs in, 50, 60–62; the plague as a marvel in, 59–60; Ser Cepparello, 58; on storytelling for combating the plague, 26, 63
deception, 141, 141n. 34
De coelibatu liber (Barbaro), 105, 105n
De contagione et contagiosis morbis (Fracastoro), 76–83; composition of, 73; on *fomes,* 74, 79–80, 81, 83; Fracastoro wanting to surpass the ancients with, 24; germ theory of disease anticipated in, 19, 78; poetical science in, 20; poets and physicians distinguished in, 75; on *seminaria contagionum,* 74, 77–79, 82, 83; similitude in, 80–83; on syphilis, 83–88, 97
De differentiis febrium (Galen), 77, 77n. 8, 83

Dehio, Ludwig, 103
De legationibus libri tres (Gentili), 151
De legato libri duo (Maggi), 120–27; Barbaro's *De officio legati* contrasted with, 126–27; and classical culture, 24; in context of existing literature on ambassadorial work, 108; as humanist work, 20–21; Odysseus as model for ambassador in, 21, 23, 108, 125–26, 127; on perfect ambassador, 20, 108, 122, 123–24; as Platonic, 108; on travel making for prudence, 124–25; Venice as influence on, 20, 24, 107, 122–23
Della dissimulazione onesta (Accetto), 178, 180
Delle navigationi e viaggi (Ramusio), 84
Del perfetto cancelliere (Piccolomini), 163
Del secretario (Tasso), 184–93; on ambassadors, 189; antiquity and Renaissance contrasted by, 23, 187; and Castiglione's *sprezzatura,* 190, 191; on Cicero as model for secretaries, 22, 23, 25, 185–87, 189, 192; classical orators and Renaissance secretaries compared, 22–23, 24, 188–89, 193; at end of Renaissance, 1; letters accompanying, 194; publication of, 19; on secretary's knowledge, 191–92; on tacit persuasion, 190–91, 193; on Bernardo Tasso, 187–88; Vannozzi on, 181, 188
Del segretario (Persico), 172–73
De morbo Gallico (Leoniceno), 87
De morbo Gallicus opus (Hock von Brackenau), 87–88
De officio legati (Barbaro), 108–20; as Aristotelian, 108, 111; on Barbaro as ambassador, 113, 114, 115–16, 117, 119, 120; Barbaro's father Zaccaria in, 113, 113n. 29, 114, 115, 116, 117; on brevity, 116; calculated indirection in, 117; and classical culture, 24, 119; composition of, 105; as encomium to Venetian ambassadorial work, 112; as exclusive rather than inclusive, 109; and existing literature on ambassadorial work, 107, 109; as first treatise on ambassadorial work by a humanist, 20, 107; the ideal ambassador in, 111; influence of, 107–8; Maggi's *De legato libri duo* contrasted with, 126–27; movement from public to private in, 110; as patrilineal in conception, 113; patriotic asides in, 112; Platonic reading of, 111; as *ritratto,* 114, 127; *supervenire* in, 117–18, 120; three sections of, 109–10; Venice as influence on, 20, 24, 112, 113–14, 119
De officio legati (Dolet), 107–8, 120–21
De oratore (Cicero), 22, 185–86
De rerum natura (Lucretius): Fracastoro's *De contagione et contagiosis morbis* influenced by, 83; Fracastoro's *Syphilis sive morbus Gallicus* influenced by, 20, 24, 89, 95; Tasso borrowing from, 195; on wonder and ignorance, 96, 96n. 49
De re uxoria liber (Francesco Barbaro), 105
De sympathia et antipathia rerum (Fracastoro), 73, 76, 77, 83, 90
Discorso (Costo), 178
Discorso di Logrogno (Guicciardini): political importance of, 132n. 14; on reconstructing Florentine government, 132–33, 136, 137, 146; the *Ricordi* and, 135, 135n. 19
discretion, 138–40, 142, 145
disease: as metaphor, 71, 91; new diseases, 87, 87n. 34; wondrous diseases, 20, 47–49. *See also* contagion; plague; syphilis
doctors. *See* medicine
Doglio, Maria Luisa, 111
Dolet, Étienne, 107–8, 120–21
Donato, Girolamo, 105, 151
Dondi, Giovanni, 39

education: courtiers as rivals to educators, 9; humanists as teachers, 14; personal growth through humanist, 3; Scholastic contrasted with humanist, 13–14. See also *studia humanitatis*
eloquence: doctors attempting to demonstrate, 39; Dolet on false, 121; humanists in search of, 1; of Odysseus, 125
epic poetry: Fracastoro's *Syphilis sive morbus Gallicus* modeled on, 89, 90,

epic poetry (*continued*)
93; Homer, 124, 125, 196; secretaries compared with epic poets, 194–96
Epistole di M. Tullio Cicerone scritte a Marco Bruto, L' (Maggi), 106
Este, Alfonso d', 195
eutrapelia, 33

Ferdinand, King of Aragon, 141, 141n. 34, 143, 149
Ferdinand, King of Naples, 147, 148
Fernandez de Oviedo, Gonzalo, 85
Ferry Carondelet and His Secretaries (Sebastiano del Piombo), 155–58, *157*
Ficino, Marsilio, 65–70; as at center of humanist culture, xiv; *Commentary on Plato's Symposium on Love,* 68; on exemplarity, 25; on humans infecting animals, 61; on medical profession, 50; on melancholy, 70, 70n. 77; self-fashioning of, 23; synthesis of humanism and medicine in, 19. See also *Consilio contro la pestilenzia*
Figliuolo, Bruno, 115n, 117n. 35
Fish, Stanley, x, 38n
Flaminio, Marcantonio, 73
Florence: as in decline for Guicciardini, 136–37; Guicciardini chosen as ambassador to Spain, 130–31; Guicciardini on reconstructing along lines of Venice, 133, 136, 137, 146; Machiavelli as secretary for, 22, 160–64, 165–66, 170; as marginal in European politics, 142; Lorenzo de' Medici, 147, 152; Piero de' Medici, 147–48
fomes, 74, 79–80, 81, 83
Foucault, Michel, 79, 79n. 13, 82
Fracastoro, Girolamo, 71–98; and classical scholarship, 73–74; *De sympathia et antipathia rerum,* 73, 76, 77, 83, 90; education of, 72; on epic poetry, 89; *Homocentricorum sive de stellis liber unus,* 73; as humanist, 75; humanist associates of, 72–73; interests of, 72; and the literary, 26; *Naugerius,* 76, 88; on new diseases, 87, 87n. 34; as poet, 75; rhetoric and medicine in works of, 20; self-fashioning of, 23; on syphilis as wondrous disease, 70; *Turrius,* 79, 82; works of, 73. See also *De contagione et contagiosis morbis; Syphilis sive morbus Gallicus*
French, Roger, 49n. 3, 53
Fried, Michael, 158
Frye, Northrop, 30

Galen: *De differentiis febrium,* 77, 77n. 8, 83; Fracastoro reading, 72; and Fracastoro's *seminaria,* 77, 77n. 8, 78; Gentile da Foligno influenced by, 54; humanist physicians reviving works of, 67; plague as explained by Galenic physicians, 55; as writing on sympathy and antipathy, 73
Garbo, Tommaso del, 77
Garin, Eugenio, 39
Garzoni, Tommaso, 6
Gaza, Theodore, 105
Gentile da Foligno, 50–57; Avicenna as influence on, 54; *consilia* of, 51, 51nn. 9, 12; *Consilium contra pestilentiam,* 51; on conversation as causing plague, 55, 63; death from the plague, 56–57; Ficino's *Consilio contro la pestilenzia* referring to, 50, 67; medical training of, 53; on the plague, 49–52; professional status of, 53; as scholastic physician, 19, 50, 53–54, 67; on telling stories to alleviate melancholy, 69
Gentili, Alberico, 131n. 7, 151
Georges d'Armagnac and His Secretary (Titian), 158–61, *159*
Georgics (Virgil), 28, 30–31, 89
Gerusalemme liberata (Tasso), 26, 181–84, 186, 195–96
Gesualdo, Giovanni Andrea, 43
Gilbert, Felix, xivn. 11
Giustiniano, Antonio, 150, 151
Godman, Peter, 162n. 14
Goodwin, Charles, 11
Gorgias, 128, 132, 144–45
Grafton, Anthony, xiiin. 8, 13, 17n
Gramigna, Vincenzo, 175, 176–77
Grünpeck, Joseph, 91, 92
guaiacum, 93, 95–96
Guarini, Giambattista, 177–78
Guazzo, Stefano, 168, 168n. 29, 171–72, 177

Guicciardini, Francesco, 128–52; as ambassador to Spain, 21, 128–32, 142; *Consolatoria,* 134; on exemplarity, 25, 151; humanism as influencing, xiv, xivn. 11; and the literary, 26; *Oratio accusatoria,* 130; pessimism increasing in, 21–22, 137; *Report from Spain,* 128–29; *Ricordanze,* 129–30; self-fashioning of, 23. See also *Discorso di Logrogno; History of Italy; Ricordi*
Guy of Chauliac, 52

Hale, John R., 9n. 19
harmony of nature, 90
Harrison, Fraser, 60
Henderson, John, 49n. 3
Hippocrates, 47–48, 73
Hispaniola, 94
History of Italy (Guicciardini): ambassadorial work in, 146–52; Guicciardini introducing himself into, 132, 146; Guicciardini's ambassadorial experience reflected in, 145–46; on office revealing the man, 134; on Sforza's attempt to manipulate Italian ambassadors, 146–49
Hock von Brackenau, Wendelin, 87–88
Homer, 124, 125, 196
Homocentricorum sive de stellis liber unus (Fracastoro), 73
Horace, 34
humanists, 1–4; on ambassadorial work, 122; as ambassadors, 15, 16, 109; applying timeless models of antiquity to historically determined present, 192; and classical literature, 1–2, 24; coining of *humanista,* 14n. 32; dates of humanism, xiv; as elitist, xiii; on exemplarity, 2–3, 24–25; humanism's advantages for professionals, 13; and the legal profession, 14; and the literary, 25–26; medical humanism, 48–49, 49n. 3; and medical profession, 15, 16, 49, 66–67, 71; medicine attacked by, xii, 16; and notaries, 14; the past as understood by, 2; Petrarch as first, xiv, 1, 18; professions shaping identity of, xi, xv; protohumanists, xiv, 19; Scholasticism contrasted with humanism, 13–14, 15; secretarial office as ladder to success for, 17–18, 164, 171; as secretaries, 15, 16–17, 176; self-fashioning of, 23; self-reflexive turn in literature of, 4; and *studia humanitatis,* 1, 14n. 32; success of humanism, xii–xiii; theory and practice brought together by, xiii; Venetian humanism, 104, 104n. 11

Inferno (Dante), 60, 64, 92
Ingegneri, Angelo, 175, 178
Isidore of Seville, 60

Jacobus, Johannes, 62n. 56
Jardine, Lisa, xiiin. 8, 13
Javitch, Daniel, 11
John the Evangelist, St., 32–33

King, Margaret L., 104n. 11, 120n, 126
Kirkham, Victoria, 64
Klibansky, Raymond, 70n. 77
Kristeller, Paul Oskar, xvn, 14, 15n. 35

laughter, 59, 76, 83, 86
laurel branch, 34–35
legal profession, 14
Leoniceno, Nicolò, 66–67, 87, 87n. 34, 97
Leto, Pomponio, 105
Libellus de mentulagra alias morbo Gallico (Grünpeck), 91
libro del cortegiano, Il (Castiglione), 6–11, 190, 191
Lopez de Villalobos, Francisco, 92
Lucretius: Fracastoro reading, 72; philosophical detachment and serenity of, 90. See also *De rerum natura*
Luigini, Luigi, 77n. 8

Machiavelli, Niccolò: as exemplary secretary, 22, 173–74; humanism as influencing, xiv, xivn. 11; on humans becoming beasts in behavior, 4; Persico on, 172–73; as secretary, 22, 160–64, 165–66, 170; secrets disclosed by, 22, 173; self-fashioning of, 23–24; and Titian's *Georges d'Armagnac and His Secretary,* 159–60. See also *Prince, The*

Maggi, Ottaviano: on ambassadors and wonder, 102; Barbaro contrasted with, 126–27; biographical sketch of, 106–7; diplomatic experience of, 106–7; *L'Epistole di M. Tullio Cicerone scritte a Marco Bruto,* 106; on exemplarity, 25; and the literary, 26; as never serving as an ambassador, 21, 123; Plato and Cicero translated by, 106; as pushing classical models to their limits, 122; Ruscelli on, 106n. 14; self-fashioning of, 23. See also *De legato libri duo*
Malatesta, Maria, 5, 11n. 26
Malpiglio, overo de la corte (Tasso), 191n. 12, 193
Mann, Thomas, 47, 59
Manzoni, Alessandro, 184
Markulin, Joseph, 140n. 32
Marzari, Giacomo, 164–65
Marzi, Demetrio, 165n. 23
Mattingly, Garrett, 102, 103n. 8, 122
Maximilian, Emperor, 149, 150, 156, 167–68, 168n. 28
Mazzeo, Joseph, 190
McClure, George, 6, 19, 40
McVaugh, Michael, 48, 49n. 3
Medici, Lorenzo de', 147, 152
Medici, Piero de', 147–48
medicine, 45–98; Avicenna's *Canon,* 54, 54n. 25; Boccaccio's *Decameron* on, 19, 50, 57–59, 63–65; Bologna's medical school, 56, 64; Ficino on, 50; Hippocrates, 47–48, 73; humanist interaction with, 15, 16, 49, 66–67, 71; humanists attacking, xii, 16; in Italian university system, 15, 19; Leoniceno, 66–67, 87, 87n. 34, 97; long medical Renaissance, 48–49, 49n. 3, 67; medical humanism, 48–49, 49n. 3; metaphorical discourse in, 78–79; nascent professionalism of, 56; particular and universal as concern of, 65; Petrarch on, 16, 39, 65–66; the plague not damaging standing of, 56; and poetry in Fracastoro, 75; poets and doctors on the wondrous, 49; poets and doctors thinking through similitude, 79; and rhetoric, 82, 82n. 17; and social mobility, 17; three reactions to the plague, 47–70. *See also* disease; Ficino, Marsilio; Fracastoro, Girolamo; Galen; Gentile da Foligno
melancholy, 69, 70, 70n. 77
Merula, Giorgio, 105
messaggiero, Il (Tasso), 181, 189
Millar, Fergus, 165n. 21
Miller, David, 155, 173, 174, 180
Miraulmont, Pierre de, 165, 165n. 21
Mocenigo, Alvise, 106, 107, 122, 123
Montaigne, Michel de, xv
Mussato, Albertino, 37

Nati, Andrea, 164, 172, 173
Naugerius (Fracastoro), 76, 88
Navagero, Andrea, 72, 101–2
Nigro, Salvatore, 171, 175, 178–79
notaries, 14
Nutton, Vivian, 78

Odysseus, 21, 23, 108, 125–26, 127
Olson, Glending, 33
Oratio accusatoria (Guicciardini), 130
Oration on the Dignity of Man (Pico della Mirandola), 3, 62
Orator (Cicero), 22, 185, 186
oratory: ambassadors employing, 16, 21, 108, 109; Quintilian's definition of orator, 21, 24, 132, 135, 137; Tasso on the secretary's knowledge of, 192; Tasso's *Del secretario* comparing classical orators and Renaissance secretaries, 188–89, 193. *See also* eloquence
Oresme, Nicole, 33

paideia, 3
Palmer, Richard, 52
Panofsky, Erwin, 70n. 77
Park, Katharine, 56
Pascale, Giovanni, 87
Persico, Panfilo, 172–73
Peter Martyr, 84, 96, 101, 102
Petrarch, Francesco, 27–44; as ambassador, 40–42, 40n. 22, 44; and Augustine's rhetoric of silence, 190; *Canzoniere* (rima 168), 42–43; as at center of humanist culture, xiv; and classical culture, 24; dedication to *studia humanitatis* as defined by, 18; on exemplarity, 24–25; as first humanist,

xiv, 1, 18; as first of his age to receive the laurel, 36–37, 38; and the literary, 25, 26; on medicine, 16, 39, 65–66; oratorical and letter-writing traditions distinguished by, 185n. 8; as physician to the soul, 40, 44; and the priesthood, 35; *Privilegium laureae,* 37, 37n. 17, 38; and the professions, 38–44, 38n; Rome chosen over Paris by, 38; on secretaries, 42–44; self-fashioning of, 23, 193; on solitary retreats for poets, 35–36; and the university, 38. *See also* coronation oration of Petrarch

piazza universale di tutte le professioni del mondo, La (Garzoni), 6

Piccolomini, Bartolomeo Carli, 163, 163n. 17

Pico della Mirandola, Giovanni: and Barbaro, 104; *Oration on the Dignity of Man,* 3, 62; on the self, 3–4

pigs, in Boccaccio's *Decameron,* 50, 60–62

plague: becoming commonplace, 69–70; Boccaccio's *Decameron* on, 19, 50, 57–65; conversation as causing, 55, 63; Ficino's *Consilio contro la pestilenzia* on, 67–70; food chain in transmission of, 62; Gentile da Foligno on, 49–57; melancholics as less affected by, 69; as new and unheard of, 52–53; prevailing explanation of, 55; three reactions to, 47–70; as wondrous disease, 48, 53, 55

Plato: *Apology,* 68; on Homer, 124; Maggi translating, 106; Maggi writing in imitation of, 126; *Republic,* 196; *Symposium,* 68

play, 32–36

Pliny the Elder, 66

Pliny the Younger, 187

Plutarch, 72

Pocock, John G. A., 132n. 14

Poetics (Aristotle), 88

poets: and doctors on the wondrous, 49; and doctors thinking through similitude, 79; medicine and poetry in Fracastoro, 75; metaphorical discourse in medicine, 78–79; Petrarch creating yet refusing official professional status for, 36–44; Petrarch's coronation oration on profession of, 30–36; and philosophers taking pleasure in causes of things, 88–89; Socrates on, 196; Tasso as poet, 193–96; Tasso contrasting ambassadors with, 182. *See also* epic poetry

Pole, Reginald, 173

Poliziano, Angelo, 105

Polybius, 72

Pomponazzi, Pietro, 72

Pontano, Giovanni, 76, 105

prattica e theorica del cancelliere, La (Marzari), 164–65

Prince, The (Machiavelli), 161–74; as acknowledging knowledge of secrecy, 173–74, 180; antibureaucratic attitude of, 170; and classical culture, 24; envisioning the writer as a secretary, 162–64, 169–70; Machiavelli reconceptualizing his past in, 160; as political program not advice literature, 170; the secretary as seen in, 22, 164; on secretiveness in princes, 166–68; on spectacle as means of control, 166–67; Tasso's Aladino compared with, 182–83

Privilegium laureae (Petrarch), 37, 37n. 17, 38

professionisti, I (Malatesta), 11n. 26

professions: in Castiglione's *Il cortegiano,* 6–11; courtiers as professionals, 9, 10–11; humanism's advantages for, 13; humanist identity shaped by, xi, xv; jurisdictional disputes among, 12, 27; legal profession, 14; melancholy as disease of professionals, 70; in Middle Ages, 5; Petrarch on play and, 35; Petrarch on professionalism, 38–44, 38n; professional deformation, ix–xii; in Renaissance Italy, 4–13; rhetoric used to persuade public of legitimacy of, 12–13; routine work delegated by, 12; self-authenticating discourse in, 11–12; sociological approach to, 11; specialized knowledge in, 12; structural and relational theory of, 12–13; term as polysemic, 5, 6. *See also* ambassadors; medicine; poets; secretaries

Proteo segretario (Benvenga), 183–84

protohumanists, xiv, 19
prudence, 124–25, 138–39, 176

Queller, Donald E., 103
Quintilian: and *meraviglia* elicited by the courtier, 10; on the orator as good man who speaks well, 21, 24, 132, 135, 137, 159
Quondam, Amedeo, 168n. 29, 177n. 59

Ramusio, Gianbattista, 73, 74, 84, 85, 94, 102
rationes seminales, 95
Rebhorn, Wayne, 9
relazione, 103
Renaissance: dates of, xn. 3; medical Renaissance, 48–49, 49n. 3, 67; the professions in, 4–13; the self as conceived in, 3–4; Tasso contrasting antiquity with, 23, 187; viewed as advance over Middle Ages, 15. *See also* Florence; humanists; Venice
Report from Spain (Guicciardini), 128–29
Republic (Plato), 196
resident ambassadors. *See* ambassadors
rhetoric: Augustine's rhetoric of silence, 190; in Barbaro–Pico della Mirandola debate, 104; Fracastoro bringing together medicine and, 20; Fracastoro on rhetorical force of poetry, 75; and medicine, 82, 82n. 17; Petrarchan, 39n. 18; Petrarch on medicine and, 39–40; professions using to establish legitimacy, 12–13; speech and action needing to correspond in, 135–36, 137; Tasso on tacit persuasion, 190–91; as unifying *studia humanitatis,* 1. *See also* oratory
Rhu, Lawrence F., 184n. 4
Ricordanze (Guicciardini), 129–30
Ricordi (Guicciardini): advice for future ambassadors, 142–45; and classical culture, 24; composition of, 18–19, 20, 132n. 11; on deception, 141, 141n. 34; on discretion, 138–40, 142, 145; discretion required for reading, 140, 140n. 32; on double perspective for ambassadors, 143–44; Guicciardini's ambassadorial experience reflected in, 131–32, 140–41; on ignorance in ambassadors, 144–45; pessimism of second early version of, 137; on public service in building a reputation, 130, 130n. 5; reading in light of ambassadorial work, 132–46; on secretiveness, 138, 138n. 25, 168n. 29; on the wise man as a good citizen, 135–36
Robert, King of Naples, 29, 36, 40
romance, 26, 30, 31–32, 34, 38
Rosier, Bernard de, 109, 138
Ruscelli, Girolamo, 106n. 14

Saccone, Eduardo, 10
Salutati, Coluccio, 66
Sansovino, Francesco, 160, 170–71, 179
Saxl, Fritz, 70n. 77
Scala, Bartolomeo, 161
Scaliger, Julius Caesar, 73
Scarano, Emanuella Lugnani, 135n. 19
Scholasticism, 13–14, 15, 104
Sebastiano del Piombo, 155–58, *157*
secrecy: as characteristic of secretaries, 22, 171–74, 178–80; Guicciardini on secretiveness in ambassadors, 138, 138n. 25, 168n. 29; Machiavelli on secretiveness in princes, 166–68; Tasso as secretive poet, 195n
secretaries, 153–96; as "*a secretis,*" 164–66, 165nn. 21, 24, 170; Benvenga's *Proteo segretario* on, 183–84; counselors compared with, 174–76; epic poets compared with, 194–96; humanists as, 15, 16–17, 176; as insiders, 177–78; late Renaissance treatises on, 160; Nati's *Trattato del segretario* on, 164, 172, 173; Petrarch on, 42–44; the place of, 155–80; as professionals in Renaissance Italy, 4–5; Sansovino's *Il segretario* on, 171; in Sebastiano del Piombo's *Ferry Carondelet and His Secretaries,* 155–58, *157;* secretiveness and silence as characteristic of, 22, 171–74, 178–80; as servile functionaries by late sixteenth century, 17, 174, 175, 176–77; and social mobility, 17–18, 164, 171; Tasso's *Gerusalemme liberata* on, 183–84; in Titian's *Georges d'Armagnac and His Secretary,* 158–61, *159. See also* Machiavelli, Niccolò; Tasso, Torquato

segretario, Il (Sansovino), 171
segretario dialogo, Il (Guarini), 178
Seigel, Jerrold, 190
selfhood, Renaissance notion of, 3–4
seminaria contagionum, 74, 77–79, 77n. 8, 82, 83
Seneca, 39
Sforza, Ludovico, 115–16, 118, 133, 147–48
Sigismondi, Sigismondo, 176
silence: Augustine's rhetoric of, 190; and secretiveness as characteristic of secretaries, 22, 171–74, 178–80
similitude, 79, 80–83
Siraisi, Nancy, 48, 49n. 3, 53
Socrates, 19, 25, 67–69, 196
Solerti, Angelo, 193
somario de la medicina, El (Lopez de Villalobos), 92
Sontag, Susan, 71, 91
sprezzatura, 9–10, 190, 191
Stallybrass, Peter, 61
Steber, Bartholomaus, 86–87
Stephens, Walter, 195n
Struever, Nancy, 38n. 18, 82n. 17, 170, 179
Struthius, Josephus, 77
studia humanitatis: Castiglione's courtiers grounded in, 8, 9; Petrarch as defining dedication to, 18; and practical knowledge as a citizen, 142; rhetoric as unifying subject within, 1; secretaries as trained in, 160, 176, 177; term "humanist" and, 14n. 32
Sufhoff, Karl, 53n. 19
Symposium (Plato), 68
syphilis: as *flagellum dei,* 85; Fracastoro's *De contagione et contagiosis morbis* on, 83–88, 97; Fracastoro's *Syphilis sive morbus Gallicus* on, 88–96; guaiacum as cure for, 93, 95–96; literary representation of, 85–86; myth of origin of, 94–95; naming, 87, 97–98; as new disease, 83–84, 86–88; New World origins of, 84–85; sin linked to, 85; as venereal disease, 85; war associated with, 91–92; as wondrous disease, 48, 53, 70, 86, 87–88, 90, 97
Syphilis sive morbus Gallicus (Fracastoro), 88–96; and classical culture, 24; composition of, 18, 73; on guaiacum as cure for syphilis, 93, 95–96; heroic imagery in, 89, 90, 93; hybrid character of, 20; Lucretius's *De rerum natura* influencing, 20, 24, 89; medicine determining structure of, 75; as *medicum laborem,* 95, 96; on myth of origin of syphilis, 94–95; threefold Christian pattern of, 96; Virgil's *Aeneid* influencing, 24, 90–91, 93–94

tacit persuasion, 190–91, 193
Tasso, Bernardo, 181, 187–88
Tasso, Torquato, 181–96; on Barbaro, 101; Barbaro's *De officio legati* influencing, 111; as at center of humanist culture, xiv; disparate elements brought together by, 185; on exemplarity, 25; *Gerusalemme liberata,* 26, 181–84, 186, 195–96; and the literary, 26; *Malpiglio, overo de la corte,* 191n. 12, 193; *Il messaggiero,* 181, 189; as poet, 193–96; as secretive poet, 195n. See also *Del secretario*
theater, as metaphor for life, 134
Themistius, 105
Thomas Aquinas, St., 33–34
Titian, 138–39, 158–61, *159*
Traité de la Chancellerie (Miraulmont), 165
translation, 106
Trattato del segretario (Nati), 164, 172, 173
Turrius (Fracastoro), 79, 82

Valla, Giorgio, 105
Vannozzi, Bonifatio, 175, 177, 181, 188, 194
Vella, Giorgio, 86
Venice: Barbaro influenced by, 20, 24, 107, 111, 112, 113–14, 119; in diplomatic history, 102–4; Guicciardini on reconstructing Florence along lines of, 133, 146; in Guicciardini's *History of Italy,* 149–50; humanism in, 104, 104n. 11; Maggi influenced by, 20, 24, 107, 122–23; myth of, 104, 122, 123; patriciate of, 103, 124; patrilineal social structure of, 113. *See also* Barbaro, Ermolao
Vera, Juan Antonio de, 108n. 19
Vico, Giambattista, 98
Villani, Giovanni, 52, 52n. 18

Villani, Matteo, 57
Virgil: doctors quoting, 39; Fracastoro reading, 72; *Georgics,* 28, 30–31, 89; on the laurel branch, 34; Petrarch as symbolic son of, 29. See also *Aeneid*
vita activa, 2
Vocabolario degli accademici della Crusca, 5

White, Allon, 61
White, Hayden, 71, 75, 79
Wilkins, Ernest Hatch, 18, 37
Witt, Ronald, xiv, 14, 41n. 24, 185n. 8
wonder: ambassadors and, 102; epistemological dimension of, 75–76; Fracastoro on, 76–77; and ignorance in Lucretius, 96, 96n. 49; poets and doctors on the wondrous, 49; poets and philosophers as inclined to, 88–89; syphilis eliciting, 86, 87–88; travel writers experiencing, 102; wondrous diseases, 20, 47–49

Xenophon, 122, 126

Zatti, Sergio, 195
Zinano, Gabriele, 172, 175–76

KING ALFRED'S COLLEGE
LIBRARY